D0571746

Interdisciplinary perspectives on modern history

Editors
Robert Fogel and Stephan Thernstrom

Avenues to adulthood

Avenues to adulthood

The origins of the high school and social mobility in an American suburb

REED UEDA

WITHDRAWN

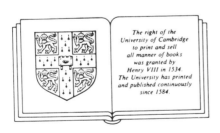

The right of the
University of Cambridge
to print and sell
all manner of books
was granted by
Henry VIII in 1534.
The University has printed
and published continuously
since 1584.

CAMBRIDGE UNIVERSITY PRESS

Cambridge
London   New York   New Rochelle
Melbourne   Sydney

Published by the Press Syndicate of the University of Cambridge
The Pitt Building, Trumpington Street, Cambridge CB2 1RP
32 East 57th Street, New York, NY 10022, USA
10 Stamford Road, Oakleigh, Melbourne 3166, Australia

First published 1987

Printed in the United States of America

Library of Congress Cataloging-in-Publication Data
Ueda, Reed.
Avenues to adulthood.
Includes bibliographies and index.
1. High schools – United States – History.
2. Social mobility – United States.   I. Title.
LA222.U34   1987   373.73   86–28371

British Library Cataloguing in Publication Data
Ueda, Reed
Avenues to adulthood : the origins of the
high school and social mobility in an
American suburb.
1. Social mobility – United States –
History   2. Education, Secondary –
United States
I. Title
305.5′ 13′0973   HN90.S65

ISBN 0 521 32770 9

To my mother and father

Contents

Acknowledgments

In the process of writing this book I have accumulated debts that I cannot possibly repay in full. As a partial accounting, I wish to thank several institutions for their support and a number of individuals for their assistance. An award from the Joseph A. Grossman Fund at Harvard University enabled me to launch this study as a doctoral thesis. A Mellon fellowship from Tufts University and an American Council of Learned Societies fellowship provided the time to prepare the thesis for publication. Dean Mary Ella Feinleib of Tufts also provided help at a key juncture. My research was expedited by the knowledgeable staffs of the Massachusetts State Archives, the State Library, the Boston Public Library, the Somerville Public Library, the Harvard College Library, the Federal Record Deposit Archives in Waltham, the New England Historic Genealogical Society, the Somerville Historical Society, and the administration of the Somerville High School. My research assistants at Tufts, especially David Le-Blanc, Lisa Spezzaferro, Jean O'Connell, and Le Jen Chen, made an invaluable contribution. My editors at Cambridge University Press, Frank Smith, Rhona Johnson, and Louise Calabro Gruendel, skillfully guided the manuscript into print. I am obligated to Carl F. Kaestle, Oscar Handlin, Bernard Bailyn, Robert W. Fogel, Patrick J. Blessing, Joel Perlmann, Jane Hunter, Nathan Glazer, and Sheldon White for their insights and interest in my work. This book could not have been written without the direction of Stephan Thernstrom, whose scholarship and clear judgment have taught me what I know of historiography. All these individuals deserve credit for the merits my book might possess and do not share in the responsibility for its lapses. Finally, I would like to thank Peggy, Mildred, Goro, Nancy, and Eddie for their forbearance and devotion.

Introduction

In Paris, at the great World's Exposition of 1900, thousands of observers from all nations marveled in fascination at the educational achievements of democracy heralded in the American Educational Exhibit. They drew around the special showcase for the high schools of Somerville, Massachusetts, a Boston suburb. Exhibited there were "interior and exterior views" of the Latin High School, a display of the English High School "in all its cosmopolitan branches from art to science, from studio to laboratory," and a copy of a school yearbook.[1] The American high school represented by Somerville became a symbol of the civilizing and technological progress of modern times celebrated by the world's fair. How the American high school developed a consequential role in social change, widely recognized in late industrial society, is the subject of this community study of Somerville.

Historians and sociologists possess only a preliminary understanding of the public high school's role in the forming of the industrial social order.[2] This study, therefore, seeks to throw light on the function of the modern American high school in the currents of migration and social mobility generated by the industrial revolution. The high school served as a pathway for various social groups to white-collar and professional jobs. If so, did it serve to promote the formation of a middle class and to define its characteristics? Moreover, did it recruit the children of immigrants and manual workers into these forms of employment? This study reconstitutes the life courses of three generations of high school students to determine if John Goldthorpe's finding that education promoted the social mobility of British workers has an American parallel, or whether, as Samuel Bowles and Herbert Gintis argued, schooling reinforced the social inequalities of capitalist society.[3] In the end, empirical evidence emerged providing some concrete elements of support to both these general theses.

The high school's role in the evolution of the civic life of the modern city is another focus of investigation. Support for this institution expressed the shifting balance of political power between natives and immigrants, businessmen and workers.[4] The achievements of high school students served as a source of pride in the hometown. Above

1

all, the high school acted as a symbol of community in a sprawling city of impersonalized social relationships.[5]

These developments are addressed from the perspective of students and their parents. The experience of youths who went to high school and its effects on their families and their adult lives form the mainspring of historical action. Family resources and strategies determined the extent of support given to secondary education for youngsters.[6] The peer-group culture of the high school supervened the family to introduce students at an impressionable age to new values and habits that affected their aspirations in adulthood. The conformist pressures of high school youth culture catalyzed the sense of unique generational identity among turn-of-the-century adolescents.[7] Finally, by using their education as a qualification for desirable jobs, high school students promoted the importance of meritocratic credentials for social advancement.[8]

Educators and policymakers are also discussed, but chiefly in relation to the influences of their social origins upon their public actions. This volume is a social history that treats the American high school as it was centered in a matrix of community and population. It seeks to counterbalance the tendency of historians to treat American education as a projection of an elite group of reformers and schoolmen.

The site of this study – Somerville, Massachusetts – evolved from a farming district into a commuter "streetcar suburb" of Boston between 1800 and 1930. It was a "zone of emergence" for mobile natives and immigrants who migrated from the central city by following the street railway lines to new homes. Somerville also grew from a heavy influx of immigrants from northern New England, Canada, Great Britain, northwestern Europe, and Ireland, who sought better living and working conditions in the American city.

Somerville had one of the highest and fastest growing high school attendance rates of the ten largest cities in Massachusetts in 1910. It is a logical choice as a historical laboratory for identifying the social, economic, and cultural forces that produced the first expansion in high school attendance at the turn of the century, when secondary schooling was popularized among the middle class and the upper working class.

Somerville offers unique advantages for the comparative study of the relationship between social structure and education because of the rich historiography of its locality. The development of the social structure of metropolitan Boston has been closely examined by Oscar Handlin, Stephan Thernstrom, Sam B. Warner, Jr., Elizabeth H. Pleck, and Peter R. Knights,[9] and the evolution of public schooling in this area has been explored by Michael B. Katz, Stanley K. Schultz, Marvin Lazerson, Carl F. Kaestle, and Maris A. Vinovskis.[10] These studies have reconstructed a broad historical context of urbanization and educational innovation against which the social impact of the high school in Somerville can be gauged.

Statistical data drawn from the U. S. federal census, the Massachusetts state census, and student records are used to reconstruct group behavior and patterns in the social structure. The conclusions reported here were reached with tentativeness and circumspection. Above all, this volume must be seen as an exploratory study. Undoubtedly, other researchers will refine the methods and interpretations presented here. Finally, this work is not designed to build models for social policy. Rather its purpose is simply to show that the historical significance of the American high school lay in how students and parents made it part of their lives in an urban milieu.

1   *Farm village to commuter suburb*

When George O. Brastow took the oath as first Mayor of the newly chartered City of Somerville in 1872, he crowned an Algeresque career that coursed this Boston suburb's avenues to business success and political power.[1] The highest honor of the community he helped found in 1842 as a selectmen-run town went to the former country lad from the Massachusetts village of Wrentham. Brastow had risen an entrepreneur in Somerville's residential real estate boom and a Whig leader elected one of the town's first selectmen and school committeemen. Service in the Civil War interrupted his public career, but Brastow returned as a hero. The ambitious booster climbed to loftier heights as a Republican in state politics, winning terms as representative and senator, and serving as president of the Senate before his installation as mayor.[2]

In his inaugural speech, the sixty-one-year-old civic patriarch looked back fondly on Somerville's "small and humble" childhood as a rural district of Charlestown that was partitioned into a township in 1842. He catalogued the streets, railways, water and sewer lines, fire and police departments: the ligatures developed by the vigorous growth of the suburban population. Above all, Brastow placed the public schools at the forefront of the civic accomplishments he unfurled before his rapt audience. The public schools, proclaimed Brastow, always served as the advance agents of "progress in wealth and population." He praised the wisdom of his fellow citizens, who made Somerville highest among all Massachusetts towns in school expenditure per pupil for several years. Casting his eyes toward a glowing future for the city, the new mayor proclaimed that Somerville would continue to attract newcomers as long as "the high character of our schools" was sustained. Brastow pledged that his administration would do its utmost to keep the schools from receding "from their present high position."[3]

The citizens who heard their mayor's confident words knew from Somerville's short history that this formula had worked and could serve as an agenda for future prosperity. Somerville's emergence as a focal point for Boston's metropolitan growth was due to the development of a middle-income housing market concerted with a disci-

4

plined sponsorship of a public school system. Opportunistic boosters such as George Brastow had coordinated these two factors to transform a farming village into a middle-class zone of urban growth.

The process of suburban development

When the new town of Somerville was formed in 1842,[4] it became the youngest child of Charlestown, "that honored ancestor" of the communities fanning out along the Mystic River Valley in eastern Massachusetts. Settlers had filled the valley's hilly farmlands since colonial times, carving out Woburn, Stoneham, Winchester, Burlington, Malden, Everett, Medford, and Arlington from Charlestown's ample bounds that once covered the entire region.[5] The west district of Charlestown that became Somerville, called by colonials "Beyond the Neck," had been a sleepy countryside occupied by a handful of dairy farmers.[6] At the time of its incorporation as Somerville it was still a sparsely populated hinterland containing fewer than 200 dwellings.[7] The most notable feature of the infant town was the McLean Asylum for the Insane established there by the Massachusetts General Hospital.[8]

In the half century since the Revolutionary War, however, the sprouting of cities and manufactories in Massachusetts had gradually altered the character of West Charlestown's economy.[9] As Boston builders shifted from wood to brick structures to shelter it's swelling population, brickyards sprang up in west Charlestown where the soil contained both superior clay and sand. For years brickmaking flourished as the chief industry of the district, as the kilns "smoked the days and illumined the nights."[10] Livestock raising and dairy farming also expanded, for the multiplying inhabitants of Boston and its spreading suburbs required more food supplies. Capitalizing on the development of textile and manufacturing in nearby towns such as Waltham and Lowell, entrepreneurs established a bleachery in 1821 that in 1845 employed 37 hands who processed $315,000 in cotton goods.[11] Other businessmen opened a pottery plant, a grist mill, a distillery, a cordage manufactory, and a spike works in west Charlestown.[12] A historian of the region has identified it as part of Boston's vital "fringe economy," "an array of specialized village economies" in "scattered centers" marked by "the absence of dense settlement, the fuzziness of boundaries, the bucolic appearance of the landscape."[13]

The district's residents watched the first trains steam from the farms into Boston in 1835, when the Lowell railroad line was pushed through their pastures.[14] Many who wished to preserve the rural character of the region opposed the railroad, which gobbled up a large swath of land spanning the town and pockmarked it with station depots. The next year, however, another railroad, the Charlestown line, laid down its tracks. Later incorporated as the Fitchburg Railroad Company, its cars carried ice to the piers of Charlestown for transshipment to sweltering ports around the world. The inhabitants of west Charlestown discovered quickly that the locomotive brought a large flow of commerce into their neighborhood that accelerated the pace of economic growth.[15]

Businessmen and clerks came to work in the offices along the tracks, while laborers from Ireland and British Canada flocked to the brickyards and railyards.[16] The sons of farmers from depressed rural areas of northern New England drifted toward west Charlestown in search of employment.[17] Population mounted and a sense of local interest intensified. Gradually, the people of west Charlestown began to see themselves as a separate community, but social tensions arose within. Protestant workers resented the unfamiliar Irish immigrants who moved from the center of Charlestown to crowd into their neighborhood. Resentment turned into furious violence when in 1834 they burned the Ursuline Convent near their homes. They had eyed the convent as a symbol of encroaching papism and the competition of Celtic laborers.[18]

West Charlestown was beginning to feel the tug of forces that were bursting the ancient fabric of Anglo-Saxon society in Massachusetts. The economy that appeared to rest securely on the cargo-filled traders sailed by New England merchants around the world[19] was toppled by the contraction of Boston's hinterland market and the surpassing growth of rival entrepots in New York City and Philadelphia.[20] The merchants shifted their enormous capital out of the collapsing sphere of commerce to reinvest in industry, railroads, and canals. The textile factories of Haverhill, Lowell, Waltham, and Fall River, empowered by $100,000,000 of Boston finance capital,[21] drew young farmwomen to operate the looms who were replaced later by immigrants from British Canada and Ireland.[22] The spiraling demand for labor welcomed the arrival of the famine-starved Irish immigrant. In Charlestown itself, from 1830 to 1850, the flood of foreigners entering the city, composed mainly of Irish newcomers, grew almost nineteenfold.[23] Population doubled in Charlestown, in that period, from 8,783 to 17,216.[24] West Charlestown was a rural island encircled by surging waves of industrial expansion and urban migration.

Charlestown was polarized by social change into two different communities: The eastern half resembled a neighborhood of Boston and the western half remained mostly rural. Many Bostonians streamed over the Charles River Bridge into east Charlestown to take advantage of rents there that were half the price asked in Boston.[25] The building of the toll-free Warren Bridge linking east Charlestown and Boston hastened settlement.[26] That urban district, integrated with the social life of the sprawling metropolis, seemed increasingly alien to the people of west Charlestown.[27] After 1820, the wealthiest property holders among the outlivers, feeling they received inferior services and aiming to initiate real estate and industrial development, agitated for separation. When they gained incorporation as the new town of Somerville, in 1842, the delighted inhabitants celebrated with a festive banquet graced by dancing and saluted by cannon fire.[28]

The township contained four square miles of hilly land with few improvements. The handful of schools Charlestown had supported were dilapidated; the roads suffered from years of neglect.[29] Not even a meetinghouse or church stood within the town's boundaries.[30] In colonial times, the founding of a parish usually was the precondition for the emergence of a new town, but Somerville lacked a religious institution to serve as the formative nucleus of community life.

Somerville was an overspill of the spreading metropolitan population with no coherent social form. What all Somerville residents had shared, however, was a desire to attain their own municipal status separate from Charlestown and neighboring communities. They resisted the political gravity of Boston that was pulling Brighton, Charlestown, Roxbury, and West Roxbury into its municipal boundaries.[31]

Like these towns, however, Somerville contained the potential to grow into a mixed community of commuters and locally employed workingmen. It lay within the "pre-streetcar metropolis," two to three miles from Boston, which could easily be linked to the city by commuter transport. Also, like the other towns outlying Boston, Somerville afforded inviting opportunities to venturesome capitalists as a site for manufacturing and commercial activity.[32]

When Somerville was incorporated in 1842, the townspeople were employed in farming, brickmaking, and commerce. But "new times demand new manners and new men," announced advertisements placed in Boston newspapers by Somerville promoters wishing to attract laborers, mechanics, and businessmen to the infant town.[33] In 1845, entrepreneurs operated three cordage manufactories, a tin works, and a paint manufactory.[34] A line of the Boston and Maine Railroad joined Somerville with Boston in that year, giving Somerville two railroad linkages with the city. The capacious transport facilities of the town lured new industries. By 1855, several more manufacturing enterprises boosted the output of finished products pouring from Somerville. Two rolling mills churned out sheets of iron; a plant fashioned steam engines and boilers; a foundry produced thousands of brass tubes; and a glass factory employing 100 workers made window panes for the buildings spreading across the metropolitan area. From 1845 to 1855, the old bleachery increased its cloth output by fivefold and doubled its work force.[35] The Commonwealth's policy of granting general incorporation helped industrialists penetrate the field of enterprise.[36]

As industries multiplied, the production of Somerville's chief agricultural goods slackened. Five thousand seven hundred bushels of potatoes were harvested in 1845, but only 1,400 bushels were gathered in 1855; hay production in those years dwindled from 985 tons to 630 tons. Brickmaking also tapered off from 27,566,000 bricks produced in 1845 to 17,000,000 bricks in 1855. Brickmaking employed 349 men in 1845, but engaged only 220 hands ten years later.[37] The fields and brickyards of Somerville gradually gave way to looming factory buildings and belching smokestacks.

The influx of newcomers seeking business opportunities was quickened by the growing industries, and also by the development in 1854 of commuter travel by hourly steam car to Boston.[38] In 1857, the Somerville Horse Railroad Company began service that carried passengers to main junctions in Somerville.[39]

The rush of settlement forced the town's population upward at dizzying speed. From a rural village of 1,013 in 1842, its population climbed to 3,540 in 1850, to 8,025 in 1860, and to 14,685 in 1870.[40] In three decades, Somerville's population multiplied by over fourteenfold. As the newcomers filled to capacity the town's available dwelling places, a wave of housing construction mounted. Land held for generations by a single family began to change hands regularly. The Massachusetts industrial census of 1855 reported that in the past ten years, "a large part of the farms in this town have been cut up into house and building lots."[41]

The town's valuation was boosted by the rise of population and the construction of new buildings. From $988,513 in 1842, the town's valuation leaped to $2,102,631 in 1850, $6,033,053 in 1860, and $15,775,000 in 1870.[42] With abundant unimproved land situated next to Boston and surrounding suburbs, the potential for housing development seemed limitless. Farmers holding large tracts, such as the Tufts family, began to speculate in real estate, as they realized the future of Somerville lay in residential development.[43]

With the advent of the building boom, the town government initiated physical improvements to make Somerville an attractive alternative to life in the central city. The Charlestown Gas Company ex-

Table 1.1. *Country of origin of Somerville's population, 1855, 1865*

	1855		1865	
	N	%	N	%
United States	4,171	72	7,050	75
English Canada	160	3	221	2
Ireland	1,305	22	1,729	18
England, Scotland, Wales	128	2	258	3
Germany and Holland	27	—	41	—
France	8	—	8	—
Italy	2	—	1	—
Other countries	5	—	32	—
Unknown	0	—	13	—
Total	5,806		9,353	

Sources: [Nathaniel B. Shurtleff], *Abstract of the Census of . . . Massachusetts . . . 1855 . . .* (Boston, 1857), pp. 118–19, Oliver Warner, *Abstract of the Census of Massachusetts, 1865 . . .* (Boston, 1867), pp. 72–3.

tended its pipes into Somerville in the 1850s, bringing convenient lighting to every part of the town.[44] The dependence of residents on wells ended in 1866, when arrangements were made with Charlestown to supply water from Mystic Lake.[45] Open drainage courses disappeared as the town undertook the construction of an extensive sewer network.[46]

A beckoning suburb with inexpensive homes and thriving manufactures was spreading next to Boston. The town attracted newcomers from several foreign lands, especially Ireland, Great Britain, and English Canada, who toiled in the brickyards, the railyards, the factories, and the construction sites. In 1855, 1,305 Irish immigrants lived in Somerville, comprising 22 percent of the population; by 1865, 1,729 Irish immigrants made up 18 percent of the town's population (Table 1.1). Migratory laborers from Nova Scotia and Newfoundland boarded with families, while Scottish and Welsh artisans set up their own households.[47] Only a handful of blacks established residence in Somerville from 1850 to 1870.[48]

The majority of newcomers, however, came from other parts of Massachusetts and neighboring states. Thirty-three percent of all adults in Somerville had come from other Massachusetts towns by 1875, and 26 percent had migrated from other states, chiefly from Maine, New Hampshire, and Vermont.[49] Other arrivals were mobile craftsmen and white-collar workers who escaped from crowded Boston neighborhoods to build homes on the green hills of Somerville. From there, it was a short commute to shops, factories, and offices in the metropolis.

The bulk of Somerville's population growth was produced by the arrival of immigrants and natives from outside the town. By 1875, these people accounted for 85 percent of the population increase since incorporation. Natural increase generated a fraction of population growth and reflected different rates of childbirth between native and foreign-born mothers. Whereas native mothers gave birth an average of 3 times each from 1855 to 1865, immigrant mothers each gave birth almost 5 times.[50] The immigrants of Somerville, due to the coming of the "famine Irish," comprised a quarter of the town by 1865[51] and were reproducing faster than the natives; but this natural increase was restrained by their high susceptibility to disease and devastating infant mortality.[52]

The family was the basic unit of habitation in the industrializing town. Newcomers frequently arrived as married couples; many came with two or more children. The gender ratio was nearly balanced in 1850 and 1860, reflecting the preponderance of conjugal units in the population.[53] The newcomers found Somerville a place where children could be raised in pleasant surroundings, away from the disease and disorders of the great city. Also, they were still within a short ride on the railroad or street railway to office or factory. Somerville was a hospitable setting for middle-class family life. A town of families also was a town of children: In 1865, 3,297 of the town's 9,353 inhabitants were under fifteen years of age.[54]

Household structure in 1850 varied according to property wealth and the occupation of the head of the family (Table 1.2)[55]. Households headed by white-collar workers often contained more children than those headed by manually employed fathers. White-collar households also had the most servants and boarders, but few resident relatives. High-white-collar families owned several thousand dollars in property; they had ample resources to support many children and a servant staff.[56] Manual workers' households had fewer children, and often included relatives and boarders to generate income since they had little property and low wages.

At midcentury, household structure shifted unevenly into a gradual decline in size and complexity. From 1850 to 1860, in every occupational group, the average number of children shrank. White-collar households increased their servants and boarders, but workingmen's families reduced the numbers of resident relatives, servants, and boarders. The households of unskilled Irish laborers shrank in all components: They had fewer children and took in fewer boarders and relatives by 1860 (Table 1.3).

Table 1.2. *Structure of households, 1850, 1860*

Head of household occupation	Year	N	Mean N children	Mean N relatives	Mean N servants or boarders	Mean real property ($)
High white collar	1850	21	3.19	0.00	0.71	$12,252
	1860	15	2.53	0.00	0.73	7,333
Low white collar	1850	44	2.43	0.00	0.41	1,516
	1860	68	2.03	0.03	0.79	888
Skilled	1850	63	2.32	0.03	0.49	2,540
	1860	93	2.29	0.02	0.19	1,070
Semiskilled	1850	9	2.56	0.21	0.44	778
	1860	38	1.79	0.03	0.37	795
Unskilled	1850	39	2.26	0.21	0.44	159
	1860	56	2.21	0.07	0.04	227

Table 1.3. *Structure of households headed by Irish-born laborers, 1850, 1860*

Year	N	Mean N children	Mean N relatives	Mean N servants or boarders	Mean real property ($)
1850	31	2.32	0.26	0.55	126
1860	51	2.25	0.04	0.02	249

Industrialization and the reclustering of mobile middle-income groups in Somerville transformed the economic basis of the social structure. From 1850 to l860, the labor market moved deep into the transition from farming to industrial employment. Manual workers comprised over two thirds of employed persons (Table 1.4). Semiskilled workers increased in that decade from 5 to 25 percent of the labor force, reflecting the impact of the factory system.

As an expanding working class replaced the farming population, the distribution of real property in the social order contracted. Twenty-eight percent of employed persons owned property in 1850, but only 18 percent had holdings in 1860. Furthermore the rate of property ownership dropped most sharply among low-white-collar, skilled, and semiskilled employees (Table 1.5). Property ownership was nearly universal among high-white-collar men, but only a small minority of low-manual workers were able to acquire real estate.

Table 1.4. *Employed persons by occupation, 1850, 1860*

Occupation	Year	Number	Percent
High white collar	1850	21	6.9
	1860	17	3.6
Low white collar	1850	70	23.2
	1860	130	27.8
Skilled	1850	95	31.6
	1860	127	27.1
Semiskilled	1850	16	5.4
	1860	119	25.4
Unskilled	1850	99	32.9
	1860	75	16.0

Table 1.5. *Rate of property-ownership by employed persons, 1850, 1860*

		Property owners		Persons without property	
		1850	1860	1850	1860
Total *N*		84	87	217	382
% total *N*		27.9	18.6	72.1	81.4
Range of property ($)		500–44,000	160–23,000		
Occupation					
High white collar	*N*	20	14	1	3
	%	95.2	82.4	4.8	17.7
Low white collar	*N*	25	25	45	106
	%	35.7	18.5	64.3	81.5
Skilled	*N*	30	30	65	97
	%	31.6	23.6	68.4	76.4
Semiskilled	*N*	3	12	13	107
	%	18.8	10.1	81.2	89.9
Unskilled	*N*	6	6	93	69
	%	6.1	8.0	93.9	92.0

Although propertyholding became more concentrated at the top of the occupational pyramid, it was redistributed in smaller units. The average in all quintiles of property values shrank from 1850 to 1860 (Table 1.6). This development was due to the subdivision of large farms into housing lots that were sold to new homebuyers.

Table 1.6. *Real estate values by quintile,*
1850, 1860

Quintile	Year	Average property values ($)
1	1850	18,705
	1860	12,819
2	1850	5,172
	1860	4,762
3	1850	3,344
	1860	3,029
4	1850	1,972
	1860	1,910
5	1850	1,155
	1860	905

The social structure was being polarized into a property-owning business class and a propertyless working class by growing entrepreneurialism and the industrial expansion of a low-skilled labor system.[57] Somerville's dynamic economy had introduced a sharpening social division. At the top of the social ladder were Yankee businessmen who ventured into new enterprises and invested in the real estate market. At the bottom were the immigrant Irish (see Table 1.7). In 1860, seven out of ten Irish workers clustered in low manual jobs and nine out of ten owned no property.[58]

The ideology of industrial progress and the common school movement

Early Somerville was controlled by Whig voters who anticipated that community growth would ride along the twin rails of industrial and moral progress.[59] They expected the schools, the churches, and government to nourish the free individual's spirit of ascetic self-discipline that drove in tandem with the material advance of the whole community.[60] Whigs strongly supported educational reform as part of their overall conception of governance of the industrial polity.[61]

The Whig majority in Somerville ran "a New Model government" seeking to boost the town through vigorous and economical stewardship. The town fathers in 1845 confidently assessed the fruits of intelligent government:

> by the rapid progress of converting the farms of Somerville into streets, house-lots and squares, we see on all sides the embryo

Table 1.7. *Rate of property-ownership by Irish-born employed persons, 1850, 1860*

	Property owners		Persons without property	
	1850	1860	1850	1860
Total *N*	4	13	64	132
% total *N*	5.9	9.0	94.1	91.0
Range of property ($)	500–1,800	200–6,000		
Occupation				
High white collar *N*	0	0	0	0
%	0	0	0	0
Low white collar *N*	0	1	1	6
%	0	14.3	100	85.7
Skilled *N*	0	3	1	20
%	0	13.0	100	87.0
Semiskilled *N*	0	3	1	51
%	0	5.6	100	94.4
Unskilled *N*	4	6	61	55
%	6.2	9.8	93.8	90.2

workings of a large and popolous [sic] town; that . . . the enter-prize [sic] and energy of our own people is exciting the industrial population of the neighboring towns and cities, and many desir-able families are hoping and intending soon to escape from the dust and tumult of Boston and to enjoy the rural scenery . . . of our hillsides.[62]

Whiggery's vision of industrial progress was appealing in a com-muter suburb growing through the arrival of self-made men who pur-sued business enterprise and political leadership.

George O. Brastow had been one of the eager young men who came to make his fortune and to raise a family in the new town. Born in the village of Wrentham, Massachusetts, Brastow moved to west Charlestown when he turned twenty-seven in 1838. He helped lead the drive to turn west Charlestown into the new township of Somer-ville in 1842. He was elected a Somerville selectman in 1845 and served on the school committee from 1847 to 1862. Like many rising entre-preneurs, Brastow turned from Whig to Republican and won posts as state representative and senator before becoming Somerville's first mayor in 1872.[63] Endowed with a sense for opportunities, Brastow added success in business to his achievements in politics. He ventured profitably into real estate and home construction. He founded the Somerville Horse Railroad Company in 1857, giving the community its first street railway line. Brastow's projects powerfully stimulated the major impulses of economic change transforming the town.[64]

John S. Edgerly also exemplified the union of enterprise and public spirit exhibited in the careers of Somerville's early leaders. Edgerly was born in the New Hampshire farm town of Meredith in 1804. As a youth he struck out from the depressed countryside and headed for Boston to find better prospects. In 1836 he moved to the Winter Hill district of Charlestown, in the future area of Somerville. Along with Brastow and other prominent Whigs, he spearheaded the movement to incorporate Somerville in 1842. Edgerly became a wealthy merchant who invested in real estate. A true founding father of Somerville, he was elected to the first board of selectmen, serving for fourteen years, acting as its chairman during most of that period, and also served on the school committee. His dedication to public welfare was legendary: It was said that in a heavy snow "no night was too dark or road too bad for him to start with his lantern and shovel to break out any place that his horse could not get through, whenever there was need." The Edgerly School was named in honor of his civic deeds the same year Brastow was elected the first mayor of Somerville.[65]

George O. Brastow and John S. Edgerly were representative of the Yankee business class, whose broad mandate of civic duty included a high priority for public education. Both served on the school committee soon after Somerville was incorporated. They hoped that schooling would disseminate the knowledge and morality that enabled self-made success and good citizenship such as theirs. Their interwoven commitments to public education, government, and enterprise expressed a world-view in which the common school was part of the transforming growth forces of urbanizing communities.[66]

The half-formed sense of communal identity in Somerville presented both a problem and an opportunity for common-school promoters like Brastow and Edgerly. On the one hand, the inchoate consciousness of civic affairs in the new town had to be galvanized into an active sponsorship of public schooling. On the other hand, the absence of preestablished municipal priorities permitted willful new men to innovate in public education. The educational frontier in Somerville was still a tabula rasa. The fledgling town inherited from Charlestown neglected elementary schools overflowing with pupils. Onto the blank slate left in their hands, the town fathers projected Calvinist anxieties of impending disorder and a transcending vision of rational progress – the guiding ideology that would shape the future schools of Somerville.

The social changes they had unleashed through capitalism and suburban development filled them with profound ambivalence. They were worried by the poverty and social disorder they saw in the lives of the poor Irish in Somerville, but they were exhilarated by the pace of the community's material advancement. To overcome these contradictory tendencies, they heeded the prophetic writings of Horace Mann, the first Secretary of the Massachusetts Board of Education, whose career, as historians have observed, "mirrored the tensions of the Victorian era." Mann "glorified railroads and economic development," while deploring the concomitants of "class conflict and extremes of poverty and wealth."[67] As a solution to the contradictions of his age, he urged the common school to bridge the growing chasm between capitalist and laborer, between Yankee and Celt. Mann advised that the common school would be the "great equalizer" in an age when "fortunes increase on the one hand, and new privation is added to poverty on the other."[68] Mann and his successors as Secretary, Barnas Sears and George Boutwell, asserted that, by properly training character, schools would repair an individual's moral flaws leading to poverty and vice. They believed that education would replace ignorance with knowledge and civic values that would counteract the city's corrupting influences.

Evidence of the degeneration of the uneducated was manifest to Somerville citizens. They read the Charlestown newspapers that told them of the dangers to peace and property presented by the ignorant poor at the border of their neighborhood. In the winter of 1852, a rash of juvenile crimes struck Charlestown. The Charlestown *City Advertiser* described the disturbances and focused on the plight of "a boy of thirteen years, who was detected in stealing" and who "was sent to the Almshouse." "In this case, as in almost all those which come to our notice," observed the paper, "the boy could neither read nor write, never having been sent to school and has but just commenced learning the alphabet."[69]

From a grander perspective, schools would fulfill industrialism's promise of a more abundant life for all, by cultivating the inventive and practical intelligence of the people. Bustling newcomers on the board of selectmen and the school committee were captivated by Horace Mann's vision of "the locomotive, taking up its burden of a hundred tons and transporting it for hundreds of miles . . . ; the steamboat cleaving its rapid way, triumphant over wind and tide; the powerloom yielding products of greater richness and abundance in a single day, than all the inhabitants of Tyre could have manufactured in years."

They agreed with the great school reformer that such technological progress was not "the result of outward riches or art," but of "intelligence," an "inward force" which "has been awakened and . . . replenished . . . by . . . Common Schools."[70]

The famous chairman of Somerville's school committee from 1843–7, Dr. Luther V. Bell, clearly envisioned the civilizing mission of the common schools. Superintendent of the McLean Asylum for the Insane since 1837, Dr. Bell was regarded by his fellow citizens as "the first statesman . . . whose writings and political championship of education made him a close second to the illustrious Horace Mann." A newcomer from Chester, New Hampshire, Bell achieved a reputation as an international authority on mental disease. A humanitarian who used science to restore reason to afflicted minds, he saw the common school as the lamp guiding the rational development of industrial civilization. As chair of the school committee, Bell was in a powerful position to propagate an idealized conception of the public schools to his colleagues and to the town meeting.[71]

Envisioning public education as a key to social betterment, Somerville's fathers aimed to give it maximum popular impact. They were confident in this course. As New England heirs to revolutionary civic traditions, they inherited the Enlightenment faith in the redemptive power of popular intelligence and individual virtue. They infused this faith with the Protestant reformer's sense of mission and the Whig's confidence in government's role in social amelioration. They aimed to enlarge the republican mandate for educating the whole populace by creating a universal public school system. "Knowledge and moral culture shall no longer be confined to the few," proclaimed the Somerville school committee, "while virtue, truth, and all excellence, shall spread over the earth like the light of the sun, redeeming the world from misery and ignorance."[72]

Population growth and public-school expansion

The explosive population growth caused by suburban migration jolted the town fathers' utopian idealization of the common school into the hard ground of reality. Common-school promoters worried that teachers and scholars were handicapped in classrooms overcrowded by waves of newcomer children. The challenge to the successful conduct of school business was simple and inescapable: Would the town be able to hire more teachers, build new schools, and develop an institutional structure for the school system capable of handling the growing student body?

The rapid increase in Somerville's population thus acted as a stim-

Table 1.8. *Percentage of school-age children anually
enrolled in school compared to other towns, 1846–
70*

	School-age children enrolling (%)[a]	Rank in state
1846	65	185 out of 311
1849	66	257 out of 316
1855	83	72 out of 331
1860	80	114 out of 334
1865	81	104 out of 334
1870	91	29 out of 340

[a] In 1846, "school-age" children defined as those 4–16
years of age. In all other years it refers to children
5–15 years old.
*Sources: 11th, 14th, 20th, 25th, 30th, 35th Annual Re-
ports of the Massachusetts Board of Education,* appendixes.

ulant for educational innovation and reorganization. Rising enrollments pressured town leaders to expand and to reform the school
system. As a result of their adaptive and experimental efforts, annual
enrollment rates rose steadily.

"The rapid increase of school children in Somerville at once sur-
prises us, and demands attention," warned the school committee in
1851. Persons of school age showed "an increase of one hundred per
cent in five years." A steady rise in the proportion of children five to
fifteen years of age attending the public schools further increased school
enrollment. More and more parents were sending their children regularly to Somerville's classrooms. In 1846, only 65 percent of school-
age children enrolled, and Somerville ranked 185th out of 311 towns
in the state in percentage of the school-age population enrolled in
school. By 1870, 91 percent of those of school age were students, and
Somerville jumped in percentage enrolled to 29th out of 340 towns in
the Commonwealth (Table 1.8).

The school committee invested heavily in the construction of more
classroom buildings, but the rushing tide of newly enrolled students
still overtook the new facilities. They lamented, "Since [1845] five new
[school]houses have been erected and are now occupied by more than
three hundred and fifty pupils!"[73] Between 1842 and 1871, school
construction struggled to keep pace as the number of primary-school

Table 1.9. *Attendance at primary, grammar, and high schools, 1842–71*

	1842		1849		1861	1871
N primary schools	5		6		12	NA
N grammar schools	1		3		4	5
N subgrammar schools	0		0		6	NA
	1842		1849		1861	1871
	Winter	Summer	Winter	Summer		
N primary students	198	223	381	436	842	1,485
Avg. primary attendance	157	171	258	266	615	1,363
% attending	79.3	76.7	67.7	61.0	73.0	91.8
N grammar students[a]	74	70	278	310	782	1,305
Avg. grammar attendance	50	55	189	172	657	1,228
% attending	67.7	78.6	68.0	55.5	84.0	94.1
N HS students	—[b]		—		83	161
Avg. HS attendance	—		—		77	157
% attending	—		—		92.8	97.7

[a] Includes intermediate or subgrammar school pupils in 1861, 1871.
[b] High school did not exist.
Sources: *School Committee Records*, 1842, pp. 1–9; *Annual School Committee Reports*, 1849, p. 10; 1860, p. 102; 1861, p. 3; 1871, pp. 96–9.

pupils multiplied by seven times and the number of grammar-school students by almost twenty (Table 1.9).

The community had a variety of interests in building new schools besides the basic need for housing students. Boosterism was an important motive. Town fathers wanted attractive facilities that would give Somerville an advantage over other suburbs in the competition for desirable newcomers. Residents viewed their suburb as a hospitable refuge for the family and naturally wanted schools close to their homes so that getting to school would not be hazardous or difficult for children.[74] Groups of private citizens petitioned the town government each year for new schools to be located in their districts.[75] Lastly, residents who shared with the school committee a conception of the ameliorative potential of schooling wanted a complete system of facilities that would make elementary education truly "common," comprehensive of all groups in the town.[76]

Despite gratifying gains in attendance and the construction of a school system, the turbulence of urban growth disrupted the smooth operation of the schools. The school committee attributed the problems of retaining good teachers and instructional quality to "the disadvantages of a shifting and unsettled population." They blamed the lack of continuity in a child's educational career upon the constant movement of families and complained that many pupils entered the town at an "advanced age, or remove from it, after a brief residence." They watched teachers stagger under the repeated influx of new students who had to be absorbed in the classroom. The committeemen noted in 1854 that "more than half the scholars now attending school in town, have entered its limits within the last five [years]."[77]

To meet the spiraling demand for schoolrooms, the school committee multiplied the number of levels in the educational system, thereby relieving demographic strain on the primary and grammar schools. In 1852, the Somerville Free Public High School was opened, much to the satisfaction of the school committee, which had promoted it for several years as the necessary capstone to a public school system.[78] In 1853, an intermediate or subgrammar school was inserted between the primary school and the grammar school.[79] Pupils now spent their first three years in a primary school, three years in an intermediate school, and three years in a grammar school. This arrangement organized classes into a crude graded hierarchy where pupils of proximate ages and educational attainment learned together in one class. Still, within a single grammar school class, a teacher instructed pupils ranging in age from 10 to 13 years old. Ability and age grouping, however, helped educators install a coherent set of stages for learning. An ordered process of mental development was institutionalized in the graded structure.[80]

The creation of a middle link – the intermediate school – was more economical and provided more contact between teacher and pupil. It reduced the cost of the grammar schools by assigning a female teacher, who received one third the salary of a male teacher, to what had been the first three years of grammar schools.[81] The school committee hoped that the subdivision of the grammar school would keep class size from exceeding "the ability of the teacher to bestow upon [pupils] the considerate, motherly or personal attention, which they will require." They wished to avoid "the catastrophes of New York" that "furnish a sad argument against the collection together of such numbers of little children."[82] Thus they adverted disparagingly to the Lancastrian monitorial system of the New York City schools, in which hundreds of pupils were taught in one class.[83] The leaders of the proud young town were intent on keeping the suburban school from becoming a

Table 1.10. *Population and town valuation, 1842–70*

	Population	Increase	Valuation ($)	Increase
1842	1,013	—	988,513	—
1850	3,540	249	2,102,631	113
1860	8,025	126	6,033,053	187
1870	14,693	83	15,775,000	161

Source: Somerville, *Annual Town Reports,* 1868, p. 175; 1870, p. 113.

Table 1.11. *Average number of students per teacher,*
1846–70

	Somerville	Boston
1846	55.8	58.8
1850	52.7	55.6
1860	54.2	50.8
1870	42.1	39.9

Source: 11th, 15th, 25th, and 35th Annual Reports of the
Massachusetts Board of Education, appendixes.

factory-like urban school. "With us," they asserted, "the opposing city arguments, drawn from dense population and economy, entirely fail."

The town fathers hoped Somerville's new facilities and expanding economy would allow teachers to provide more personalized attention to the individual child. The town's valuation, which grew faster than its population from 1850 to 1870, would supply the funds to build more schools and hire more teachers (Table 1.10).[84] Nevertheless, the ever-increasing number of school-age children forced the school committee to pack the classrooms densely. Somerville's 50 to 1 student–teacher ratio was about as high as that found in the Boston public-school system (Table 1.11).

The rapid growth of the public schools in Somerville undermined private schools and academies. Two private schools taught sixty-five scholars in 1850, who paid $300 each for yearly tuition.[85] By 1860 only one private school was in operation. It enrolled only seventeen students and charged $1,700.[86] At such an exorbitant cost, only a few wealthy families supported private schools. The people of Somerville had committed their educational future to the public school system.

That the founding of Somerville coincided with the launching of the common-school movement was of utmost significance for the role of public education in the town. The common schools were adopted to stabilize and discipline the social order of the early stage of suburbanization in which wealth and power concentrated in the hands of newcomer Whig capitalists, while industrial production endangered craftsmen and proletarianized workers. The agenda for urban development gave a central place to the common-school ideology aimed at healing social disorder and restoring economic opportunity through popular schooling.

The common school catalyzed civic patriotism and communal identity in a new industrializing town. Somerville boosters like George O. Brastow took pride in their universal school system as the outstanding achievement of the fledgling community. Somerville's Albert Winship, editor of the influential New England *Journal of Education,* recalled that the first schools founded by Somerville citizens "gave them confidence, courage and reputation" and acted as "village rallying points."[87] But overcrowding constantly threatened to erode Somerville's educational advances. The high ratio of students to staff was the consequence of the gross increase of the school-age population caused by migration and the common school's success in attracting a rising proportion of children and youths. Urban growth and industrial change enlarged and stimulated the public school system. Its effectiveness would be determined by how the expansionary forces that had given it life could be turned into enduring mechanisms of institutional support and operation.

2   *The evolution of educational leadership*

In mid-nineteenth-century Somerville, the functioning of the common-school system rested unsteadily on growth from a rural community to a dynamic urban society. To secure it on a firmer foundation, the town fathers invented arguments to intensify community support for the schools, recruited able new leaders to manage them soundly, and endeavored to turn a casual collection of amateur teachers into a bureaucracy with a professional ideology and careerist occupational goals. By 1872, when Somerville obtained a city charter, the suburb had developed a permanent civic commitment to the progress of public education, a tradition of strong leadership in the school committee, and a large corps of professionalized teachers, dominated by women, who taught a curriculum that emphasized character training and practical intellectual skills.

The common school and the public interest

The common school was the forge shaping a popular conception of the public interest in Somerville. Because the town's early development was shaped by the common-school movement, educational innovation quickly became the focus of civic affairs.

In 1842, the town's first school committee inherited five ill-maintained schools from Charlestown. Four were primary schools and one was a grammar school. All were located in east Somerville, the densest center of population in the new town.[1] Students spent their first four years in primary school and four more years in the grammar school. School buildings were in very poor condition and the increasing enrollments made the construction of more facilities imperative. The town, therefore, immediately appropriated funds for the construction of two schoolhouses in the following year.

In the winter of 1842 only 68 percent of pupils enrolled in grammar school attended class, although 80 percent of enrolled primary pupils attended. The percentage of attendance changed only slightly in the next three years. In the winter of 1845, grammar school attendance rose to 75 percent and primary attendance dropped to 70 percent.[2]

23

One teacher assigned to each schoolhouse taught all the pupils in a single crowded classroom where 4-year-olds and 12-year-olds learned together. Attendance in the summer session was often lower than in the winter, as boys and girls stayed away from the school desk to help out at home, at the shop, or on the farm.[3] The school committee criticized "the withdrawal of the largest scholars" by parents who needed income or labor from their children.[4]

Faced with sluggish attendance rates, the school committee indefatigably worked at persuading the townspeople to send their children to school regularly. The commercial elite of the town – the farmers, brickmakers, and merchants – spent generously for public education, yet they did not encourage their children to make full use of the schools. The school committee publicly presented itself as a united body to impress parents with their clear resolve to raise attendance rates. In annual reports that mixed the ingredients of religious sermons and political tracts, committeemen regularly described the "uniform harmony of their deliberations, and the almost equally unanimous agreement of their decisions."[5]

Compounding the diffidence of parents was the difficulty of travel to the schools. Early Somerville was interlaced with muddy roads and cow paths, making the daily trek to the schoolhouse tiring and hazardous. Moreover, the school committee did not relocate schools to more convenient sites.[6]

The opening of housing tracts in the outer districts required that more schools be established according to the changing spatial distribution of the population. The dispersion of the townspeople pressured the school committee to build schools in outlying areas to achieve optimum geographic coverage. The town meeting first petitioned the school committee to provide more accessible schools in 1845, a demand reiterated frequently, and sometimes acrimoniously, as the inhabitants pushed their settlements toward the town's boundaries.[7]

Despite the demand for public schools, they suffered from low attendance rates. Sluggish attendance reflected popular apathy and even mistrust toward the common school. Many parents viewed the common school as an intrusive arm of government thrust into the private domain of child rearing. Others were skeptical of an expensive tax-supported institution whose usefulness was yet unproven.

A violent classroom incident in 1845 crystalized the uneasy relations between the public and the common school. A pupil's assault upon his teacher in the outlying Walnut Hill School sparked a heated debate over parents' responsibility to submit their children to the control of schoolmen. Walnut Hill School was a combined primary and grammar school lying in the western tip of Somerville where a scat-

tered population of farmers felt "considerable doubts" about the necessity for public education. The school committee had been troubled
by the school's average attendance of eighteen pupils in the winter of
1845, the lowest of all schools. During that term, Martin Draper, the
young master, was the victim of an "unprovoked and brutal attack"
by a student who was over 16 years old. Draper was the latest master
at Walnut Hill School to suffer from student misconduct: His prede-
cessor, George Swan, had also faced problems, though not as severe.[8]

During a formal inquiry, the school committee was struck by the
depth of hostility toward Draper expressed by the schoolchildren's
parents. The committee learned that even before the attack, Walnut
Hill parents, led by Jesse Kimball and Andrew Dearborn, registered
"bitter and eagerly pressed complaints against the master." Kimball
was a 27-year-old brickmaker from Maine whose 5-year-old son attended Walnut Hill School. Dearborn was 35 years old, a farmer from
New Hampshire, and had a 10-year-old boy and a 7-year-old girl at
the school.[9] Both were young men from northern New England who
were uneasy about consigning to the alien dictates of the town
schoolmaster the children they had reared in their own customs and
values. Their complaints were not explained in detail, but the inquiry
record suggests that they objected to Draper's method of instruction
and his disciplinary policy, which probably entailed corporal punishment.[10]

The dispute between teacher and parents was an outgrowth of a
fundamental conflict between a stubborn context of rural traditional
habits, called by historian Paul G. Faler "the obstinate cultural legacy
of the eighteenth century," and the newly emergent industrial morality of school reformers. Faler concluded,

> This clash of values was evidently at the root of the conflict be-
> tween school reformers and teachers, on the one hand, and a sig-
> nificantly large portion of the people of Massachusetts on the other.
> . . . If [reformers] sought to instill in children the virtues of self-
> discipline, respect for law, obedience to authority, and self-imposed
> restraints on "natural impulses," they encountered the progeny of
> an age that had, at best, been indifferent to these values or, at
> worst, had encouraged their opposites. The task of the teacher in
> gaining respect, maintaining attentiveness, stimulating interest and
> teaching children to curb their impulses is difficult enough for the
> instructor whose efforts are duplicated and reinforced by others.
> The task is infinitely greater if the instructor is seeking to change
> habits of behavior and values that the student shares not only with
> his peers but with his parents and much of the society in which he
> lives.[11]

But this clash of values went beyond the conflict between traditional and industrial conceptions of personal discipline. It also involved the views of parents on the proper relation between the sphere of family government and the sphere of communal government. A vehement minority of parents sharply disagreed with the school committee on how much authority should be ceded by parents to an officer of government, the teacher. Many families found it uncomfortable to turn over their children to a stranger who treated them according to the officious standards set by the school committee.[12]

At the Draper inquiry, plaintiffs, the defendant, and concerned citizens testified in a raucous atmosphere. The school committee secretary lamented the absence of reasoned cooperation by all parties, declaring that "obstacles and difficulties have been wantonly and unreasonably interposed to nullify every effort to have an orderly and successful session."[13]

When completed, the inquest unanimously found that "nothing had appeared in the conduct of the teacher indicating the slightest blameworthiness in him. . . ."[14] Instead, the school committee chastized the townspeople for their failure to cooperate with schoolmen. Indeed, the school committee warned that "the spirit of depreciation and dislike of any teacher is easily carried from the old to the young."

They also blamed the "black days" of the Draper affair on the admission policy for older students. The committeemen were not prohibiting a person over sixteen years from taking a seat in the common school. Rather, they felt that a school such as Walnut Hill did not have facilities or the staff to instruct and discipline adolescents properly. The school committee thus took its inquiry as an opportunity to urge that a public "High School of our own" be established to remedy this condition.

The Draper affair had implications beyond the classroom, for it challenged the civic consensus the young town government had sought to establish through popular participation in building a public school system. The school committee responded vigorously to the incident, because at stake was not only the success of the common-school movement but also the ability of town government to create and command a conception of the public interest.[15] Thus the school committee used the Draper affair as a means to lecture the populace on their obligation to submit their private concerns to the control of a public institution. They turned an educational controversy into a civics lesson. They declared it was the obligation of parents trustfully to yield their children to the charge of school officers. "Society has rights in each youth," explained the committeemen, "and duties in relation to him from which it cannot escape, which the parent cannot assume and which he ought not to interfere with."[16]

All school officers acted as "trustees" of the town's interest in its population of children. Moreover, they had a commission upon which civility itself rested. The schools were "essential to a republican form of government"; they required every citizen's support "because society must be protected from the dangers of ignorance and vice."[17] The social consequences were so enormous that parents must stop acting as if "they have rights to prescribe or dictate" educational policy. The public interest demanded that "when a scholar enters one of the public school-houses and his name is registered as one of its members . . . , he becomes under the guidance of the laws of the land, completely removed from the control of his parents and guardians . . . both as to discipline and instruction."

Although that pronouncement sounded Draconian to some parents, the school committee assured them that this arrangement would not produce "tyranny." The political process would guarantee the influence of parents. "If the Trustees of the Public do not fulfill their trust adequately and faithfully," the committeemen reminded them, "they are answerable to the law and to a public will, speaking in annual elections."[18] The spread of free public schools required the populace understand that the public interest was in the interest of every individual citizen, and by participating in its formulation they protected themselves against governmental infringement.

Furthermore, the school committee pointed out schoolteachers had a clear duty only to execute the public trust that reposed in them. They had to operate above the particular claims of "any self-constituted body or individual parent, whether he pay much or little in his share of public burdens." The educator would not recognize the special status of parents who paid more in support of the schools, but would regard all parents equally and obtain their cooperation. The school committee affirmed that the teacher knew "the true interests of a scholar" and should never surrender "to the wrong judgments of selfish interests of any human being, whether connected by the ties of consanguinity or not." Common-school reformers emphasized that the time had come when expert professionals knew better how to educate children than their own parents.[19]

The school committee of 1845 also stressed the public's duty to pay taxes for support of the town schools. They described a tradition extending back to the Plymouth Colony enjoining every inhabitant to sacrifice personal stakes for the common weal. "Those who have no children," announced the committeemen, "or who would prefer to

Table 2.1 *School expenditure compared to other Massachusetts towns, 1846–70*

	Rank in per pupil expenditure	Rank according to percent spent on schools of taxable valuation
1846	10 out of 311	NA
1849	16 out of 316	NA
1855	4 out of 311	3 out of 320
1860	6 out of 333	23 out of 334
1865	11 out of 335	3 out of 334
1870	9 out of 336	1 out of 330

Sources: 11th, 14th, 20th, 25th, 30th, 35th Annual Reports of the Massachusetts Board of Education, appendixes.

educate them at their own firesides, or elsewhere, are compelled to assist in educating the children of others." They scolded meddlesome parents who "hold out the idea that the schools are theirs . . . because they pay a large tax." That attitude would be as improper as thinking a citizen could interfere with the operation of a court of common law. The public school and the court of law, alike, were trustees of the civil order that required disinterested fiscal support.[20]

The general consequence of the Draper affair was the school committee's campaign to formulate and polemicize a civic rationale for popular support of a public school system. For the next two decades, they reiterated these claims on behalf of the public interest with increasing effectiveness. The people of Somerville came to regard the generous funding of the public schools as a cardinal civic necessity. Few towns in Massachusetts consistently appropriated a higher share of their annual budget to schools or spent more on each student than Somerville (Table 2.1). As the willingness to finance the schools grew, more and more parents came to view the schools as an investment in the town's welfare and as a trust for future generations. They sent their children more regularly to obtain the fruits of their tax dollars. Somerville climbed steadily in school-attendance rates from one of the lowest ranking towns in the Commonwealth after the Draper affair to the highest decile of towns by 1870.[21] It took over twenty years of promoting the common school for the town leaders to popularize the institution as a trustee of the public interest, to convince the people that it was as necessary for communal welfare as a court of law.

Table 2.2. *Expenditures on schools and roads, 1842–65*

Year	Town budget ($)	Amount spent on schools ($)	% spent on schools	Amount spent on roads ($)	% spent on roads
1842	5,652	1,288	23	2,077	37
1843	6,585	3,394	52	1,630	25
1844	6,574	2,761	42	1,910	29
1846	13,862	9,712	70	2,179	16
1849	19,545	5,475	28	2,419	12
1855	42,045	12,821	30	7,626	18
1860	42,375	16,819	40	6,589	16
1865	92,123	23,980	26	12,023	13

Source: Somerville, *Annual Town Reports.*

*Social origins of educational leadership: selectmen and the school
committee*

The ideology and policies that popularized public education were
produced by a changing leadership elite. The local oligarchy of farmers, merchants, and brickmakers who had organized the movement
that incorporated Somerville in 1842 took seats on the first board of
selectmen and the school committee. These founders were also the
religious pillars of the town, organizing Somerville's First Congregational Society in 1844.[22] Economic, political, and religious leadership
were concentrated in the hands of a small faction.

The first selectmen made the improvement of Somerville's roads[23]
and schools, which had suffered from years of neglect by the Charlestown city government, the highest priority. Thus they obtained from
the town appropriations of $2,077 for highways and $1,288 for schools
out of the first annual budget of $5,652.[24] In the next two decades,
public education and transportation remained the top fiscal items,
receiving over one half of the town's annual expenditures (Table 2.2).

The school committee became the most active organ of town government. Flowery reports of its business were issued annually to pub-
licize its work, whereas annual reports of the board of selectmen were
not published until 1857.[25] Four of the first eight school committeemen were charter members of the First Congregational Society of Somerville.[26] Religious leadership affected their sense of educational
mission: Protestant stewardship went hand in hand with supervising
the schooling of the town's children. As a result, the church elders
on the school committee acted to prevent the teaching of overexuber-

ant "pagan" classical literature, and instead exhorted the classroom
reading of exemplary literature tinged with Protestant moralism.[27]

During the 1840s, the school committee and selectmen cooperated
actively to promote public schooling. Three selectmen simultaneously
served on the school committee, thereby uniting the policy goals of
both organizations. The early custodianship of the public schools
hinged on an alliance between the farmer gentry and business entrepreneurs. Of town leaders from 1842 to 1850 who could be traced to
the manuscript records of the U.S. Census, five of fourteen selectmen
were farmers and six were merchants or dealers; six out of eighteen
school committeemen were farmers and four were merchants or dealers (Table 2.3). This partnership in support of the common school was
the outgrowth of the reshuffling of elites in the town as industrialization and urbanization altered the social structure. Both leading
farmers and businessmen banked upon public education to provide
social stability.

Newcomer politicians were quick to take part in the town government. Even in the 1840s, eleven of fourteen selectmen and eight of
eighteen school committeemen came from another Massachusetts town
or another state. In the 1850s, seven of thirteen selectmen and ten of
twenty-three school committeemen were newcomers; and in the next
decade eleven of thirteen selectmen and nine of twelve school committeemen had migrated to Somerville. A new mixed elite of merchants, businessmen, professionals, and artisans pushed the old
agrarian elite from the seats of municipal government. After 1850,
only one farmer served on the board of selectmen and none sat on
the school committee. Both selectmen and school committeemen came
from the wealthiest class, the highest quintiles of taxpayers and real-
property owners in Somerville (Tables 2.4, 2.5, 1.6: chapter 1). Mobile
settlers, wishing to be led by men like themselves, elected successful
newcomers who had a stake in growth and who were willing to take
bold initiatives to achieve it.[28]

Newcomer politicians were especially eager to participate in forming policy on the school committee. Ambitious "new men" won school
committee posts with such frequency that no consistent leadership
could sustain control of that organization. "Since 1852," observed the
1857 Annual Report of the school committee, "there have been several sweeping changes in the constitution of the school committee
. . .: In 1853, when the majority of the board was composed of new
members; in 1854, when nearly all of the board of the preceding year,
was changed, and in 1856, when every member save one of the board
of 1855 was displaced."

Complaints rose about the discontinuity in leadership and policy

Table 2.3. *Social characteristics of selectmen and school committeemen, 1842–70*

	Selectmen			School committeemen		
	1842–50	1851–60	1861–70	1842–50	1851–60	1861–70
N traced	14	13	13	18	23	12
N untraced	4	3	4	4	5	5
Mean age at first term	46	42	46	43	38	44
Mean N children	3.7	3.4	3.5	3.6	2.5	2.6
Place of birth:						
Massachusetts (locality unspecified)[a]	3	6	2	9	13	4
Massachusetts (outside Charlestown/Somerville)	3	2	6	1	3	4
Other state	8	5	5	7	7	5
Foreign	0	0	0	0	0	0
Unknown	0	0	0	1	0	0
Selectmen also on School Committee	3	1	0	1	0	0
Occupation:						
Farmer	5	0	1	6	0	0
Merchant	2	3	3	1	2	2
Dealer in goods	4	1	4	3	2	1
Manufacturer	1	0	1	1	1	1
Professional	0	0	1	4	9	5
Other business	1	2	2	1	3	1
Clerical	0	1	0	0	4	0
Skilled	1	6	1	1	2	2
Semiskilled	0	0	0	0	0	0
Unskilled	0	0	0	1	0	0
No occupation	0	0	0	0	0	1

[a] Could include Charlestown or Somerville.
Source: Manuscript schedules for Somerville of the 1850 and 1860 U.S. Census; Samuels and Kimball, eds., *Somerville Past and Present*, "Biographies"; Hamilton Hurd, *History of Middlesex County, Massachusetts*, p. 775–7.

formation. The school committee realized that "the result" of these sudden shifts in leadership was "hazardous to the welfare of the schools" and had "defeated all hope of a regular and consistent system of school management." To end the commotion, the town passed

Table 2.4. *Property taxes paid by members of the school committee and board of selectmen, 1842–70 (in $)*

Year	Rate per $1,000	School committee, mean tax per member	Selectmen, mean tax per member
1842	4.29	24.80	49.39
1844	4.15	38.74	45.02
1846	3.12	27.75	45.82
1848	4.68	53.88	41.15
1850	5.65	53.58	54.12
1852	5.73	32.82	40.01
1854	5.00	18.35	48.30
1856	5.80	45.77	73.54
1858	6.60	44.63	108.42
1860	5.70	28.23	73.41
1862	9.00	50.90	82.68
1864	11.50	39.62	122.75
1866	17.00	92.29	255.64
1868	19.00	198.12	317.30

Source: Somerville, *Annual Town Reports,* 1868, p. 175.

Table 2.5. *Real property owned by selectmen and school committeemen*

Year elected		N	Mean real property holdings ($)
1842–50	Selectmen	14	18,186
	School committeemen	18	10,900
1851–60	Selectmen	13	4,385
	School committeemen	23	4,817
1861–70	Selectmen	13	7,231
	School committeemen	12	2,311

Source: U.S. Census manuscript schedules 1850, 1860.

a law permitting only one third of the committee to be replaced each year.[29]

Although both the board of selectmen and school committee were captured by rising newcomers, their memberships differed in significant ways. A comparative analysis of the characteristics of individual selectmen and school committeemen reveals that the latter were socially positioned so as to have developed a greater interest in education prior to holding office. The school committee drew many professional men, differing markedly from the board of selectmen, on which only one professional served from 1842 to 1871. In contrast, eighteen professional men – physicians, lawyers, clergymen, and educators – sat on the school committee. These members of the school committee knew profoundly the value of education, since they had had unusual training to attain their callings. Furthermore, some of the professional men on the school committee had first-hand experience, such as lawyers Oren S. Knapp and Charles S. Lincoln, who had worked as schoolmasters before joining the bar.[30]

Another significant difference was that school committeemen were substantially less wealthy than selectmen, owning roughly half as much property (Tables 2.4 and 2.5). They were striving for social mobility with smaller material advantages. Perhaps this is why they also seemed to have practiced family limitation, having fewer children than the selectmen. Limiting family size could help invest more attention and resources in each child. Furthermore, because they had less resources to pass on to their children, they were more concerned than the selectmen that a free public school system be available to supply effectively the knowledge and character training needed to succeed in life. That school committee members had a fundamentally different orientation in town affairs than selectmen was also revealed by a pattern of separate officeholding. From 1850 until 1870, only one individual obtained a seat in both organizations.

Curricular innovations: functionalist intelligence and character training

Because they believed that public education had to supply useful knowledge to be truly popular and beneficial, the school committee created a curriculum designed to nurture practical mental skills. Parents too had insisted on useful learning, but the school committee maintained ordinary citizens did not have the broad vision required to plan the curriculum of the common school. To illustrate this point, the committeemen published a story about a youth who had come to class with an arithmetic book tucked under his arm and orders from his parents that this should be the sole subject of his study. The schoolmaster urged the lad to study writing, reading, and geography as well. But the youth refused, "No I calculate to cart brick from Somerville to the city all my life – it needs no great knowledge of geography to find the way over there!" This tale showed a case of ignorance suppressing talent. The boy's reply "indicated a quickness of perception, perhaps the external index of a mind capable of adorning the council chambers of the land." But because of his parents' limited horizons the boy's response told "a sad tale . . . of that still earlier training, which could have bound a soul to aspirations of mental attainment no higher than he felt."[31]

Judging themselves to be solely qualified to reform teaching and learning, the school committee constructed a curriculum for the new age of industry and urban growth. Its fundamental aim was basic literacy and numeracy. Common-school instruction in literacy and computation standardized these abilities and, indirectly, redefined character education to fit the conditions of urban life and industrial work. A standard written language was needed to foster the nexus of communication that underlay orderly social and economic relations in an impersonal, urbanizing society. But the teaching of literacy in itself inculcated forms of self-discipline and industriousness. Historian Harvey J. Graff has argued that teaching literacy "could ease the transition and assimilation of the working class and the poor to industrial and 'modern' social habits" and cites R. P. Dore's conclusion that "widespread literacy" in a developing country "at the very least . . . constitutes a training in being trained."[32] Instruction in basic mathematics developed the precise quantitative sense that enabled people to judge the number, scale, and dimensions of objects, goods, and services, an essential competence for dealing with the constituents of the built environment and the commodities of economic exchange.[33] But learning arithmetic, like learning grammar, instilled the habits of self-discipline, orderly behavior, and industry that facilitated survival in a competitive economy and familiarity with the regimen of industrial work. Carl F. Kaestle and Maris A. Vinovskis agree that the common-school era is "where the work–discipline thesis best matches specific and deliberate developments in schooling with the human capital needs of the economy." However, they intelligently warn against overestimating "the tightness of the links between economy and education."[34] For instance, the interest in time–work discipline was possibly a response to a general perception of social disorder, not specific manufacturing requirements.[35]

Reinforcing the characterological effects of teaching basic literacy and numeracy was a general classroom emphasis on habits of punctuality. Educators believed punctuality advanced scholarship and bred competence for adult responsibilities. The school committee extolled the salutary consequences of "the formation of those ineradicable habits of punctuality, of doing every duty at its proper time, of never deferring the duty of the present moment to a future period, which are to follow [the child] through the grammar school, the high school, the college, the workshop, the family and the legislative halls."[36]

The most visionary aim of the new curriculum was to strengthen the student's analytic powers so that he or she could solve problems in any context. To achieve this end, the curriculum had to center on the process of thought rather than the transmission of a body of knowledge. The school committee ordered that instruction should not make the pupil "acquire learning, but the means by which that object can in the future be secured." School subjects were likened to "tools in acquiring a mechanical trade." The "degree of dexterity" an apprentice attains "enable[s] him to apply it to any and every form, quality and extent of work which may be required."[37]

School committees of the 1840s predicated curriculum on a "faculty psychology." Reading, spelling, arithmetic, and geography constituted the courses that exercised the analytic faculties of young minds. Developed faculties could then be applied generally to the solution of a variety of problems. But this path of learning was not intended to lead to esoteric knowledge, which the school committee disdained. The committeemen considered "philosophy, history, the [classical] languages, music . . . and perhaps declamation" to be ornamental in nature, not "instrumental" for faculty development.[38]

When the school committee conducted public examinations of pupils, they did not test for speed or mnemonic accuracy of recital, but "how thoroughly they comprehend."[39] They cautioned that "word memory and glib repetition" are frequently mistaken "as the proof of good scholarship" because teachers, parents, and pupils "are all stimulated to wish a school to appear well."[40] The school committee, therefore, opposed mimetic exhibitions that did not stretch the minds of students. The duty of schoolmen was to steer learning around meretricious scholastic display, toward independent thinking. Consider the school committee's description of a good examination performance:

> The committee examine a class in geography. They ask the pupil the first common question which occurs to them out of the book; he hesitates, his mind labors, his attention is thrown inward upon the recollection of his atlas; the thing is in his mind, after a while he gives vent to his opinion. Names may be miscalled, great points omitted, yet it is perfectly apparent that a purely intellectual effort has produced the result desired.

Like Horace Mann, the school committee of Somerville held that "intelligence is the grand condition," not imbibing received knowledge.[41] The town fathers who brought the railroad, commerce, and the factory sought to foster through the common schools the independent ability to manipulate information to solve new practical problems.[42] As static customs and traditional beliefs ceased to be adequate guides to action in an urbanizing community, the townspeople needed to have a functional, problem-solving intelligence, operating for self-interest, to chart their behavior.[43] But despite high expectations, the dulling grind of teaching and uninspired students usually reduced lessons to rote learning. Nevertheless, the development of autonomous cognitive abilities became a permanent official objective of the public-school curriculum.

The mission of the teacher

The school committee directed the schools to educate intelligent, virtuous people. Parents supported this effort, but they also wished to insure considerate treatment of their children. The common-school teacher needed the ability to keep these two objectives in balance.

To prepare the next generation for "their part in the great drama of human life," the school committee stipulated that "those they appoint as teachers shall not only be competent to teach the several branches of knowledge . . . but also to render the pursuit of knowledge attractive to the pupil." Besides intellectual skill and inspiration, teachers had to have keen moral sensitivities. "A paternal regard for those under their care," the committeemen explained, "the gentleness that shall win their confidence, firmness to maintain proper discipline, a degree of enthusiasm for their calling and a sense of the responsibility of their station, are essential in those who would succeed as instructors of youth."[44]

The school committee regularly praised individual teachers who desisted from using the rod.[45] In a community marching forward to the beacon of liberal progress, the barbarity of force had to be banished from the school. Able teachers mingled affection with discipline to cultivate a self-regulating moral will that would serve as a personal compass in the town's maze of temptations.[46]

Educating Somerville's future citizens in accordance with the ambitious goals of the common-school movement was decidedly a demanding job. A new kind of teacher was needed who would fill the common school with intellectual energy and moral idealism, thereby turning it into an engine of social reform. To this calling were attracted many young women recently graduated from the newly established women's colleges, seminaries, and high schools of Massachusetts. They were eager to try their talents in one of the few professional fields accessible to women in the mid-nineteenth century.

Their chief rewards would be the spiritual gratification of Protestant stewardship, of social service in a profession that was "perhaps the most prostrating of any in its effects upon body and mind."[47] A teacher's patient struggle to teach the son of an illiterate Irish laborer would be rewarded when she heard the boy read aloud in clear tones the mysterious letters in the schoolbook. While treating her pupils with affection and sympathy, she had to master the art of imparting knowledge, a duty that "may well task the powers of the ablest and most gifted minds."[48] The teacher had to monitor personal comportment rigorously because it inevitably affected the quality of her instruction. The school committee insisted that each teacher be "a model of honesty, frankness, sincerity and virtue" or else her "words, however fitly and religiously will fall upon stony ground."[49] A small salary and the knowledge their task was "one of the highest and noblest that falls to the lot of humanity" was recompense for the teachers' arduous duties.[50]

The need to practice economy accelerated the movement to hire female teachers. Throughout Massachusetts, women could be hired at less than one-half the salary paid to men.[51] Horace Mann noted that because female teachers cost less, towns had recruited many more women into their teaching staffs. By 1847, women constituted nearly seven out of ten teachers employed in the state's public schools.[52] Since they had not usually attended the few normal schools then in existence and were believed to have natural maternal sympathies, they were often appointed to the primary schools. As historian Michael B. Katz and his colleagues noted, according to the regnant Victorian ideology of domesticity "the moral and spiritual role assigned to women not only justified but made imperative their entrance into classrooms as surrogate mothers."[53]

In 1842, the year Somerville was incorporated, all female teachers in the town's system taught in primary schools (Table 2.6). By 1849, however, four women had posts in the grammar schools, equaling the number of male grammar-school teachers. The fear that women could not discipline older boys subsided as women proved their ability to control their classes.[54] By 1861, women outnumbered men at all levels of the school system, including the high school. In 1871, nearly all, fifty-nine out of sixty-four teachers in the Somerville system, were women. The vaunted "paternal regard" of teachers demanded by the school committee had become a "maternal regard."

The burdens of teaching – the pressures to meet high character standards, to win the confidence of anxious parents,[55] to edify rowdy children, and to survive on a slender income – combined with powerful social expectations to marry at a desirable age, generating a high rate of turnover in the ranks of teachers. No primary-school teachers from 1842 remained in 1849; no primary teachers from 1849 taught in 1861; and only 15 percent of the primary teachers of 1861 remained in

Table 2.6. *Number of teachers in the school system, 1842–71*

	1842	1849	1861	1871
Female primary teachers	4	6	13	26
Female grammar teachers	0	4	11	29
Female HS teachers	—[a]	—	2	4
Male primary teachers	0	0	0	0
Male grammar teachers	2	4	4	3
Male HS teachers	—	—	1	2
% primary staff remaining from previous noted year	NA	0	0	15
% grammar staff remaining from previous noted year	NA	0	25	20
HS staff remaining from previous noted year	—	—	NA	0

[a] High school did not exist.
Sources: School Committee Minutes, 1842, pp 1–9; *Annual School Committee Report,* 1849, p. 11; 1861, p. 13; 1871, pp. 96–7.

1871. Grammar school staffs exhibited only slightly more stability. In 1861, 25 percent of the grammar teachers of 1849 were still in their posts; in 1871, 20 percent of the staff of 1861 were still teaching. Public-school teaching became a major professional career for women by the time of the Civil War, but occupational pressures and the marriage priority made their careers short-lived.

High rates of teacher turnover were especially damaging to the work of instruction.[56] Teachers with valuable experience were lost.[57] In the classroom, "harmony is destroyed, and progress impeded." Each year, the school committee was forced to engage in a frantic search for qualified replacements to fill vacated slots.[58] All too often, replacements were found only by luring teachers from school systems in other towns. The school committeemen and the townsfolk frowned on this recourse, because they felt that a local resident, familiar with the community, would be a more effective educator.[59]

The school committee labored to maintain high standards for teaching while reducing the rate of staff turnover. The members did not hesitate to fire incompetent teachers, because "a removal, however unpleasant," was "simply an act of justice to all concerned." Their chief effort to stem the exodus of experienced teachers was to raise salaries and to install a schedule for promotional increases.[60]

Notwithstanding the problems engendered by the growth and professionalization of the staff, the city fathers came to regard the school teacher as the personification of civic spiritedness. Albert E. Winship, editor of the well-known New England *Journal of Education*, proudly noted that Somerville's teachers were leading members of the city's voluntary associations, such as the Masons, the Odd Fellowship, and religious and charitable organizations. According to Winship, they were the chief exemplars of the highest ideals of local boosterism, "representative of the best reading and thinking, of the highest purpose and noblest aspiration of the city."[61]

The town leaders who campaigned to make the common school a public trust and who transformed the teacher's role into a female-specialized profession of social reform were mobile newcomers in commercial and professional pursuits whose major civic objective was the material growth of Somerville. Practical, aggressive men managed the evolution of the school system, and they conceived it as an investment in the long-range prosperity and order of the community. Fully believing that education would create a better world,[62] they sought to make the schools an instrument for propagating knowledge and habits useful for adjustment to urban life and industrial work. Somerville students would be taught in a basic way to read, to write, to count, to be self-disciplined, to think autonomously and pragmatically; in sum, to act as independent agents in an orderly manner within a society where the rise of industry had created impersonal and functional social relations. The communal leaders who sponsored urban growth constructed new bases of support and operating mechanisms for the public school system, but they believed that only when a free high school was established would their reforms fulfill their highest potential for social amelioration.

3   *The free high school*

The fledgling suburb of Somerville entered the wave of secondary-school reform sweeping Massachusetts before the Civil War, when the town meeting voted with "complete unanimity" in 1850 to prepare the establishment of the first Free Public High School.[1] The record of a unanimous vote for the high school in Somerville contrasts sharply with opposition to the institution in nearby Beverly, Massachusetts, later in the decade.[2] Were the townspeople enthusiastically united behind the high school, or could Somerville's unanimous vote have reflected a consensual deference to the will of the selectmen and school committeemen, a symbolic act affirming communal respect for leadership, as in colonial town politics?[3] The question is germane, for evidence of underlying friction exists. The remarkable George L. Baxter, who was headmaster of the high school from 1867 to 1911, recalled, "It required strong, persistent efforts by friends of education to overcome the reluctance of the people to tax the entire community for the higher education of a small portion of it."[4]

Unfortunately, no contemporaneous records of individual voting survive to shed more light on these issues. Thus, to proceed to a closer analysis of popular support for the high school, this study perforce focuses on the period of operation immediately after its establishment. It also depends on an examination of the characteristics of students and their families to assess the basis of sponsorship for secondary schooling. Nevertheless, these social data probably reveal more about deep-seated popular attitudes toward the high school than a single act of voting.

Expectations of the high school

When the Free High School of Somerville was finally constructed in 1852, the Boston suburb became one of sixty-five towns founding public high schools in the 1850s, a decade that witnessed the establishment of 60 percent of the high schools existing in the Commonwealth by 1860.[5] The state had ordered towns of 500 families to establish high schools since 1827, but the impulse to comply came from social and

40

economic change rather than obedience to law.[6] Many towns adopting the higher institution were at the forefront of urban development and the industrial revolution. Their leading citizens aggressively promoted local policies to increase community wealth and accelerate growth.

To the boosters of these expanding towns, the establishment of a public high school culminated the mission of the common schools.[7] Proponents of the new institution outlined the principal benefits it would provide. First, it would strengthen "republican equality," preventing "social caste," by affording means for people of all origins to enjoy the rewards of advanced schooling. In Somerville, the school committee declared that a public high school offered "the advantages which a poor man's child may very much desire, and can nowhere else procure, without money and without price!" Second, the high school would be the means of "discovering and developing genius and talent" in all social classes, and thus supply the "gifted minds and energetic characters" who will improve society.[8]

Like many other towns in the state, the commuter suburb of Somerville was impelled by material growth and soaring hopes for public education's role in local development to found the Free High School. The town fathers aimed to make that institution, like the common schools, a place to prepare students for practical life and to contribute to social progress. There, students would "gain an acquaintance in studies more accurate and practical" and would not be directed toward "recitative dexterity." School committeemen glorified the practical high school curriculum, which they compared invidiously to the abstruse "classical studies" of academies and seminaries that produced merely formal learning.[9]

Pragmatism and local pride dominated their view of the opportunities to be afforded by the high school. The best students were not "prodigies capable of working incomprehensibly and mysteriously, and sure to stop at a fixed point, but, strong, progressive, well-balanced faculties which it would be an honor to our town . . . to train to distinction and usefulness, without calling for foreign aid."[10] The high school accommodated subjects of "most immediate practical value to a young man or young woman." Even the sequence of courses was adjusted to facilitate the departure of scholars for work. "Thus, mathematics, history, natural science, physiology, etc., – subjects which every one will wish to study, – have been placed among the special branches for the first two years" while "the other studies required by law," languages and philosophy, were shunted into the last two years.[11] Students could take immediately the courses that provided communication skills and knowledge useful for white-collar work, and then leave. As a result, from the time of its founding, the Free High School did not produce a single graduate for ten years.[12]

The growing number of middle-class parents who were developing a Victorian cultural preference for keeping their children at home late into adolescence also looked forward to a town high school. Parents no longer needed to send youths to boarding academies or high schools in neighboring towns to supply a superior education.[13] The chairman of Somerville's school committee in 1847 pointed out this benefit of the high school: "We have the conviction that High School pupils could be carried to a better grade of education at home than would be practicable under the mixed training of academies or with the changing pupils of private seminaries."[14] A public high school would keep parents and their older children together, thus prolonging family unity. Youths would not have to suffer "separation from the influences of the domestic fireside."[15] Furthermore, from this perspective, a public high school would attract parents to Somerville who wished to give advanced schooling to their children while keeping them at home.

Constraints on the popularity of the high school

Although born amidst glowing publicity, the high school struggled to attract students in its first decade. Ironically, the low enrollment at the high school was caused by the forces of social mobility and economic growth it had been designed to foster. In the 1850s, the multiplication of factories, shops, and small businesses enlarged the local job market for youth employment. Adolescent sons of merchants and artisans were lured away from the classroom into offices and shops that needed apprentices.

The new economic opportunities reduced the proportion of children who went to school at all levels of the social structure (Table 3.1). In an 1850 sample of Somerville's population, over 90 percent of elementary school age children from families in every occupational stratum attended school at some time during the year. A much smaller proportion of 16- to 19-year-old children attended school. Since no high school existed in Somerville in 1850, most of the older students entered an upper grammar grade while others went to a private academy or public secondary school in Boston or Cambridge. In the 16- to 19-year-old bracket, 40 percent of the children of high-white-collar parents and 30 percent of the children of low-white-collar and artisan parents attended school, as compared to none of the children of semiskilled parents and 20 percent of the children of unskilled parents.

Table 3.1. *Children of employed persons attending school, 1850, 1860*

Parent's occupation	Year	Grammar school age children[a]	High school age children[b]
High white collar	1850	91.4	40.0
	1860	62.3	22.2
Low white collar	1850	91.1	30.8
	1860	63.0	22.2
Skilled	1850	97.7	30.8
	1860	71.3	11.5
Semiskilled	1850	100.0	0
	1860	73.8	0
Unskilled	1850	91.1	20.0
	1860	59.0	25.0

[a] 4–15 years old in school (%).
[b] 16–19 years old in school (%).

In general, parents with high-paying jobs and more than the average number of children were more likely to prolong schooling for their children.

The percentages of children who attended school during the year declined sharply in every occupational stratum from 1850 to 1860, a decade when enrollment rates in schools paradoxically climbed from 66 percent of school age students to 80 percent (Table 1.8, Chapter 1). This complex pattern was the outcome of three separate developments. First, a high percentage of enrolled students were transients, not regular attenders. Second, it seems cultural attitudes toward sending to school very young children changed: hardly any 4-year olds attended school in 1860, whereas many had in 1850. Third, a higher percentage of older students were dropping out to go to work as Somerville's growth expanded the labor market by creating more jobs and providing mass transportation to them.[16] The proportion of attenders among high-school age youngsters dipped to 22 percent of youths from white-collar backgrounds and 11 percent of those from artisan backgrounds.

A striking exception to the pattern of decline was the percentage of 16- to 19-year-old attenders from unskilled families, which climbed to 25 percent. However, the records of the Free High School show that only one child of a laborer was enrolled there from 1856 to 1861. Nearly all the high-school-age sons of laborers who attended school went to a grammar school, probably while waiting for a job to turn up. School attendance for them represented a response to unemployment, rather than capitalization on educational opportunity.

The growing flow of students leaving the classroom for jobs severely hampered the growth of high school attendance. Enrollment fluctuated throughout the 1850s and hardly grew at all. Seventy-six scholars enrolled when the high school opened in 1852; only 83 were enrolled in 1860.[17]

The stagnant business of the high school aroused many public criticisms. Some parents blamed its unpopularity upon the poor quality of instruction. A disgruntled group averred that the school was too small to merit operation. Desperate for a way to defend the institution, the school committee feebly pointed out that a town of Somerville's size was obligated by state law to run a high school.[18] Overworked teachers criticized the abilities of students entering the high school, who were inadequately prepared by the grammar schools.[19] Although the high school was built in Somerville's geographic center next to the town hall, the growing dispersion of the suburban population contributed to low attendance and undermined the "cooperation of all classes and conditions in its support." In certain neighborhoods of the town, the school committee admitted it was "far more convenient for many pupils to attend school in Charlestown, or in Boston, than to attend the High School."[20] Even after streetcars linked the districts of Somerville, many parents were unwilling or unable to pay for their child's long ride to the high school.

The problems of the high school divided the community into three groups. The first did not see the necessity for more education than that afforded by the grammar school; a second preferred to send their children to private schools; and the last was "deeply solicitous that a High School . . . shall be faithfully maintained." The school committee remonstrated with the first group, pointing out that education for the public welfare should not be obstructed by a limited conception of its role. To the parents who supported private institutions over public schools, the school committee explained the undemocratic character of the former, which confined "the highest advantages to those only whose parents can afford to pay for them." "And he who nobly pours out his treasure like water to buy choice opportunities for his own flesh and blood," sternly exhorted the committeemen, "must not marvel that a republican form of government . . . should divert some of the beneficent streams of private wealth into the large public channel, which passes by and waters the homes where indigence, involuntarily sits in ignorance."

For supporters of the high school, the school committee extended

its profound gratitude and discussed attempts to improve attendance, financing, and instruction.[21] The committeemen presented the
same public-interest rationale to elements disappointed with the high
school that they utilized to justify the entire school system. They engaged the townspeople in a civic dialogue that viewed the high school
as it affected the whole community, as part of a framework of republican institutions that guaranteed equal opportunity. The ethical authority they invoked, however, could not override the economic
changes limiting sponsorship of secondary schooling to a select group
of mobile middle-class families.

Origins of high school students

High-school attendance was the result of a collective family decision
that involved parents and children.[22] The chief sponsors of high-school
education in the 1850s and 1860s were parents in white-collar occupations (Table 3.2). Of the fathers of scholars entering in 1852 and
1853 who could be traced from student records to the 1850 U.S. Census schedules, 55 percent held white-collar jobs.[23] The white-collar
occupational class was heavily overrepresented in high school sponsorship, since only 30 percent of the town's workers held white-collar
jobs. Merchants and commercial farmers were especially eager to send
their youngsters to the Free High School. Out of twenty-eight white-
collar fathers, thirteen were merchants and twelve were farmers. (Somerville farmers were chiefly involved in commercial agriculture; because they were entrepreneurial proprietors, they are classified in the
white-collar class.) [24] Three of the twenty-eight white-collar fathers
were industrialists. Parents who sponsored a high school education
sprang, like the selectmen and school committeemen, from an elite
composed of leaders of the rural economy as well as harbingers of the
new urban economy.

A group of artisans were next in support for secondary schooling.
Thirty-one percent of the fathers of high school students worked in
skilled trades. They sent children to high school in proportion to their
numbers in the community, since they comprised 32 percent of the
town's work force. As historian Carl F. Kaestle has suggested, "because of changes from craft to factory production, some members of
this upper artisan group may have felt anxious about their positions
and their sons' futures."[25] This insecure "labor aristocracy" sought to
enhance their families' status by sponsoring schooling to a greater
extent than other workers.[26]

Low-manual workers were least able or willing to send their children to high school. Only four semiskilled fathers and two unskilled

Table 3.2. *Fathers of entrants to Somerville High School,*
1852–3, 1856–61, 1859–61

	White collar	Skilled	Semiskilled	Unskilled	Unemployed
1852–3[a]					
N	28	16	4	2	1
%	55	31	8	4	2
1850 Somerville (male labor force)					
%	30	32	5	33	
1856–61[b]					
N	74	26	0	1	10
%	67	23	0	1	9
1859–61[c]					
N	37	23	0	1	2
%	59	37	0	2	3
1860 Somerville (male labor force)					
%	34	31	17	18	

[a]Fifty-one of all fathers of 122 entrants were traced in the 1850 U.S. Census schedules for Somerville, Massachusetts.
[b]One hundred eleven of all fathers of 181 entrants. Tabulated from Michael B. Katz, *The Irony of Early School Reform* (Cambridge, Mass.), Appendix C, Table C-2, p. 271.
[c]Sixty-three of all fathers of 119 entrants were traced in the schedules of the 1860 U.S. Census.

fathers gave their children a high school education. Only 4 percent of the fathers of high school students were unskilled, although they comprised 33 percent of the labor force.

Almost a decade later, from 1859 to 1861, white-collar and artisan fathers still displayed the strongest sponsorship of secondary schooling for their children. Fifty-nine percent of the fathers were white-collar men, although the white-collar stratum was only 34 percent of the work force. Only one father was a member of the professions. Thirty-seven percent were skilled employees, although artisans were only 31 percent of the work force. But in contrast with the early 1850s, only six farmers (less than one-sixth of all white-collar parents) sent their children to high school; and not a single semiskilled parent had a child in high school, although semiskilled workers had expanded to 17 percent of Somerville's labor force. Unskilled fathers continued to show little ability or interest in supplying their children with a high school education. Of sixty-three identified fathers of students, only one was a laborer. Learning algebra in a high school classroom was an irrelevant luxury for their children, whose work was needed to help keep a poor family fed and sheltered. As industrialization and suburban development proceeded forward, farmers and low-skilled workers fell far behind in sponsorship of secondary schooling.

For the Irish laborer, the Free High School was a distant place whose workings were not for his son or daughter. Not one of the students from 1852 to 1853 and from 1859 to 1861 traced to the census schedules was the child of an Irish-born worker. The Irish immigrant's meager wages made him dependent on his children's employment. As a day laborer in the railroad yards, construction sites, or factories, he made seventy-five cents a day.[27] Lay-offs frequently idled him. To supplement his income, the Irish parent had to send the children to work as soon as the law allowed. After attending grammar school – often, before completing it – the Irishman's son toiled at his father's side, in the railyards, the brickyards, the factory, or the bleachery. His daughter helped out at home or was hired as a housekeeper. Furthermore, the mental horizons of the laborer born in rural Ireland centered on achieving family security, not investing in schooling as a tool for social advancement.[28] A high school education was not a steppingstone leading out of poverty for the second generation of Somerville Irish.

When the 1852–3 and 1859–61 samples of parents are compared with the sample of parents of Somerville high school entrants from 1856–61 tabulated by Michael B. Katz in his seminal study, *The Irony of Early School Reform*, a consistent pattern of sponsorship emerges: a disproportionately high representation of white-collar fathers including hardly any professionals, a substantial proportion of artisan fathers, and a very small fraction of low-manual fathers. During its first decade of operation, the Somerville Free Public High School was attended almost exclusively by the children of a white-collar occupational class and a transitional artisan stratum that emerged in the process of industrial development.

How did the occupational distribution of secondary-school sponsorship in Somerville compare to that found in the wider context of early industrial society? Studies of sponsorship in two other cities in the United States indicate that Somerville was a fairly representative antebellum community (Table 3.3). The job profile of parents in Somerville fundamentally resembled those of the New York City public

Table 3.3. *Distribution of occupations of parents of students in the New York City Free Academy, 1849–53; the high schools of St. Louis, Missouri, 1860–2; and secondary schools in France, 1860s*

New York City Free Academy	1849–53 (%)	Total NYC labor force (%)
White collar	47.8	21.3
Professionals	12.9	3.7
Other white collar	34.9	17.6
Manual	46.0	75.0
Artisans and factory workers	35.4	41.2
Other manual	10.6	34.8
Total	816	

St. Louis high schools	1860–2 (%)
White collar	66.3
Professions	10.0
Other white collar	56.3
Manual	33.7
Skilled	13.7
Semiskilled	8.9
Unskilled	11.1
Total	730

Secondary schools in France	1860s (%)
White collar	77.0
Professions	18.6
Other white collar	58.4
Artisans	6.1
Peasant farmers	12.3
Workers	1.9
Noncommissioned military	1.3
Other	1.4
Total	12,603

Sources: Retabulated from Carl F. Kaestle, *The Evolution of an Urban School System: New York City, 1750–1850* (Cambridge, Mass., 1973), p. 107, Table 16; Selwyn K. Troen, *The Public and the Schools: Shaping the St. Louis School System, 1838–1920* (Columbia, Missouri, 1975), Appendix A; Patrick J. Harrigan, *Mobility, Elites, and Education in French Society* (Waterloo, Ontario, Canada, 1980), Table 1, p. 14.

Free Academy and the high schools of St. Louis: White-collar employees were the most heavily represented, but a large minority were manual workers. However, for the New York City and St. Louis institutions, more parents were professionals and low-skilled workers, possibly because these cities were major cosmopolitan centers with a larger professional and laboring population.

The parents of Somerville High School students and their counterparts in New York City and St. Louis can also be juxtaposed with parents of secondary-school students in mid-nineteenth-century France, identified in another study, to reveal patterns of similarity and contrast between the United States and an industrializing European society.[29] The sources of data and treatment make it impossible to achieve exact comparability, but three important comparative generalizations can be made. First, that a small fraction of low-skilled workers appeared in both the American and French samples. Second, in the American samples, a larger proportion of these parents were artisans. Third, white-collar sponsorship, especially by the professions, appears to have been more prominent in France. In early industrial society of the trans-Atlantic world, the lower classes did not participate in secondary-school sponsorship. Rapid industrialization in the United States may have made more artisans fearful of displacement by the factory system, and one of their responses to shore up their family position was to support advanced schooling. The greater involvement in France of white-collar and professional parents may have stemmed from the historical entrenchment of a bureaucratic class, and possibly, although insufficient historical evidence makes this a very tentative hypothesis, by lower levels of popular education and social mobility in French society.

A finer picture of the conditions affecting high school attendance is obtained through an analysis of students according to gender and the characteristics of their households (Table 1, Appendix III). Both boys and girls who entered high school in 1852-3 and 1859-61 predominantly came from property-owning families with at least four children. The large majority of students had fathers who pursued a business career or a skilled trade, and who were born in Massachusetts or a neighboring New England state. The proportion of students with parents employed in manual work was higher than the proportion of manual workers among the parents of high school students (Table 3.2). This differential indicated that skilled workers often sent more than one child to high school.

The families of high school students sent a majority of their children, 12 to 20 years old, to school (Table 3.4). High school boys came from families where sons attended school at a higher rate than daugh-

Table 3.4. *Status of sons and daughters in families of high school students who entered in 1852–3, 1859–61 (%)*

	Sons 12–20 years old			Daughters 12–20 years old		
	School	Work	Home	School	Work	Home
SHS[a] 1852–3 Families of						
Boys	72.2	22.2	5.6	62.5	0	37.5
Girls	56.0	44.0	0	84.8	0	15.2
SHS 1859–61 Families of						
Boys	72.7	21.2	6.1	68.4	0	31.6
Girls	66.7	20.0	13.3	83.1	0	16.9

	Children 4–15 years old		Children 16–19 years old	
	In school	At home/work	In school	At home/work
1860 Families of				
Semiskilled heads	73.8	26.2	0	100.0
Unskilled heads	59.0	41.0	25.0	75.0

	All 13–16-year-old males			All 13–16-year-old females		
	School	Work	Home	School	Work	Home
All families of Hamilton, Ontario						
1851	30.1	14.9	55.0	25.6	3.1	71.3
1861	51.5	9.4	39.1	52.0	1.8	46.2

	Families w/ boarders	Families w/ servants	Families w/ relatives	Total N
SHS 1852–3 Families of				
Boys	81.2	0	0	16
Girls	61.1	0	0	36
SHS 1859–61 Families of				
Boys	56.0	36.0	0	25
Girls	38.6	36.4	0	44

Table 3.4. (*cont.*)

	Students with sibling 16–20 years old				Students with sibling 12–15 years old			
	% with work-ing brother	N with brother	% with work-ing sister	N with sis-ter	% with work-ing brother	N with brother	% with work-ing sister	N with sis-ter
Mid-nineteenth-century cohort Somerville High 1852–3								
Boys	50.0	6	0	6	0	4	0	7
Girls	82.4	17	0	10	0	15	0	20
Somerville High 1859–61								
Boys	80.0	5	0	9	0	7	0	7
Girls	66.7	6	0	13	16.7	12	7.7	13

[a] SHS, Somerville High School.
Sources: Computed from records of the Somerville High School and the manuscript schedules of the U.S. Seventh Census of 1850 and the U.S. Eighth Census of 1860; Michael B. Katz et al., *The Social Organization of Early Industrial Capitalism* (Cambridge, Mass., 1982), p. 255.

ters, and high school girls came from families where the reverse pattern held. In all these families, a substantial fraction of sons in these families went to work, while none of the daughters did.

The capacity to send older children to school with exceptional frequency differentiated the families of high school students from others in the industrial social order. Youths 12 to 20 years old in high school students' families attended school about as frequently as grammar-school-age children 4–15 years old in all workingmen's families, and much more often than youths 16 to 19 years old in these families. Youths in the families of Somerville High School students also attended school at a higher rate than youngsters around the age of secondary-school entry in the general population of another urbanizing North American community – Hamilton, English Canada – in 1851 and 1861.

Important differences distinguished the students of 1852–3 from those of 1859–61, signifying a change in the social basis of high school sponsorship. Among the former, 83 percent of boys and 68 percent of girls came from families with four or more children. Also, 87 percent of the boys and 83 percent of the girls came from property-owning families; furthermore, over half the boys came from the wealthiest group of property-owning families. But among students entering in 1859–61, less than 60 percent of the boys and girls came from families holding property; over a third of the boys and girls came from small families with one to three children. Significant differences in birthplaces of students' fathers also developed. In the 1852–3 cohort, over 90 percent of the students had native-born fathers, and over a third of these had fathers born in a neighboring New England state. In the 1859–61 cohort, nearly half the boys had fathers born in another New England state and and over a fifth had foreign-born fathers; almost a third of the girls had fathers born in another New England state.

After the first decade of the high school's operation, the social origins of students moved away from the wealthiest, largest households to small and medium-sized households owning smaller amounts of property. Also, by the 1860s, the proportion of the sons of foreign-born parents, chiefly immigrants from Great Britain, had grown considerably. A common feature of both 1852–3 and 1859–61 cohorts, however, was the large proportion of high school students with fathers born in another New England state. A high school education increasingly became the goal of youngsters from smaller nuclear households modestly endowed with property, and headed by a newcomer white-collar worker or artisan.

Another significant change occurring between the two cohorts was that the timing of a child's entry into the high school became more exact. In the opening years of the Free High School, entry ages varied enormously: a few children started as young as 11 or 12 or as old as 19. By 1860, however, the range of entry ages narrowed considerably. The majority of entrants from 1859 to 1861 started high school at 14 or 15 years of age, and none was over 16. During the 1850s, Somerville educators had established age grading and a more uniform curriculum that prepared a growing number of students for high school admission at the age of 14 or 15. A more basic change contributing to age narrowing was that Somerville families decided in the 1850s that secondary schooling should fit into their household life cycle immediately after their children's elementary schooling and just before the time they left home. The custom of prolonging dependency and insulating children from the external community, characteristic of Victorian family culture, replaced the habit of semiautonomous experimentation, the repeated movement of youths between family and independent livelihood, found among American families of the previous generation.[30]

Different gender-role expectations in the mid-nineteenth-century urban household linked birth order of a child and the likelihood of high school attendance. To account for the different treatment of gender in the transition to adulthood, the birth order of high school students was determined for this study according to all resident siblings of similar gender. Over 60 percent of boys were either the sole or first-born son in their families in both the 1852–3 and 1859–61 cohorts. In contrast, the majority of girls entering in 1852–3 and 43 percent of those entering in 1859–61 were the second-born daughter in a family with two girls, or the middle-born or last-born daughter of a family with three girls.[31] Some boys who went to high school were the eldest sons in the households, because older brothers had moved out to live on their own. But many sole and eldest resident sons did not have nonresident older brothers. These lads probably came from families that invested resources to support their only, or first, upcoming male income-earner through high school, to improve his prospects for white-collar employment and to give him the prestige of advanced education. As he had no younger brothers or sisters who were employed, he received parental resources only (Table 3.4). A girl high school student was often a younger daughter, because oldest daughters stayed at home longer than oldest sons.[32] After the oldest daughter finished her schooling (some had attended high school), she helped keep house until she married, so that younger sisters were free to attend high school.

Most boy and girl students with an older brother relied upon him to supply the income margin that permitted them to attend high school, a form of short-term role exchange designated here as family instrumentalism.[33] Fifty percent of the boy students with an older resident brother entering in 1852–3 and 80 percent of those entering in 1859–61 depended on his employment to be allowed to enroll (Table 3.4). But they were not helped by an employed older sister. Likewise, no female high school student had older sisters who went to work: They were all at home handling domestic chores. But most girls with an older brother were assisted by his employment to attend high school.

The majority of the students' families of the early 1850s took in boarders who helped supply the additional income that freed a child to attend high school (Table 3.4). They were also not encumbered by the need to support servants or resident relatives who could be identified.[34] Some boarders probably provided service or labor. In the 1860s, fewer families had boarders and 36 percent had servants. Although household structure had grown more complex by the addition of servants, family resources, such as the employment of a sibling, could be readjusted to permit a child to go to high school.

The fact that girls greatly outnumbered boys in the Free High School suggests that parents' motivation for sending their children was more complex than a desire for providing useful linguistic and computa-

Table 3.5. *Number of male and female high school entrants, 1852–67*

	Male	Female	Total
1852	23	61	84
1853	17	17	34
1854	22	21	43
1859	11	22	33
1860	9	49	58
1861	13	18	31
1865	10	25	35
1866	15	19	34
1867	22	29	51
Total	142	261	403

Source: Records of Somerville High School.

Table 3.6. *High school students by parent's occupation, entered 1852–3, 1859–61*

Parent's occupation		1852–3			1859–61		
		Boys	Girls	Total	Boys	Girls	Total
White collar	N	11	22	33	11	23	34
	%	33	67		32	68	
Manual	N	12	21	33	13	23	36
	%	36	64		36	64	

tional skills. Parents in both white-collar and manual employment sent twice as many daughters as sons to high school (Tables 3.5 and 3.6) in a Victorian age when girls were groomed for their proper place as wives and mothers.[35] Of course, some parents hoped that their daughters, too, might be aided in employment by an advanced education. For example, only five years after its founding, the Free High School had prepared nine women for teaching posts in the town.[36] But probably these, too, were expected eventually to marry.

For the large majority of girls, however, the Free High School was chiefly valued as a place where they could be properly "finished" with a genteel cultural sophistication. This expectation was part of a transformation of women's role in middle-class society that occurred in the mid-nineteenth century. The historian Joseph Kett has clarified the principal features of this change:

> During the middle decades of the 19th century, the world of novels and poetry became as much a part of the sphere of women as the tasks of child rearing and school teaching. As a corollary, girls were not merely to be educated but educated thoroughly, to the point where fluttering eyelids would no longer conceal a vacant mind. Foreign travelers in America often commented that American girls were better educated than American men and far more sprightly in conversation, just as they observed that American fathers made sacrifices for their daughters that they would not think of making for their sons. Possession of an educated daughter became a sort of prestige symbol, a crude form of conspicuous consumption.[37]

Moreover, parents hoped that the high school would give their daughters the cultivation that might make her a more attractive spouse to a business or professional man. A further inducement was the reasonable opportunity cost[38] of polishing a daughter's graces at the high school. Since a working daughter could earn only half what an employed son could earn due to the lower wage scale of female workers, the opportunity cost of her "finishing," in income forgone for the family due to school attendance, was much smaller. To parents concerned about status, an educated daughter who brought prestige to the family and enhanced her marriageability was well worth such a cost.

An ambitious young man often left the Free High School after a year or two to begin a career in clerking, business, or law. The proliferation of trade and manufacturing in mid-nineteenth-century Massachusetts multiplied openings for office apprentices. The purposive lad could "learn the ropes" and climb to a position as manager or partner, or leave to start his own business.[39]

The masters of the Free High School kept a desultory record of scholars departing from the halls of learning that displayed the lure of early employment (Table 3.7). Of fifteen discharged boys who were recorded, eleven left to try their fortunes in the world of work. None left for an institution of higher learning. Charles Brastow, the son of George O. Brastow, attended high school but dropped out in 1859 to go to work in the Boston firm of Horatio Harris Company. Seventeen-year-old Augustus White did not have a post waiting for him, but still left high school to take his chances "in search of business." Frank Brackett, 16 years old, yearned for adventure on the high seas and left to sail on the *Garnet*, a ship bound for New Orleans.

The extremely different paths traveled by "little women" from school

Table 3.7. *Boys and girls leaving the Free High School before graduation, 1855–60*

	Boys	Girls
Remarks on leaving		
Course not completed	1	6
To go into business	10	0
To go to sea	1	0
Moved	2	4
Personal illness or infirmity	1	11
Illness in family	0	2
Entered another school	0	2
Needed at home	0	3
No reason given	0	6
Total	15	34

to early adulthood are revealed by the the records of thirty-four girls who dropped out of the Free High School. In stark contrast to the boys, none of the girls left school to go to work. Eleven of the girls left because of the strain of study. Educators, physicians, and parents in the mid-nineteenth century believed that the adolescent girl easily fell to a host of maladies. Hard mental work, it was believed, wracked her weak frame; frayed nerves could plunge her into debilitating illness.[40] The parents of Esther Ross and Mercy Hood preferred that they withdraw when they became ill, rather than risk aggravating their conditions.

The call of family duty also enjoined girls to forsake the high school diploma. In 1860, 16-year-old Ellen Henderson withdrew to take care of her sick sister. Emma Hill, 15 years old, dropped out the same year because of illness in her family. Three other girls left to lend a helping hand at home or to take care of younger siblings. A girl's work as housekeeper, nurse, or babysitter often took priority over schooling. A small fraction of girls who withdrew, however, sought to advance themselves through education. In February 1860, Charlotte Light, 14 years old, left to enter the Normal School in Boston. But Charlotte was unusual: Most girls who wanted a teaching career in the 1860s finished high school before proceeding to a teacher-training institution.

The multiplication of entry slots in the occupational structure for sons and the claims of domesticity on daughters were the principal forces pulling scholars out of high school before graduation. The advent of the Civil War also carried away students. Albert Mitchell, who

Table 3.8. *Graduates of Somerville High School, 1862–71*

	Total	Boys	Girls
1862	6	3	3
1863	6	2	4
1864	12	1	11
1865	11	4	7
1866	7	4	3
1867	7	4	3
1868	17	7	10
1869	25	5	20
1870	16	5	11
1871	33	11	22
Total	141	46	94

was admitted in 1856, died in combat; a classmate, Frederic Glines, died a prisoner of war.[41]

Finally in 1862, after a decade of operation, the Free High School had its first graduates, three boys and three girls. In the years following the graduation of these scholars, the graduating classes fluctuated in size, but always remained small (Table 3.8). From 1862 to 1871, the largest class of graduates had thirty-three members. In that span of years over twice as many girls as boys received diplomas. A sample of seventeen fathers of scholars graduating from 1862 to 1865 suggests which parents sponsored their children to finish high school.[42] Nine fathers held white-collar posts, five were in skilled jobs, and three were unemployed. None was a semiskilled or unskilled worker. After the first decade of the high school, graduation as well as attendance was achieved almost exclusively by children of white-collar and artisan parents.

The town fathers and citizens of Somerville established the Free High School to popularize public secondary education among all social classes. The school committee designed it to be a major supplier of useful higher knowledge to the future generations of businessmen, clerical workers, and technicians. But the Free High School fell far short of these lofty expectations in its first two decades. The unanimity of the town-meeting vote to found the Free High School was probably a consensual affirmation of the decision-making authority of selectmen and school committeemen, rather than an expression of total support for educational innovation. If the vote reflected pervasive communal enthusiasm, it quickly waned when parents and students began to take advantage of new employment opportunities generated by Somerville's expanding economy and by its linkage through commuter travel with the job market in Boston and Cambridge. The Free High School's enrollment grew sluggishly and graduation rates were very low. In the 1850s and 1860s, popular participation in public education was achieved only at the elementary levels of schooling.

The high school served a segment of the native business elite and the artisan occupational class; it scarcely affected the children of low-manual workers or of Irish immigrants. Gradually, however, newcomers from other parts of Massachusetts and New England started small families and homes in Somerville and joined in sponsorship of secondary schooling. Eldest and sole sons and daughters frequently attended high school. But many students, especially girls, were younger siblings helped out by employed brothers to go to high school. Boys gained linguistic and mathematical skills useful for white-collar work, as well as the cultural badge of advanced schooling. Most girls attended to enhance the cultural sophistication attractive to a desirable marriage partner, due to their severely limited job opportunties and the Victorian family's practice of socializing girls for motherhood through prolonged dependency. Girls were twice as numerous as boys at the high school, because the opportunity cost of sending daughters to high school for "finishing" was much lower than that for educating boys, who sacrificed substantial income and rapid career entry.

The Free High School functioned as a seminary for the children of the elite and the prosperous artisan families, but even among these groups it was only a finishing school with very limited popularity. The high school primarily cultivated and confirmed the genteel culture of a minority of privileged youths. White-collar and artisan parents rarely conceived of a high school education as a device for occupational mobility. Their sons frequently left the high school to prepare for adult careers through an office or shop apprenticeship, and their daughters dropped out to prepare for marriage by learning their domestic duties at home. For the vast majority of youngsters in mid-nineteenth-century Somerville, the job or the household, not the high school, was the avenue from adolescence to adulthood.

4 *The rise of Yankee city and the prolongation of schooling*

After the Civil War, a Republican city government widened opportunities for home ownership in Somerville by keeping taxes low, expanding municipal services, and extending rapid transit. By providing attractive living conditions, the suburb helped relieve the pressures generated by competition for housing in the Hub City of Boston. Postwar prosperity made the Republican fathers optimistic about the consequences of their public policies.

Growth, however, had introduced new ethnic and class tensions. Besides receiving mobile white-collar employees who built new homes, Somerville attracted a swelling population of Irish Catholics and low-skilled workers who toiled in the burgeoning factories. Correspondingly, the labor market experienced an expansion of white-collar jobs and semiskilled industrial employment, while skilled posts failed to grow as rapidly.

Citizens worried that a dynamic economy alone could not assure the smooth growth of opportunity and the maintenance of social order. Poverty and inequality threatened to increase under intensifying population pressure, the depersonalizing of human relationships, the proletarianization of workers, and the fear dividing Yankees and immigrants. City fathers believed that the public school's role had to be expanded to preserve economic opportunity and to heal social divisions. The schools had to reach more students from a greater diversity of backgrounds and, most importantly, lengthen their educational careers to provide the extensive preparation to face life in an industrial society. In pursuing these goals, educators systematized the learning experience to inculcate in the future generation of city dwellers common standards of judgment and habits of thought that would promote ordered patterns of coexistence.

Toward a city charter

The Civil War slowed Somerville's population growth by recruiting over a thousand male inhabitants for the Union cause, but the town's economy gained momentum from the conflict.[1] Manufacturing enterprises were stimulated by the wartime demand for "various articles

59

for the armies and general commerce."[2] The iron-casting factory's output tripled from ten years earlier; the brass works multiplied production by six times; and the glass factory's outflow of goods increased over fourfold. The relentless building of homes, shops, and factories ate away at the once plentiful meadowland of the town. By 1865 only 10 acres of unimproved land remained in Somerville.[3]

Returning soldiers and a pent-up flow of migrants streamed into the suburb with the coming of peace. While Somerville's population only increased from 8,025 in 1860 to 9,353 in 1865, it spurted to 14,865 by the end of the decade.[4] From its original nucleus in east Somerville near the Cambridge line, the town's population radiated northward to Winter Hill and westward to Arlington. Boosters eager to attract newcomers and to promote business were excited by the outward signs of growth. "Such rapid increase of population as this [town] Census [of 1867] shows," the selectmen remarked, "and such a financial record as the Report of the treasurer gives us, must certainly be most encouraging of all good citizens."[5]

The extension of settlement, however, engendered neighborhood interests that threatened to divide the town. In the final year of the Civil War, the residents of west Somerville agitated to join their district with Cambridge. Citizens dissatisfied with the schools in that neighborhood, led by S. C. Whitcher, a 40-year-old flour dealer who had migrated from New Hampshire, petitioned the General Court for annexation to Cambridge. Wishing to keep west Somerville for future real estate and commercial development, the selectmen went before the legislature and defeated the motion. To win back the insurgents, the selectmen advised the town meeting "to decide whether they will give the required [school] accommodations."[6] The following year the town elected Whitcher to the school committee, where he helped plan new schools to be established in west Somerville. The local residents were satisfied.

Discontentment with the quality of public education precipitated the first major challenge to the municipal framework. The annexation movement revealed the high premium newcomers to the suburb placed upon the kind of schooling afforded their children. The people of Somerville were able to accommodate dissidents by including them politically in the process of formulating educational policy, and by acceding to their demands for school reform.

The expansion of the town, however, was continuously creating new constituencies that would intensify demand for basic municipal services. The drive for commercial development thrust the Lexington and Arlington Branch railroad through west Somerville in late 1870. The open fields were covered by churches, schoolhouses, stores, and depots as the railroad brought new settlers in its wake. A new urban center formed in west Somerville, stretching out the fabric of settlement that was once compactly woven around east Somerville.

Somerville had grown into a sprawling community that required modernized institutions to support the welfare of its diversified populace. A permanent professional police department was established in 1870, replacing the antiquated village constabulary. A town newspaper, the Somerville *Journal*, was founded that same year to unite the community through the first daily medium of information addressed to its concerns.[7] In 1871, a large new high school building was erected adjacent to the old structure, which was converted into a town hall.[8]

Elements within the citizenry began to fear that the town meeting form of government could not keep pace with the demand for effective municipal management of an expanding city. Complaints over the inadequacy of the town government system cropped up. Two unsuccessful petitions for division of the town appeared before the General Court in 1867,[9] and a movement to join Somerville to Boston or Charlestown surfaced in 1869, but subsided quickly for lack of popular support.[10] Finally, when the 1870 U.S. Census recorded that Somerville's population had pierced the 10,000-inhabitant threshold required to qualify for a city charter, the community successfully obtained official city status from the General Court of the Commonwealth.[11] Somerville became one of many Massachusetts towns securing city charters after the Civil War to manage the problems of growth through larger, comprehensive, and more powerful municipal governments. Conversions from town to city rippled across the Bay State, bringing 60 percent of the population under the governance of city charters by 1890.[12]

A Republican machine

The ruling elite of Yankee businessmen made a smooth transference of power from town to city government. The new city charter supplied them with centralized instruments of administration and job patronage. A mayor, board of aldermen, and common council supplanted the slow-moving town-meeting system. Two aldermen and four councilmen were elected annually to represent each of the city's four wards (Fig. 4.1).[13]

Yankee Republicans shrewdly manipulated Somerville's government to build a partisan supremacy that went unchallenged until the following century. They fastened a lock on both the board of aldermen and the common council, which together framed legislation as

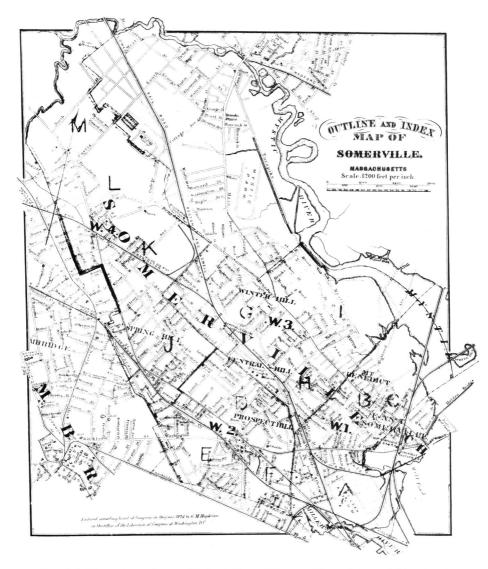

Fig. 4.1 Map of newly established City of Somerville and its neighborhoods showing the four wards, 1874. *Atlas of the City of Somerville, Massachusetts.*

the city council. Of the aldermen and councilmen elected in the early 1880s whose party affiliation was identified, over 80 percent were Republican.[14] A decade later, Republican power became even more imposing. In 1891, seven of the eight aldermen were Republicans; in

Table 4.1. *Occupations of aldermen, common councilmen, and school committee members, 1880–4*

	Aldermen		Common councilmen		School committeemen	
	N	%	N	%	N	%
White collar	18	82	32	68	16	84
Professions	0		2		12	
Business[a]	17		21		3	
Clerical and other white collar	1		9		1	
Blue collar	4	18	15	32	0	0
Skilled	2		9		0	
Semiskilled	2		6		0	
Unskilled	0		0		0	
Housewives	0	0	0	0	2	11
Unknown	0	0	0	0	1	5
Total	22		47		19	

[a]Includes proprietors, manufacturers, commercial agents, inventors, salesmen, and dealers.
Source: Somerville, *Annual Reports*, 1880–4; *City Directory.*

1893, twenty-two out of twenty-four aldermen and common councilmen were G.O.P. members.[15] Above all, an unbroken succession of stalwart Republican mayors blocked the rise of an Irish executive who could have unleashed the minions of Celtic Democracy. After the Irish immigrant Hugh O'Brien vaulted into the mayor's office of Boston in 1884, the Republicans were keenly vigilant to keep the Democratic contagion from spreading to the suburb.[16]

Republican political culture was also expressed as a popular devotion to temperance. The local civic associations and Republican clubs that hailed Somerville as the "Banner Republican City of the Commonwealth"[17] also pointed proudly to the ban on liquor licenses ritualistically renewed each year by the city's voters.[18] Virtuous boosters accorded Somerville the added honor of "Banner Temperance City of the Commonwealth."[19] The compilers of the Massachusetts Census of 1885 observed that the liquor prohibition was a strong attraction luring respectable people to that suburb.[20]

Businessmen spearheaded the G.O.P. and ran city hall. In the 1880s, they formed the great majority of aldermen (Table 4.1). They also

Table 4.2. *Occupations of aldermen, common councilmen, and school committee members, 1891–3*

	Aldermen		Common councilmen		School committeemen	
	N	%	N	%	N	%
White collar	16	89	31	84	14	88
Professions	1		6		8	
Business	9		16		1	
Clerical and other white collar	6		9		5	
Blue collar	1	6	6	16	0	0
Skilled	1		4		0	
Semiskilled	0		2		0	
Unskilled	0		0		0	
Housewives	0	0	0	0	2	13
Unknown	1	6	0	0	0	0
Total	18		37		16	

Source: Somerville, *Annual Reports,* 1891–3; *City Directory.*

captured more seats on the common council than any other occupational group. A sizable contingent of artisans and semiskilled workers, however, helped to deny them equal domination of the lower legislative branch.

The school committee differed sharply in occupational profile from the board of aldermen and the common council. Only white-collar men and a couple of housewives sat on the school committee from 1880 to 1884. Few businessmen were elected to that post. Professional men – chiefly doctors, lawyers, and educators – controlled the management of educational affairs, as in the years before Somerville received a city charter.

A decade later, the occupational distribution of Somerville's politicians exhibited even greater dominance by white-collar men. In the early 1890s, 89 percent of the aldermen and 84 percent of the councilmen came from the white-collar class; most were businessmen and clerical workers (Table 4.2). The share of blue-collar workers among both aldermen and councilmen declined from the early 1880s. The occupational distribution of the school committee, however, closely resembled the one found in the 1880s: only white-collar workers and a few housewives sat on that body, and professionals were heavily represented.

New faces appeared more often on the board of aldermen and the common council than on the school committee. None of the twenty-two aldermen and only two out of forty-seven councilmen from the early 1880s held office in the next decade. However, seven out of twenty-two school committee members were serving again in the early 1890s.[21] A relatively stable group of professional men were returned to office from year to year to act as the custodians of educational policy.

The Republican machine rotated its candidates between the board of aldermen and the common council, thereby gaining wide influence over public affairs. Over half of the aldermen sampled from the 1880s and 1890s also gained election to the common council. Only one school committeeman, however, served on one of the legislative bodies. Political mobility was high between the board of aldermen and the common council, but almost nonexistent between those organizations and the school committee.

Although the school committeemen were usually Republican regulars, they contrasted in important ways with the aldermen and the councilmen. The majority of the school committee were educated professional men. They tended to hold themselves above the hurly burly of city politics. A few identified themselves as "Citizens" Republicans, a group of Mugwump-syle reformers.[22] They were regularly returned to their posts, for the public viewed them as a custodial elite, qualified by their education to run the schools in a spirit of service detached from political interest.

Intensifying patterns of urbanization

From 1872 to 1900, the thriving Yankee city of Somerville was one of the most desirable suburbs for middle-class people in metropolitan Boston. The number of inhabitants more than tripled in thirty years, but Somerville's social structure was cushioned against acute stresses by the city's ample residential space, the region's expanding economy, and an influx of immigrants that was small compared to Boston's.

The huge family estates of the Tufts, Irelands, Hawkins, Bentons, and Wyatts in the hilly central section were parceled to real-estate speculators. Rows of single- and multiple-family dwellings shot up on a rectangular gridwork of blocks carved out of the rambling farmlands.[23] Home construction surged ahead through the 1880s and peaked in 1892 before the onset of a nationwide depression. The number of building permits issued by the city rose from 91 in 1882 to 651 in 1892.[24] The building boom was furious in the outlying west wards of Somerville, wards three and four, and especially around the hills of Tufts College, which had been founded by a grant from the Tufts family in 1852.[25]

Controlling the city government through the Republican machine, Somerville's business and professional men boldly reshaped the city's environment. They expressed their faith in the progress of industrial civilization by constructing a physical plant that would promote the welfare of the whole population generations into the future. From 1872 when Somerville became a city to the turn of the century, they laid out hundreds of miles of new paved streets, reclaimed marshy lowlands, enlarged the water supply and the sewage system, installed electric street lights, added new public buildings to house a professional police department, a fire department, and a mass-circulation library, and built over a dozen new schools. The costly construction of Broadway Park out of sixteen acres of marshy open sewerage in 1875 symbolized the indefatigable dedication of the city fathers to modernization. "It met with fierce opposition, and its effect on local politics was volcanic, resulting, in 1876, in a complete overturn of the city government which inaugurated it," recalled a Somerville writer. Notwithstanding the political retaliation of taxpayers disgruntled with the $75,000 construction cost, the Republican machine weathered the storm and was credited for eliminating a health hazard, improving the value of surrounding real estate, and supplying the city with a recreational park.[26]

By the 1880s, the city had sufficiently contained debts incurred by building projects to lower tax rates. Yankee businessmen, whose taxes constituted the foundation of municipal finance, tightly reined the budget by establishing strict priorities. Somerville's Republican mayors lectured the city council each year on the necessity of efficient spending. In his inaugural address of 1881, John A. Cummings expressed a theme that was frequently repeated by his successors:

> Our first duty is economy. The money of the city should be expended with the same prudence and care exercised in the management of private affairs. While it is obligatory upon us to promote the material welfare of the city by providing for the support of schools, for the protection of life and property, for the comfort and convenience of good streets, sidewalks, street lights, pure water, and all necessary health-securing measures, it is our duty to accomplish all this with the least possible outlay of money. . . . A

public debt is not a public blessing, and believing this, we are annually reducing ours.

Through a policy of wise budgeting and loan financing, the Republican regimes lived up to mayor Cummings' challenge. They lowered
the city's funded debt from $1,600,000 in 1877 to $860,000 in 1888. In
that span of time, the property tax rate was cut sharply from $2.07
per $1,000 to $1.28 per $1,000 of valuation. [27]

After 1870, projects to upgrade the physical plant took a growing
share of expenditures, while the school system took a shrinking percentage. In addition, the adoption of "sinking funds" to finance municipal debt meant that school allocations henceforth were further
limited by a balance for repaying long-term loans. Although per-capita
school expenditure rose from $13.30 in 1880 to $18.98 in 1895, Somerville fell from its lofty perch as one of the state's top ten municipalities
in school spending. [28] By 1895, with the city budget depleted after a
depression, Somerville dropped to 72 out of 353 towns and cities in
per-capita expenditure.

The administrative, engineering, and financial innovations of the
Republican machine barely managed to keep pace with the needs of
a constantly expanding population. The tide of European immigrants
to the Boston area subsided after the Civil War, but the natural increase of their colonies took over as a generator of population growth.
In addition, migrants from neighboring states and Canada continued
to pour into eastern Massachusetts. Farm families and rural laborers
from Vermont, New Hampshire, and Maine arrived in Somerville in
search of new opportunities. The spread of fisheries from Canada
southward, as well as growing commerce between Canada and New
England, drew people from Nova Scotia, Prince Edward Island, and
the other maritime provinces to the cities of the Bay State. [29]

Somerville reflected the changes in immigration patterns and natural increase. The share of foreign-born peoples leveled off at 27 percent of the city's population in 1875 and 25 percent in 1885 (Table 4.3).
From 1875 to 1885, the percentage of Irish immigrants dwindled from
15 percent to 11 percent, but the proportion of newcomers from English Canada edged ahead slightly from 7 percent to 8 percent.

A dynamic new element in Somerville was the emergence of the
second-generation Irish. A key index to the rapid development of this
group was the high birth rate found among foreign-born mothers. In
1875, nearly three fifths of foreign-born mothers, most of whom were
Irish, had more than three children, while only one third of native-
born mothers had given birth to more than three children. [30] Also, a
mixed Irish-and-American generation resulted from the growing

Table 4.3. *Somerville population by country of origin, 1875 and 1885*

	1875		1885	
Country	N	%	N	%
U.S.	16,002	73	22,471	75
English Canada	1,504	7	2,329	8
Ireland	3,176	15	3,431	11
England, Scotland, Wales	697	3	949	3
Germany	189	1	195	1
Italy	18	—	78	—
Sweden, Norway	77	—	136	—
Other	205	1	382	1
Total	21,868		29,971	

Sources: Massachusetts Census 1875, Vol. I, pp. xxxix, 287–339; *Massachusetts Census 1885,* Vol. I, pt. 1, p. 534.

number of young adults who crossed the most intimate boundary separating Irish from Yankee, Catholic from Protestant, and foreigner from native.[31] By 1890, one out of four marriages involved an immigrant and a native partner. Many offspring of these mixed unions were raised in the Catholic faith and identified strongly with their Irish heritage.

The second-generation Irish climbed higher than their immigrant parents on Somerville's social pyramid. Many became artisans and white-collar employees, and some entered the professions. In addition, Irish immigrants arriving in the late nineteenth century found better jobs than their forebears who had fled the famine. In 1885, 20 percent of all Irish-born male employees had white-collar posts and 25 percent worked in the skilled trades. Since only 10 percent of Irish-born employees in Boston had white-collar jobs, Somerville appears to have experienced an earlier consolidation of an Irish middle class.[32]

As the Irish moved upward gradually on the occupational ladder, they began to disperse from their colonies in "the Patch" – the rail-yard district – and "Brick Bottom" – the center of brick manufacturing. The successful ones left the decrepit shanties in those districts for the inexpensive homes rising on the hillsides. By 1890, the second-generation immigrants, many of whom were Irish, comprised 27 percent of the population in ward one and 31 percent of ward two.[33] They penetrated even into westernmost ward four, comprising 22 percent of the population of an area that had been a bastion of comfortable gentry families such as the Tufts, who had had considerable holdings there.[34] Also merging into the flow of Somerville Irish moving to new locales were the second-generation Boston and Charlestown Irish, who crossed to the suburb in search of better housing.

The proliferation of manufacturers in the Boston area and Somerville was a powerful magnet pulling immigrants and their children into the suburb to take low-skilled industrial jobs. Although slowed by the Panic of 1873, the pace of industrial growth was steady, leaving Boston the nation's fifth largest manufacturing city in 1880 and the sixth largest in 1890.[35] The prosperity of the Hub City and its neighboring cities rested upon the operatives who manned the increasingly complex machines producing metal parts, clothing, confectionaries, printing supplies, and building materials.[36] In the self-employed artisan's eyes, the growing army of semiskilled workers symptomized the loss of independence and the erosion of craftsmanship by technological innovation. To middle-class reformers, it portended a growing polarization of classes and ethnic groups worse than the social divisions of the past.

In Somerville, new industries such as meat packing swelled the ranks of workingmen. The suburb's eastern fringe adjoining Cambridge and Boston became the site of New England's largest meatpacking and -dressing industries. The output of the J. P. Squire Company, North Packing Company, and the New England Dressed Meat and Wool Company soared from $3,700,000 in 1880 to $15,700,000 in 1899.[37] The colossal North Packing Company alone occupied five- and nine-story buildings on thirteen acres of land and employed more than 1,200 men.[38] Somerville was the home of a diverse range of other large industries: the Fresh Pond Ice Company, the Derby Desk Company, the Sanborn Brickmaking Company, the Middlesex Bleach, Dye, and Print Works, the American Brass Tube Works, the Leavitt and Henderson Carriage Manufactory, the Somerville Iron Foundry, the West Somerville Moulding Mill, the Cushman Shade Roller Manufactory, the Carr Jewelry and Novelty Company, the Union Glass Company (the only glass factory in the Boston area), and the Hurn Carpet Cleaning Company (the largest in New England). The clothing and building supplies industries of Somerville added to the city's output, which rose from $5,900,000 in 1880, to $7,300,000 in 1890, to $20,000,000 in 1899.[39]

The expansion of local industry created hundreds of jobs for semiskilled laborers who crowded into Somerville. Their share of the male labor force had declined to 8 percent in 1875 as the number of skilled construction workers grew faster in the postwar housing boom, but the new wave of mechanization and factory installations of the 1880s increased the proportion of semiskilled workers to 16 percent in 1885

Table 4.4. *Occupational distribution of the male labor force, 1875, 1885, 1900*

	1875		1885		1900	
	N	%	N	%	N	%
White collar	1,500	34	3,992	50	8,438	46
Professions	124	3	220	3	1,006	5
Other white collar	1,376	31	3,772	47	7,432	40
Blue collar	2,849	66	4,058	50	10,009	55
Skilled	1,634	38	2,208	27	4,775	26
Semiskilled	360	8	1,257	16	3,905	21
Unskilled	855	20	593	7	1,329	7
Total	4,349		8,050		18,447	

Sources: Massachusetts Census 1875, Vol. I, pp. 531–2; *Massachusetts Census 1885*, Vol. I, pt. 2, pp. 262–6; *U.S. Census 1900*, Vol. II, pt. 2, pp. 590–3.

and to 21 percent in 1900 (Table 4.4). The mechanization that heightened the demand for operatives especially imperiled the status of Somerville's butchers, metalworkers, clothing workers, furniture makers, and shoemakers. Competition from the factory system drove down demand for their skills.

Somerville's housing boom, however, continued to buoy workers in the construction trades, and prevented a severe decline in the skilled labor force.[40] Despite the proportional decrease in skilled workers from 1875 to 1900, their numbers nearly tripled from 1,634 to 4,775. Over three thousand new skilled jobs had been created. Despite the buffering effect of the growing construction trades, native artisans continued to wonder if they could maintain their position in the face of foreign-born labor and mechanization.

The fastest-growing opportunities for employment arose in the white-collar field. White-collar workers in Somerville multiplied almost six-fold from 1,500 to 8,438, growing from 34 percent of the male labor force in 1875 to 46 percent in 1900. Clerical, bookkeeping, drafting, and sales jobs multiplied most rapidly. The rise in white-collar employment also occurred in Boston, where many Somerville residents worked. White-collar employees in the Hub increased from 32 percent of the male labor force in 1880 to 38 percent in 1900.[41] Many employees moved to Somerville to find better housing and a commuter work schedule.

The creation of new local jobs by industrial and commercial expansion combined with the introduction of a double-tracked, electrified system of street railways to attract immigrants, working people, and white-collar employees who wanted a suburban residency while commuting to nearby work. After the West End Street Railway Company, formed in 1887, made these improvements, the five-cent-fare zone expanded to West Somerville.[42] A local historian in the 1890s noted with satisfaction, "Somerville has perhaps the best railway facilities of any suburb of Boston, and to this fact is largely to be attributed the phenomenal increase of that city in population and importance."[43] Indeed, even the most humble commuters could now locate in the farthest district of Somerville. The whole of Somerville was opened up to working-class people who needed cheap and efficient transportation to reach changing worksites. Carpenters and plumbers had to reach new building projects; machinists and tailors moved from shop to shop, from factory to factory, as business fluctuated. Many low-white-collar and working-class families depended heavily on regular mass transit, because they had two or three wage-earners who had to reach different workplaces. Now, these people could set up a home in Somerville.[44]

Immigrants and second-generation Irish workers followed the twisting streetcar lines into the cheapest housing districts. They pooled their resources to build the city's first Catholic institutions, including St. Joseph's Catholic Church in 1874 and three parochial schools by 1900.

Although the Irish were a small, segregated minority with little economic or political power, their presence unnerved the leaders of Yankee society. The nativist wing of the local Republican organization suspected that the influx of Irish Catholics was part of a design by priests seeking to win the suburbs surrounding Boston for the Pope. Protestants spread rumors that Boston priests encouraged prosperous "papist" families in their parish to colonize "unChristianized" Somerville. A chairman of the Republican city committee described the advice Boston clerics gave to their parishioners: "We are opening a new parish in Somerville and need your help. It's a nice place, good service to Boston – why don't you move out there?"[45]

Much to the delight of nativists, the reshuffling of Irish residential patterns actually supplied Protestant reinforcements that sustained the Yankee majority in Somerville. As the Irish pushed outward from the inner-Boston neighborhoods to East Boston and Charlestown, Yankee families in these areas fled to Somerville to escape envelopment in the Celtic surge. These displaced natives, mostly shopkeepers, merchants, and artisans, were also drawn by the attractions of the suburb, its schools, affordable housing, and salubrious spaces. The city of Somerville reported in 1880 the lowest mortality rate of eleven Massachusetts cities of comparable size.[46] Lower population densities, better sanitation, and improvements in medical treatment reduced Somerville's crude death rate.[47] In this pleasant suburb, where the Yankees were still in control, retreating natives built comfortable homes on the hills that looked across to the Boston neighborhoods whose overcrowding, pollution, and disease they had fled.[48]

Because of its strategic location, Somerville became the first bridge-head for the Yankee exodus flowing out of the central city to the "safe" Republican suburbs north of Boston. Indeed, Somerville Yankees regarded their community as a linchpin holding Middlesex County for the G.O.P.: As long as Somerville stayed Republican, they felt the Republican territory to the north would never fall to the Democrats. The Somerville *Journal*, under the ownership of the powerful banker Joseph O. Hayden, broadcast the slogan "Keep Somerville Republican." Opponents of "Romanism" operated a local branch of the American Protective Association to keep Somerville a fortress against the invading throngs of Catholics.[49]

Protected in Somerville, newcomer Yankees created an ideal of sociable life that revolved around their pride in homeownership and the cultivation of domesticity it afforded. A portrait of their lifestyle was drawn by Martha Perry Lowe, the wife of the Reverend Charles Lowe of the First Congregational Parish. When her husband received his appointment in 1859, they "built a house adjoining a large open pasture," because they were "pleased with the rural aspect of the town" and "everyone said that real estate was a safe investment here." Her chief reminiscences were the round of visits she and her husband paid to the notable citizens in their parish. She recalled the hospitality enjoyed in the Winter Hill home of Somerville founder John S. Edgerly – "a dignified house" once occupied by the great statesman Edward Everett. She fondly remembered visits to "the pretty cottage of the venerable John Boles," with a "very fine view from its piazza," and the "handsome residence of Cutler Downer on Central Street, much beloved by his neighbors and friends." She recalled hours spent at the mansion of banker Robert Vinal called "the old Spring Place," which "stood high from the street, with extensive grounds [and] large trees," where "We took tea . . . much impressed with the size and attractiveness of the old-fashioned low-studded rooms, especially the large square parlor." And she vividly related the rousing conversations at the nearby home of George O. Brastow, the first mayor of Somerville, who "was a striking personality, always hospitable, ready to oblige a friend, one who loved to joke about his experiences in the war, and tell how he graduated at Bull Run."[50]

Outside of their homes, Yankee white-collar families revolved their social activities around the city's numerous religious institutions and secular voluntary associations. Twenty-six Protestant churches – eight Congregational, five Baptist, four Episcopalian, four Methodist, three Universalist, and two minor denominations – provided a varied religious network for communal interaction. But churches alone were insufficient for expressing the sociable energies of bustling Yankees. Twenty-three men's associations, eighteen women's associations, and three mixed associations afforded a wide range of opportunities for social recreation and civic activism.[51] Fraternal lodges for Masons and Odd Fellows and gaming clubs were popular among businessmen who sought to make connections with the powerful and the prestigious. The Central Club Association enrolled the leading lights of Somerville government and commerce, such as councilman Frank E. Dickerman and banker and Somerville *Journal* publisher Joseph O. Hayden. At "The Central," it was said the pillars of the G.O.P. "meet frequently in a social way, and take an active interest in whist, billiards, pool and bowling." Social climbing was an important part of club activity, but the general benefit of membership was satisfying camaraderie. The competitive newcomers in a large, changing community found relaxing fellowship and mutual support in these associations. As the reporter of the "Webcowit Club" explained, "The object of the Club is the promotion of social intercourse, and the encouragement of kindly feeling and good-fellowship among its members."

The wives of businessmen and white-collar employees organized associations parallel to those of their husbands, but focused more sharply on charitable affairs. The Erminie Lodge, a woman's auxiliary for Odd Fellowship, exemplified the humanitarian impulses of Victorian Yankee women. Florence Hurn, a leading member, summarized one year's achievements: "The lodge has furnished a room in the Somerville Hospital, and replenishes the furnishing as often as is required. It has also furnished a room in the Odd Fellows' Home at Worcester, and at Christmas time sends a box of useful articles for distribution among the inmates. . . . The visitation and care of the sick are carefully attended to."[52]

For the many Somerville residents who sought edification, three cultural and literary clubs ran a busy schedule of activities. The Hillside Club attracted numerous dilettantes. Many were graduates of Somerville High School who had acquired a taste for sophisticated culture. There they formed a community of amateur artists, authors, and scientists. Helen J. Sanborn, the Club President in 1896 glowingly described its business:

> The constituency of the Club is the same as that of a large family in which there is not only a difference in age and sex, but also a wide difference in tastes, in natural gifts and attainments. There are mature and immature minds; the scholarly man and the "sweet girl graduate"; there are those who can produce papers that would grace any society of "literati," and those who, with fear and trembling, can but read that which another has written. Some of the best literary work from the pen of the present mayor of Somerville has been prepared especially for the Hillside, of which he has long been a member. Some find in it their only opportunity for the investigation of a new subject, and the writing of an original paper. Others make use of their musical talent, for music often serves as an illustration, and always gives an added pleasure to the program. An opportunity for social converse is a part of each evening's plan. A private house as the meeting place adds an air of refinement and the charm of hospitality, and an "outing" in May tends to promote friendly feeling and good-fellowship.[53]

Through the Hillside Club, the burghers of Somerville demonstrated that economic progress enabled them to develop cultural leadership as well.

The array of voluntary associations symbolized the social dominance of the Yankee middle class. They intertwined with the branches of city government and business enterprises to form the controlling framework for the life of the community. The Yankees had unified Somerville's institutions into a single medium for their interaction and the exercise of power and leadership. The growth of diversified social opportunities was another attraction bringing to Somerville Yankee families from Boston and Charlestown who felt harassed by foreigners and urban impersonality. In the suburb, they could enter a secure world of their own people firmly in command of the surrounding community. Their ethos embraced an ideology of escape and insulation from the profane city that enshrined the suburb as the locus of "the highest culture and morality."[54]

Policies to prolong schooling: standardizing group achievement and an empirical world view for the built environment

The Yankees of the Gilded Age suburb recognized that their web of dominance woven from politics, enterprise, and voluntarism would be fortified by an expanded role for public schooling. A more complex, pluralistic community needed revitalized public education to train intelligent and productive citizens who would support the institutional order. The key to a more effective school system, middle-class Yankees believed, lay in increasing the years of schooling for students.

How did Somerville schoolmen formulate a policy to prolong schooling? They started first from a clear recognition of the limiting material circumstances that impeded students from gliding smoothly up the grade ladder. They agonized over the poverty of working-class families, dependent on their children for a quarter to a third of their annual income,[55] which propelled youngsters out of school prematurely into the low-skilled job market. They understood the conflict between penury and sponsorship of schooling. They knew that economic forces, not moral failing, was the major cause of early departure.

Nevertheless, they implored parents "thus circumstanced [to] submit for a while to personal sacrifices, and heroically endure hardship, and absolute want even." The high cost of educational opportunity, they assured, would be an investment repaid with valuable skills that would secure "more lucrative and desirable positions in life."[56] When they turned to the children of prosperous families, educators worried that the allurements of "immediate pecuniary compensation" in business enticed these youngsters out of the classroom. It was also feared that some affluent youths left before graduating because they could see no personal gain in finishing grammar school. Schoolmen felt, however, that even these boys should recognize that rising qualifications for white-collar and professional careers made advanced schooling increasingly advantageous.[57] As the school committee expounded on the profitability of acquiring more education, they publicized the idea that the opportunity for higher levels of schooling was a rewarding family investment.

The school committee advised the prolongation of schooling as a way of ensuring the public character of education.[58] By lengthening educational careers, they claimed to "furnish what the great mass of our people want, and all they want for the training of their children," lest they withdraw and public schools turn into eleemosynary institutions.[59]

The schoolmen felt that their arguments were reaching a more receptive public, as industrialization restructured the economy of Somerville and the surrounding Boston metropolitan region. Business management increased the demand for personnel who could track complex economic exchanges by compiling statistical records and who could accurately transmit ideas and information in a business organization. These were the daily tasks of the Yankee white-collar employees whose mathematical and linguistic skills were gained from advanced schooling or training on the job. They logically associated their standard of living and status in the community with these abilities, and therefore sought the means to transfer them to their children.[60] The offerings of the public school system were an inexpensive and convenient opportunity to do so. Thus, white-collar Yankees were anxious that their sons enter the public schools and be promoted to courses that cultivated the language and calculating skills demanded increasingly by businesses. These abilities were also highly important for entering college and the professions, which were raising their qualifications in the last decades of the century.[61]

The skilled workers of Somerville had an interest in prolonging their children's education, but for reasons connected with their changing economic position. They were still a vital part of the city's economy, but industrialization had dimmed the prospects for manual self-employment. Factory mechanization and the minute subdivision of work that rendered skill less valuable,[62] the difficulty of finding apprenticeships, which caused widespread complaints,[63] and the susceptibility of numerous crafts to seasonal unemployment[64] made many workers feel that their status was declining relative to white-collar workers, whose opportunities were expanding. Even the flourishing building trades of Somerville faced recession as housing development reached the city's physical limits. Moreover, these construction workers were especially vulnerable to seasonal layoffs. Confronting a changing and insecure labor market, many artisan fathers took precautions to improve their sons' prospects by sending them to school for the skills needed in white-collar employment. They looked harder to the public schools for the training their sons needed to have the *option* of leaving manual work for secure white-collar occupations.[65]

In coordination with a public campaign for prolonged sponsorship of schooling that struck responsive chords with both white-collar and artisan parents, the schoolmen reformed the curriculum and the procedure of evaluating for promotion. Somerville's educators discovered that if they standardized coursework and the criteria for promotion to accord with practical needs, more pupils would finish grammar school, and many would move on to high school.

To propel more students to higher grade levels required a promotion procedure based on standard group achievement. In theory, the grade to which a student was promoted was a convenient aggregation of pupils with similar amounts of knowledge and learning capacities because of previous training and common age. In fact, however, any given grade, especially in primary or grammar school, displayed a broad spectrum of ages and aptitudes. For example, the first grade of grammar school had children as young as eight and as old as twelve. Many students from other cities transferred into class; they usually had prior schooling that failed to match their new classmates'. Teachers faced a bewildering diversity of ability levels.

As the school committee became more conscious of the interdependency between effective instruction and a standard level of group learning, they established a uniform grading system to produce a common procedure of evaluation used by all instructors. Thus all pupils assembled in the next grade would possess the same level of achievement as defined by the grading system. All distinctions between passing and failing work became based on the impersonal concept of "average ability." Teachers arranged lessons according to what the majority of the students could handle. A teacher's instructional technique was to be flexible enough to deal with the problems of individual pupils, but the content of lessons was governed strictly by her estimate of her students' "average ability."

In the view of the school committee, an individual teacher's determination of a grade's lesson content was convenient but potentially chaotic. The first-grade class of Teacher A had to acquire the same knowledge as that of Teacher B. Otherwise, as students advanced to higher grades where they often combined into the same class, the discrepancies in preparation would hamper instruction and common promotion to the next grade level. The school committee cooperated with teachers, therefore, to formulate syllabi, predetermined "Courses of Study" to be employed uniformly in each grade of every school in the system.[66] The introduction of these syllabi would insure homogeneous achievement and equal opportunity to advance to higher grades.

Schoolmen regularly revised the syllabi to raise the standard average ability to manipulate words and numbers.[67] Higher verbal and mathematical skills were needed in the expanding white-collar fields to monitor increasingly complex commercial exchanges. Bookkeeping was introduced in the grammar schools in 1882 to prepare students for one of the fastest growing occupations in the city.[68] The demand for able bookkeepers outstripped the supply. Businessmen asked that the schools require more "number work" to "meet the demands of the countinghouse."[69] More generally, the city dweller living amidst the profusion of signs, printed media, and rapidly changing daily news needed effective communication skills. In 1886 courses in English-language skills occupied half the study time of grammar school grades; arithmetic was the second most-studied subject.[70]

Educators valued verbal accuracy and speedy computation over intellectual creativity. Manipulative skills superseded the common-school reformers' insistence on cultivating independent faculties and judgment a generation earlier. In the Somerville schools after the 1870s, pupils focused on laborious transcription of sentences from dictation; they spelled and defined all words used in their textbook. The first grammar school lessons in composition were designed to mould writing into a clerical format, rather than to cultivate literary artistry. Students' first assignments were "business papers . . . orders, bills of purchase, receipts, promissory notes, drafts, advertisements, invitations, etc."[71] In arithmetic, students spent less time in analyzing concepts and more in "gaining familiarity with processes and quickness in computations."[72]

Somerville's scholars were turning into facile manipulators of numbers. The school committee noted in 1884, "In rapidity of abstract computations, there has been a decided gain within the past few years." They also admitted, however, that the emphasis on operation resulted in a loss of "ability to reason, to apply principles to concrete examples, and to solve problems requiring close thinking."[73]

The Massachusetts civil-service exams of the 1880s reveal that these technical skills, no matter how superficial and uncreative, were increasingly demanded in white-collar jobs. Applicants for clerical posts were asked to compute rapidly and accurately railroad passenger fares, insurance premiums, and interest rates. They were asked to add five columns of five-digit figures, to copy a rough draft of a letter filled with interlineations and abbreviations, to write down from memory an oral communication. Speed, accuracy, and precision of verbal and mathematical operations were indispensable to process the growing mass of data confronted in business, management, and clerical work. The establishment of these qualifications for white-collar work encouraged students to stay in school longer to develop the skills necessary to meet them.

An important innovation that encouraged scholastic progress was the free provision of textbooks. This service especially helped youngsters from poor families to extend their schooling. In the 1870s, teachers assigned *Sargent's Readers and Spellers*, *Greenleaf's Arithmetic*, and *Harper's School Geography*, but because these books had to be purchased by students they were used in a limited fashion.[74] After a visit to the New York City public schools, the school committee advised that Somerville adopt New York's practice of supplying free textbooks, which would enable many poor students to continue their studies.[75] At last, in the 1880s, the city schools provided all textbooks free of charge, as this service was mandated by state law.[76]

The dissemination of textbooks heightened the tension between creative thinking and rote memorization. Throughout the 1870s and 1880s, the school committee complained of the "arbitrary exercise of the memory," especially in grammar recitations, history, and geography courses.[77] As each course pivoted on an assigned textbook, critics asserted that the textbook was a crutch to teachers, who had "a class recite *verbatim* what is set down in the book."[78] Despite these fears, the number and the variety of textbooks grew, as teachers, principals, and a special textbook committee ordered new books year after year.[79]

Administrators and teachers were besieged by salesmen eager to capitalize on the lucrative market for new textbooks. In 1888, the school system spent $4,284 in book purchases from twenty-six publishers; in 1899, expenditures rose to $5,665 for texts purchased from twenty-one publishers.[80] The multiplicity of books that usually served as the reference points for study complicated the problem of standardizing the learning process. Teachers selected different basic texts and supplementary readers for each subject. Many students not only parroted routine textbook lessons; they were also memorizing widely divergent lessons.

A centralized examination system helped to standardize learning units in the face of individual teacher preferences and the variety of textbooks. All questions for tests in the grammar school were approved by all the principals in a school district, and checked by the superintendent of schools. The superintendent periodically administered his own tests. These were designed to "ascertain the degree and kind of development resulting from the instruction, and should tend to unify the system of teaching."[81] A standard set of tests compelled teachers of different classes to adhere to the syllabus that prepared for success on the exam. A minimum passing score of 70 out of 100 on all exams was required to advance to the succeeding grade in all grammar schools.[82]

An impersonal standard that applied to every pupil regulated movement up the educational ladder. Assessing achievement in numerical form, it was hoped, would replace the idiosyncratic judgment of different teachers with an objective measure. Educators felt that an averaged numerical score would make promotions more fair, because it would make evaluation more consistent. Moreover, they believed that taking a numerical average of a series of exams would filter out the constant ability level hidden by fluctuating performance.

The new curriculum that formatted educational achievement according to a measurable group standard also introduced a new program of studies that subtly inculcated a common worldview suited for a built, technological environment. Known as manual training or "hand-learning" and once confined to the handicapped and retarded, it evolved into one of the most innovative courses in Massachusetts schools after the Civil War.[83] Courses in drawing, woodwork, and sewing were espoused for an assortment of reasons. In the early 1870s, some proponents explained that by providing "prompt, speedy, and ample . . . education for the manufacturing or mechanic operative," manual training was an "investment promising a vast pecuniary return." A few years later, other advocates contended that it inculcated a salutary respect for labor and its products.[84] By the 1890s, educators added that manual training conditioned the higher nervous functions to cultivate intelligence, will power, and moral judgment.[85]

Somerville's manual training courses, however, gave only the most superficial acquaintance with mechanical techniques. They provided little opportunity for shopwork. In 1894, Somerville had no courses in metalwork and only one year of woodwork. No cooking courses were offered, although sewing was taught from the fourth to the seventh grade.[86] Clay modeling, paper cutting, and drawing comprised the bulk of Somerville's manual curriculum – hardly a thorough preparation for mechanical work. By contrast, Springfield taught six years of woodwork and Waltham five years in their grammar schools, with an additional course in high school. Boston and New Bedford offered three years of woodwork in grammar school and a year in high school. Haverhill supplied two years of woodwork in grammar school and another year in high school. Boston, Cambridge, and Waltham high schools also offered training in metalwork.

Although these cities had more comprehensive programs in manual training than Somerville, there was no consistent correlation between the extent of industrialization and the level of manual training. Heavily industrialized centers such as Lawrence, Lowell, Lynn, and Fall River had only modest manual programs, very similar to Somerville's. Manual training did not diffuse evenly into every industrial community. It served different educational purposes in different cities.

In Somerville, manual training was valued primarily for its effects on cognitive development rather than as a specialized preparation for industrial work. Educators agreed that manual training raised the quality of scholastic work by improving perceptual and imaginative faculties.[87] Drawing was introduced for the general purpose of cultivating "the constant necessity to represent objects."[88] Drawing, sewing, and clay modeling were not intended "to graduate carpenters, blacksmiths, and machinists," but, instead, to gratify the child's "natural, inborn desire to do, to create, to express." After inspecting Philadelphia's manual training courses in 1888, Somerville educators were convinced that manual training strengthened powers of expression and formal representation.[89]

Accurate reproduction rather than creativity, however, was the chief outcome of Somerville's manual training program. Children in the earliest three grades drew spheres, cubes, and cylinders, "the three forms which seem to lie at the foundation of all form." After drawing a sphere, for example, a child then "modelled" out of clay a sphere "as nearly perfect as he is able," and learned the words to describe his achievement. Miss L. A. Herrick, Somerville's special drawing teacher, explained that by his sequence of activities "the child is learning his first lessons in accuracy and truth, truthfulness in seeing, in thinking, in doing, and in speaking." In the higher grades, students drew more complex, but still geometric forms, and from 1890, they learned the techniques of mechanical drawing.[90] Drawing in school was narrowed to "object drawing." Its goal was to depict formally rather than to interpret subjectively.[91]

The techniques of sloyd, or Swedish woodcraft, were introduced into the high school in the 1890s. Sloyd also nourished the capacity for formal reproduction. In this course, a student created wood imitations of a series of models.

In all of its manifestations, manual training cultivated an empirical sense of the built material world. The generation of pupils who drew polygons, sewed patterns, and modeled clay and wood, thereby developed their perception of proportion, size, shape, and quantity. The suburban youth from a white-collar family who studied out of books, who had never seen a workshop, was able to manipulate material objects and develop a feel for their physical properties. These were important lessons because educators feared that children of white-collar parents were becoming estranged from manual work and mechanical processes.[92] Without training in inductive judgment of built material objects, the generation heading into the future industrial society would be unable to understand "the facts and forces of the tangible, living, active world . . . its buildings, machinery, processes."[93]

The ability to observe closely and to communicate accurately what was observed was increasingly required at all levels of human endeavor. This demand heightened as organizations multiplied in scale; lines of communication lengthened; and diagrams, charts, maps, and blueprints were needed to comprehend parts of the built environment and the activities people had launched amidst its complexities. The Massachusetts civil-service examinations of the 1880s revealed the role for trained empirical judgment in an urban and technological setting. An applicant to the water department had to demonstrate skill in reading different types of meters. A candidate for the fire department had to display a grasp of the spatial arrangement of a city, to know the relative locations of public buildings, residences, bridges, and firehouses.[94] Candidates for street, square, and park foremen were asked: "How much should a sidewalk pitch; and how high should it be as regards the street grade?"; "What does a stake denote marked thus: $+2' - 5''$; thus: $-3' - 7''$; thus: $-3.5'?$"[95] Somerville educators believed that manual training supplied the habits of empirical judgment urban residents needed who were constantly surveying, measuring, building, fashioning, and absorbing new technological products in their daily lives.

As they created a curriculum that standardized habits of thought and an empirical world view, Somerville schoolmen realized that the impact of the new learning increased directly according to the number of uniformly experienced teachers on the staff. Rapid teacher turnover had plagued Somerville's primary schools during the early decades of town government. Once Somerville was operating under a city charter, however, the primary-school staff stabilized and grew more experienced, largely because they received salary increases bringing them to the compensation level of grammar school teachers.[96] The movement for professional accreditation of educators, directed after the 1850s by the Massachusetts Teachers Association, formalized entry qualifications and regularized the conduct of members.[97] More Somerville teachers routinely planned in advance an integrated set of lessons for each day of schoolwork.[98] Teachers began to share "professional libraries" and lists of pedagogical guidebooks, which helped develop common instructional techniques. The drive for professional standards obtained an institutional vehicle when a city Teachers Association was founded in 1888, dedicated to uniting "all teachers . . . into one organized body of professional workers."[99]

By 1890, the teaching staff contained a large number of experienced and highly trained instructors. Women numerically dominated the teaching staff, comprising 7 out of 10 high school teachers and 136 out of 143 primary and grammar teachers.[100] Nearly 30 percent of all grammar and primary teachers had taught in Somerville schools for ten or more years and over 40 percent had attended a normal school (Table 4.5). High school teachers exhibited even higher levels of career continuity and professional training. The increase of state normal school graduates facilitated the forming of a staff that shared common professional preparation, pedagogy, and educational goals.[101] The younger generation from the normal schools occasionally clashed with older teachers, but they were welcomed for propagating fresh ideas and "wider culture."[102] The school committee hailed "the great awakening in the teaching profession" that expedited the transmission of

Table 4.5. *Length of service of teachers in Somerville and highest institution attended, 1890*

Length of service of teachers	High school		Primary and grammar	
	N	%	N	%
20 years and over	2	20	5	4
10–19	3	30	33	25
5–9	2	20	34	26
4 or less	3	30	61	46
Total	10		133[a]	

Highest institution	High school		Primary and grammar	
	N	%	N	%
Grammar	0	0	2	1
Somerville High School	0	0	45	31
Other high school	1	10	17	12
Seminary or academy	1	10	19	13
Normal school	2	20	58	41
College	6	60	2	1
Total	10		143	

[a]The length of service of ten teachers was not recorded.
Source: Computed from Somerville, *Annual Reports*, 1890, pp. 220–4.

a coherent body of knowledge and raised popular literacy and numeracy to a higher standard.[103] By creating a common basis of thought
and judgment for future generations, the teachers were creating new
bonds of social order and cooperation.[104]

Toward universal elementary attendance

From 1870 to 1900, as Somerville grew from a town of 15,000 to a city
of 60,000, the school-age population increased faster than the total
population (Table 4.6). In West Somerville's ward four, the number
of school-age children swelled by 104 percent from 1875 to 1885. In
nearby ward three it grew 70 percent. The city's enumeration of school-
age children in the 1890s, based on school districts, revealed that the
rate of growth was accelerating still faster. From 1890 to 1895, school-
age children in the city increased by 32 percent in the whole city and
58 percent in West Somerville (Table 4.7). In that period, the school-

Table 4.6. *Increase in school-age population as compared to increase in total population, 1875–85*

	Persons 5–15 years old		All persons	
	1875	1885	1875	1885
Ward 1				
N	1,298	1,643	7,555	8,993
% increase		27		19
Ward 2				
N	1,277	1,901	7,265	10,077
% increase		49		39
Ward 3				
N	590	1,005	3,595	5,564
% increase		70		55
Ward 4				
N	520	1,059	3,453	5,337
% increase		104		55
Total				
N	3,685	5,608	21,868	29,971
% increase		52		37

Source: Somerville, *Annual Reports,* 1875, p. 122; 1885, p. 133; *Massachusetts Census 1885,* Vol. I, pt. 1, p. 6.

age population was increasing at the rate of 64 percent per decade for the whole city, and 116 percent per decade for West Somerville.

The rising wave of students spilled over every level of the school system. The high school population nearly doubled in the 1880s, while primary school (where students spent their first three years) and grammar school (where they studied six more years) enrollment increased by 45 percent and 59 percent respectively (Table 4.8).

A sharp drop in the rates of illness and death among school-age children helped to boost enrollment: The death rate of young people was cut in half in the last quarter of the century.[105] In the middle of the century, cholera, influenza, and dysentery had broken out in epidemic waves, seriously impairing attendance at school and killing scores of students.[106] Crowded, unsanitary schoolhouses had helped spread the contagious diseases. But by the 1880s, improvements in city sanitation and medical treatment began to counteract the ravages of disease. The school committee began to notice that the impact of contagion in the classroom was lessening. Somerville had built more

Table 4.7. *Increase in school-age population, 5–15 years old, by school district, 1890–95*

District		1890	1895
East Somerville	N	1,213	1,504
	% increase		24
Prospect Hill	N	2,477	3,089
	% increase		25
Winter Hill	N	997	1,335
	% increase		34
Spring Hill	N	976	1,311
	% increase		34
West Somerville	N	806	1,271
	% increase		58
Total	N	6,469	8,510
	% increase		32

Source: Somerville, *Annual Reports,* 1890, p. 175; 1895, part E, p. 84.

Table 4.8. *Pupils enrolled in the public schools*

		High school	Grammar	Primary
1873	N	186	1,716	1,479
1880	N	245	2,072	1,919
	% increase	32	21	30
1890	N	470	3,290	2,788
	% increase	92	59	45

Source: Somerville, *Annual Reports,* 1873, p. 89; 1880, p. 126; 1890, p. 225.

sanitary schoolhouses after the Civil War, and teachers, students, and custodians were exhorted to maintain them with hygienic standards. "Public safety," directed the school committee, "demands of all persons having in charge the interests of the schools, extreme vigilance in regard to health, and constant fidelity in the observance of such precautionary regulations."[107]

Urban growth and a healthier environment were forces producing unprecedented enrollments, but the suburb had the resources to absorb the expanding student population. Fourteen school buildings were erected from 1870 to 1894, and several old buildings were enlarged.[108]

The school committee of 1884 described the proliferation of new buildings: "There are as many schools in [the] Prospect Hill District alone, at the present time, as there were in the entire city seventeen years ago; and the number of schools in the two districts comprising the southeastern section of the city is greater than the whole number in the city in 1872, when the first city government was inaugurated."[109] Evening schools were opened in 1875 for students who worked during the day and who wished to continue their education at night.[110] An intensive recruitment campaign doubled staff size from 74 teachers in 1873 to 159 in 1890.[111] This effort reduced the number of students per teacher in elementary schools from forty-seven in 1873 to forty-three in 1890.[112]

By the 1890s, Somerville had established a more favorable balance between school staff and resources, on the one hand, and enrollments, on the other, than some nearby cities. The city of Lowell warned in 1887 that its schools could not even accommodate half of the population between five and fifteen, and New Bedford grammar schools held an average of nearly sixty students per teacher from the last quarter of the century until World War I.[113] Most significant for the attractiveness of Somerville's schools in the metropolitan area was the comparative overcrowding found in Boston classrooms. In 1891, Boston's primary schools held fifty-two students to a teacher; its grammar schools, forty-nine. Some Boston schools were swamped: Stoughton Primary School had an unmanageable sixty-eight children to a teacher.[114] Boston parents who feared the ruinous effects of overcrowding on their children's education found Somerville's schools an enticement to relocate in the suburb.

The reduction of the ratio of students to staff occurred in tandem with the stabilization of high attendance rates. In the 1870s, primary school daily attendance stabilized at 90 percent of its enrollment, grammar school attendance at 94 percent, and high school attendance at 95 percent.[115] A significant plateau had been reached: After the 1870s, attendance well over 90 percent became normal. Furthermore, by 1890, Somerville's proportion of children five to fifteen attending school reached 94 percent, a rate that was in the top 14 percent of municipalities in the state.[116]

Teachers planned their lessons according to expectations that each day would bring an almost full classroom of scholars. Although truancy was prosecuted more systematically, high attendance probably reflected the fact that more parents and children accepted public schooling as a worthwhile commitment, and together they curtailed the intermittent movement between the schoolroom and the market for casual child labor. The dependency of youths on their peer group, teachers,

and parents intensified as more went to school daily, instead of going
to work.

Educators continued to emphasize the need for high attendance,
but they recognized that it had stabilized at a healthy level. Keeping
students in school longer now became the most important concern of
the city's schoolmen. They set their sights on finding ways to get all
students to complete a grammar school education.

Like other Massachusetts cities after the Civil War, Somerville began carefully to collect statistics on the distribution and promotion of
the student population through the grade levels.[117] Statistical tabulations gave policy makers a more precise grasp of the process of movement through the school system. The charts showed that over 90 percent of all students were enrolled in the elementary grades in the
1870s.[118] Upon the elementary schools, therefore, devolved the duty
of furnishing the vast majority of young people with all the skills and
values they would possess upon entering the field of adult life.

Somerville educators were particularly worried about a statistic in
1876 that only 25 percent of all students who had entered grammar
school six years earlier were graduating that year.[119] The proportion
of entrants who managed to graduate, however, rose steadily there-
after. In 1880, 30 percent of grammar school entrants graduated, and
in 1890 nearly half the pupils who had entered the grammar school
obtained the diploma.[120] In 1891, while Somerville's grammar schools
graduated half of its entering students, the Boston grammar schools
graduated only 37 percent of their original entrants.[121] Throughout
the 1880s and 1890s, the prolongation of schooling itself was a major
cause of rising enrollment, especially at the higher grade levels.

From the end of the Civil War to the 1890s, the Yankees of Somerville turned their suburban community into a showcase of Victorian
middle-class progress. From the command point of city government,
they launched fiscal policies and building projects to promote residential development and opportunities for industrialists and businessmen. They created a network of civic, sociable, and philanthropic
associations through which they defined the cultural ideals of the
community. The most confident Yankees believed that they were
building a communal utopia whose vitality consummated the basic
principles of American democracy: voluntarism, individual enterprise, and intelligent citizenship.

The maintenance of this world required that the public schools educate the next generation to act according to these principles. Since
its founding as a town, Somerville citizens had seen their public schools
as the finest civic achievement of their community. But the industrial
and urban growth of the Gilded Age had altered the city's social

structure, ethnic relations, and its economic opportunities. The public schools had to transmit new units of knowledge and outlook suitable for the urban environment and to assimilate the increase of students from immigrant, working-class origins. Only by being educated would the future generation be equipped to use voluntarism, enterprise, and citizenship as keys to personal and communal progress.

Educators decided that such a reconstitution of learning was contingent upon the prolongation of schooling for an increasing proportion of students. They lengthened school careers by unifying the curriculum, the evaluation process, and the practice of promotions. Schooling was prolonged also by increasing its practical relevance – by emphasizing the learning of verbal-mathematical operations and an empirical sense of the world useful for living and working in the industrial city.

These reforms received strong support from the parents of Somerville in white-collar and skilled employment who comprised three-fourths of the city's labor force by the turn of the century. The town had an unusually large group of parents with the resources to send their older children to school instead of to work. They sought to transfer their status to their children in a time when employment opportunities expanded in the white-collar field and grew less secure in manual work. They were determined that their offspring receive schooling beyond the basic grammar courses to gain the skills and cultural training that could qualify them for white-collar jobs.

By the 1890s, school attendance stabilized at well over 90 percent and half of the students who entered grammar school were graduating. Graduation rates had crossed a demographic threshold that ensured a large supply of qualified applicants for high school enrollment. And more of the graduates were flocking to the high school each year. Educators concluded that Somerville High School had to be institutionally reorganized to operate in an era when secondary schooling was reaching novel heights of popularity.

5 *Popularizing high school: "the college of the people"*

The custodians of public education had promoted the offerings of the high school as the ultimate opportunity of a democratic school system, yet after the Civil War it was still avoided by most youngsters who felt jobs and home duties provided all the necessary preparation for adulthood. The high school suffered unpopularity from a nebulous definition of its role. Only a minority attended, because the rewards of a high school education seemed vague and impractical to many. It did not provide coursework that effectively trained people for attractive jobs, and its college preparatory instruction was inferior to that provided by private academies or tutors. Furthermore, a segment of public opinion continued to question its existence on the grounds of a critique of privilege. In the 1870s, many citizens still argued that the public should not bear the burden of completing the education of the elite who could afford to attend.[1]

Realizing these defects and criticisms, Somerville schoolmen broadened popular support for the high school by transforming it into a nexus with low-white-collar employment, on the one hand, and the expanding colleges of the late nineteenth century, on the other. By the turn of the century, the high school had been restructured to perform this function with a degree of rigor and specialization unforeseen by the common-school reformers who had established it in 1852. As it assumed an unprecedented role as a supply line for the labor market and a conduit to college, it attracted a student population of growing size and ethnic diversity, but one which continued to originate from white-collar and artisan families. These changes turned Somerville into a regional and national leader in the expansion of secondary schooling.

The growing demand for high school education

Beginning in 1870, Somerville educators split high school work into two parallel, separate tracks corresponding to a college preparatory course, on the one hand, and an English or "mercantile" course, on the other. Each course took four years to complete.[2] The preparatory course was subdivided in turn into a "classical" sequence – offering

89

both Latin and Greek – and a "Regular" sequence – offering Latin and science training. The English course was explicitly designed for the pupil "who is looking forward to a Bank or Counting-room for employment." Recognizing that these students usually attended fewer than four years, the high school slotted subjects such as accounts, penmanship, algebra, geometry, trigonometry, and chemistry into the first years of the English course.[3]

By establishing two separate tracks, Somerville schoolmen breached the tradition of common schooling for the entire cohort of youngsters. Massachusetts educators of Horace Mann's generation had abhorred the notion of different social groups requiring different forms of schooling.[4] Now, however, two separate groups of upper-grade public-school students were channeled toward variant destinations in life. Even elementary grade students might specialize and diverge early, by giving greater emphasis to courses interlocking with the high school track they preferred. Schoolmen in charge of the high school were altering the meaning of educational opportunity from the chance of all children for a common education to the cultivation of the separate potentials of different groups of students.

During the economic expansion of the Gilded Age in Massachusetts, Somerville High School was acceding to the popular demand for training that gave "a more intimate acquaintance with business and the duties of the counting-room."[5] A "business" course was introduced in 1877, but it was absorbed into the English course. After all, 85 percent of the class of 1876 went immediately into "the active duties of life."[6] Somerville educators felt that without this adaptation, parents would withdraw their children to send them into an apprenticeship or to a commercial school. They consoled themselves that the primary and grammar schools already furnished the common denominator of education that all youngsters required.

The introduction of practically oriented coursework preceded a climb in enrollment at Somerville High School. Substantial rises in attendance and graduation rates attested to the attractiveness of a diversified curriculum that included preparation for low-white-collar employment. Somerville High School's enrollment percentage increased from 20.6 percent of high-school-age persons in 1875 to 30.7 percent in 1905, and was consistently higher than that of the other Massachusetts urban-industrial centers that along with Somerville grew into the ten most populous cities in the Commonwealth by 1910 (Table 5.1). Somerville's enrollment percentage of 1885 was more than triple the national average of 1890; its enrollment rate of 1895 was double the national average of 1900. Somerville High School also forged ahead

Table 5.1. *Students enrolled and graduated from high school[a] as a percentage of persons 14–17 years old, in U.S. and the ten most populous Massachusetts cities of 1910*

	Persons enrolled in high school as a percentage of persons, 14–17 years old			
	1875	1885	1895	1905
Somerville	20.6	22.5	24.2	30.7
Springfield	14.4	12.5	15.4	24.0
Worcester	12.3	18.4	25.3	24.6
Cambridge	11.7	11.7	15.8	25.4
New Bedford	11.1	11.8	11.4	7.7
Lynn	6.5	8.1	17.8	17.4
Boston	9.0	9.0	12.6	18.9
Lowell	3.9	7.4	10.6	13.9
Lawrence	5.0	7.3	7.6	7.7
Fall River	na	6.7	7.3	8.7

	Percent of persons 14–17 years old enrolled in high school			
	1880	1890	1900	1910
U.S.[b]	na	6.7	11.4	15.4

	Persons graduated from high school as a percentage of persons 17 years old			
	1875	1885	1895	1905
Somerville	8.4	8.5	11.4	20.3
Springfield	na	4.7	6.1	10.8
Worcester	4.9	5.5	8.2	11.4
Cambridge	5.4	6.7	7.9	11.4
New Bedford	5.8	5.7	5.4	6.0
Lynn	6.2	3.1	14.9	14.5
Boston	7.2	7.5	9.2	18.5
Lowell	4.6	6.1	6.0	7.2
Lawrence	4.8	3.2	3.0	7.9
Fall River	na	4.0	2.5	4.3

	Percent of persons 17 years old graduated from high school			
	1880	1890	1900	1910
U.S.[b]	2.5	3.5	6.4	8.8

(continued)

of local rivals and the nation in its graduation rate (the number of high-school graduates as a percentage of all 17-year-olds in the city).

As the rate of enrollment and matriculation to graduation mounted, the high school and its facilities were quickly outmoded. The high school building constructed in 1872 was designed for 150 pupils, but by 1890 it held 487 pupils. In 1890 the size of the teaching staff was the same as in 1872; only ten teachers were available to teach classes over three times the size they could handle. For the whole school, the ratio of students to teachers was forty-nine to one, but for the lower high school grades, classes averaged nearly sixty students to a teacher. The rising enrollments that had plagued the elementary schools were now swamping the high school.

In the mid-1880s, educators and citizen activists launched a movement to build a new high school plant, and, more importantly, to create a radically specialized secondary institution.[7] They proposed to create an "English High School," a separate institution to house the modernized English "mercantile" course of the old high school. Designed specially for the non-college major, it prepared students for commercial, industrial, technical, and scientific pursuits.[8] It would not give any training in Latin or Greek.[9] It would offer chemistry and biology laboratories, intensive work in commercial arithmetic, technical mathematics, and industrial shopwork.

The English High School plan appealed to the white-collar workers and artisans who had been the primary groups using the high school since its founding. They supported the strategy to divide the old Somerville High School into a preparatory Latin High School, which would occupy the existing building, and an English High School to be housed in a modern facility. The leading spokesman of their cause was Clarence E. Meleney, an ambitious exponent of scientific educational planning, who later ascended to a professorship at Columbia University's new Teachers College.[10] Meleney insisted that separation into two specialized schools would enable each to maximize its effectiveness. Different student populations required separate administrations and forms of institutional organization.[11] Meleney stressed

Notes to Table 5.1:
[a]"High school" includes all public secondary schools: Latin high schools, English high schools, technical high schools, and commercial high schools.
[b]Figures based on public and private secondary-schools, *Biennial Survey of Education in the U.S.*, 1952–4, pt. 1, pp. 26–7.
Sources: Computed from annual city reports and the population-by-age tables of the Massachusetts Census Reports.

that the English High School was not a mere trade school, for it offered a broad education, embracing literature, modern languages, history, mathematics, science, and government, leavened by a choice of "elective" options.[12] Indeed many of its graduates would be prepared to enter higher institutions such as normal schools and technical schools.[13]

Meleney and his followers were convinced that the popular demand for an English High School form of training greatly surpassed the demand for a classical education. In 1892, Meleney estimated that, were an English High School available the next year, 64 percent of all entrants would choose to attend that institution rather than enroll in a classical program. He indicated that other cities with large high school populations had made a commitment to the English High School. Boston and Cambridge had established this institution early in the century, and they had been joined more recently by Lynn. Worcester was constructing an English High School and Lowell was seeking to secure a new building for its institution.[14] Fall River, Newton, and Fitchburg, although lacking a formal English High School, had added to their old high schools the facilities and the coursework of a modern English High School.[15]

Proponents of the English High School knew that it had boosted enrollments in Cambridge and Lynn. In these neighboring cities, most of the growth in secondary enrollment occurred in the English High School, where the student population grew to outnumber the classical high school's as much as five to three.[16] The Massachusetts Board of Education reported that the large majority of students in the state's 250 high schools pursued an English course and planned to go directly into work.[17] Aware of these trends, Meleney urged that Somerville's English High School be housed in a new plant much larger than the one for the Latin High School.

Demand was growing for an English High School because its practical curriculum supplied skills useful for entering the proliferating clerical jobs of commercial and industrial firms. Offering more secure, continuous employment, these posts paid a higher annual income than manual work. In 1900, in the nation's manufacturing companies and railroads, clerks earned $1,011 annually, whereas production workers received $435 and railroad workers $548.[18] If a lad took the commercial mathematics, business English, and bookkeeping courses an English High School offered, and, especially, if he earned a diploma, he could improve his qualifications for a desirable clerkship.

In conjunction with these developments, the minority of parents and students interested in a more specialized classical preparatory program grew significantly. They saw the proposed division of secondary institutions as a step toward tighter articulation between public high schools and college. Their growing concern that the high school become a springboard to college was revealed by a prognosis in the Somerville High School student magazine announcing that if the twentieth century were to be as full of "great events and improvements" as the nineteenth century, "we shall be inclined to agree with the one who said that people would 'need to be born with a college education in order to keep up with the times.' "[19]

Since the Civil War, Somerville High School had tinkered with various types of Latin courses – called "classical" and "regular" courses – to keep up with the changing, disparate requirements demanded by different colleges.[20] Somerville educators anxiously watched the experiments of neighboring towns to learn about the most serviceable preparatory program.[21] As colleges stepped up recruitment of applicants from public high schools in the 1890s, effective college preparation assumed heightened relevance.[22] Educators began to feel that preparatory work was so different from the commercial track and so lacking in uniformity that "those fitting for college must have special classes" apart from the English course.[23] A separate Latin High School devoted to specialized preparation seemed a desirable reform to parents and children bewildered by the variety of college entrance requirements.

The movement to create separate secondary schools for different groups of students enjoyed a wide base of support. Parents who could sponsor a college education and parents who saw high school training as preparation for white-collar work vouched for division of the high school. The former were chiefly white-collar workers who felt their children needed the advantages of a college education to surmount the intensified competition in business and the professions. The latter group also consisted of white-collar employees, but included a large contingent of artisans who hoped to use the English High School to give their children the skills to leave the blue-collar field if they chose to do so.

Somerville's growing interest in the reform of the high school was a local manifestation of a movement to transform secondary schooling that had statewide as well as national correlates. In the 1880s, the most ambitious Massachusetts educators discussed openly the possibility of turning the high school into a modern institution that was closely articulated with the world of commerce and higher education. National educational spokesmen such as Charles W. Eliot, President of Harvard, and William T. Harris, Superintendent of Schools in St. Louis, had stimulated debate on the desirability of increasing the popularity of secondary schooling and reforming its social and edu-

Table 5.2. *Occupations of aldermen, city councilmen, and school committeemen, 1892, 1893*

	Aldermen		Common council		School committee	
	1892	1893	1892	1893	1892	1893
White collar	7	7	15	14	11	11
Professionals	0	1	1	4	7	6
Business	5	4	10	7	1	1
Clerical and other white collar	2	2	4	3	3	4
Blue collar	1	0	1	2	0	0
Skilled	1	0	1	1	0	0
Low manual	0	0	0	1	0	0
Housewives	0	0	0	0	1	1
Unknown	0	1	0	0	0	0
Total	8	8	16	16	12	12

Sources: Somerville, *Municipal Report*, 1901; Somerville *City Directory*.

cational functions. Eliot chaired the National Education Association's Committee of Ten on Secondary Schools that, in 1892, published a report that influenced college recruitment of public high school students by calling for standardization of entrance requirements, and affirmed the utility of a "modern" English course track.[24]

Despite the inadequacy of the old high school and the popular interest in secondary-school modernization, Somerville's politicians were reluctant to commit themselves to the two-high-school plan. The board of aldermen and the common council usually sat in a single committee-of-the-whole (called the city council) to discuss and enact all legislation. However, since Superintendent Meleney first presented the plan for an English High School to the city in 1889,[25] they had evasively assigned the issue to special committees which produced conflicting and vacillating recommendations.

In sharp contrast, the school committee called for the immediate construction of an English High School by an almost unanimous vote in 1892. The school committee's majority of professional members held firm views on the importance of educational opportunity, since schooling had been the path to their careers (Table 5.2). Seven out of twelve school committee members in 1892 and six out of twelve in 1893 were professionals. The only dissenter was Norman W. Bingham, who believed that a "two-session plan" would effectively relieve overcrowding without requiring taxes for a new building.[26]

The two-session plan was carefully studied by the school committee in 1891 and 1892. All members, except Bingham, concluded that it had been a crashing disaster where it had been enacted. Still, a few members thought it might be adopted as a temporary expedient until the new facility was finished. The two-session plan had been employed first by the town of Woburn a few years earlier and was therefore called the "Woburn plan." It was designed to reduce the high school's overcrowding by dividing it into a morning and an afternoon session, each shift lasting only three hours.[27] Much of the schoolwork had to be accomplished through study at home.

By early 1892, virtually every educator consulted by the school committee flatly opposed adoption of the Woburn plan. Public and professional reaction had been highly unfavorable. Fitchburg reported that only thirteen of all parents polled in the town favored having two sessions. Carlos Slafter, the principal of Dedham High School, denounced it as "a very unsatisfactory plan." Dedham had tried it for one year, he ruefully recounted, and managed to complete only half-a-year's scholastic work.[28] Students failed to do the massive homework assigned to compensate for short classes. Joseph Hall of the Public High School of Hartford in Connecticut reported that while on this system the teachers of his institution were not able to finish the required assignments for four years of coursework. Nearly all those who had experienced the Woburn plan agreed that it seriously obstructed the completion of scholastic requirements.

After the Somerville school committee inspected the outside evaluations of the Woburn plan, one member, physician Dr. Thomas Durrell, summarized the majority opinion of his colleagues. He advised that Somerville reject the Woburn plan, which had had disastrous consequences for other cities and towns. He indicated that the two-session plan had discouraged attendance where it had been installed. He added, "Wherever an English High School has been established it has increased the High School attendance forty per cent."[29] The school committee, therefore, recommended in April 1892 that the city council start at once to build an English High School.[30] This decisive motion split the city council into two opposing camps.

In 1892, the city council was run, as it had been for two decades, by a group of Republican businessmen. Fifteen out of twenty-four members of the board of aldermen and the common council (which together comprised the city council) were businessmen. Only one member was a professional man. Tax records indicate that aldermen and common councilmen were wealthier, on the average, than school committeemen.[31]

The dispute over the English High School was an internal quarrel among Republican businessmen. They divided into two factions, one that desired an immediate start on the English High School, and another that wished to have a trial two-session plan.[32] Neither side was able to gain the upper hand. The committee on public property reported unanimously to go ahead with construction, but was countermanded by the committee on finance, which stipulated that no construction should start until the two-session plan had received an adequate trial.[33] The proponents of the Woburn plan were fiscal conservatives, who agreed with Norman Bingham. Bingham had advised that utilization of high school facilities be absolutely maximized before introducing "a lot of new and expensive, and generally useless innovations, by which it is proposed that the city, already heavily burdened, shall be subjected to further and oppressive burdens of taxation."[34] Woburn-plan supporters did not want to bloat the municipal debt Somerville had accumulated to service the city's physical expansion. Wealthier than school committee members and more protective of business interests, the city council retreated toward adoption of the Woburn plan when faced with conflicting reports and postponed a final decision on the English High School.[35]

The Somerville *Journal*, under the managership of the formidable Joseph O. Hayden – banker, civic activist, and officer of the Massachusetts Republican Editorial Association – attacked the aldermen and common councilmen for their inaction in 1892. The *Journal* editorials strenuously endorsed the English High School and claimed it represented the views of the public. It accused the captains of city government of "shutting their eyes" to "public demand."[36] Disgusted by a year of atrociously overcrowded classrooms under the adopted Woburn plan,[37] the *Journal* furiously charged mayor William H. Hodgkins with plotting to thwart the English High School out of personal ambition. The *Journal* labeled Hodgkins as the "chief" of a clique dedicated to the goal of erecting a new city hall and a memorial hall. The English High School threatened to divert the funds needed for these pet projects. "He does not oppose the high school . . . openly," warned the *Journal*, "but all his influence seems constantly to be exerted toward indefinite delay."[38]

To understand better the development of this political dispute, a view must be obtained of the changing social composition of the committee on public property and the committee on finance. Although these two bodies clashed in 1892, they were both controlled by busi-

Table 5.3. *Occupations of the members of the Committee on Public Property and the Committee on Finance, 1892, 1893*

	1892	1893
Committee on Public Property		
Businessmen	4	2
Professionals	1[a]	2
Clerical	0	1
1892 members remaining in 1893		1
Committee on Finance		
Businessmen	7	5
Professionals	1[a]	3
Clerical	1	0
1892 members remaining in 1893		3

[a]Same individual.
Sources: City Directory; Somerville, *Annual Reports*, 1891, p. 421; 1892, p. 517.

nessmen (Table 5.3). Each committee had only one professional as a member. Mayor Hodgkins sat on the committee on finance that opposed the English High School. In 1893, the memberships of the committees changed significantly through election and rotation of assignments. Only one member of the 1892 committee on public property remained; aside from mayor Hodgkins, only two members of the 1892 committee on finance remained. A leading opponent of the English High School, S. Walker Janes, no longer sat on the finance committee.[39] Most importantly, two out of five members of the committee on public property and three out of eight members of the committee on finance were now professionals. The larger representation on these two key committees of professionals attuned to the importance of educational opportunity helped tip the balance of power toward endorsement of the English High School.

In addition, Mayor Hodgkins began to shift his stance. Although the Somerville *Journal* had portrayed him as an implacable foe of the English High School, he began to issue conciliatory statements in early 1893. He conceded in his January inaugural address that the provision of additional facilities could no longer be postponed "without detriment to the school." He suggested that the enlargement of the current building was the most practicable step.[40]

In the fall semester, overcrowding in the high school reached catastrophic proportions despite the two shifts of the Woburn plan. Mr. Baxter's classroom overflowed with 136 pupils and Mr. Hawes's with

LIBRARY   SOMERVILLE HIGH   SOMERVILLE LATIN

Fig. 5.1 The Latin High School, the English High School, and the Public Library formed a triumvirate of buildings at the civic center after 1895. *Annual Reports*, City of Somerville.

127 pupils. The entering class was the largest in the city's history, despite the fact that the jammed conditions had discouraged many boys and girls from enrolling.[41] Overcrowding had grown so acute that many youths were denied their right to schooling.

For several weeks before the fall term, the city council still cautiously debated the addition of an English High School. But when the shocking reports of unprecedented overcrowding poured forth in the new semester's first week, the city council swiftly authorized the immediate construction of a $275,000 English High School.[42] The shift in membership of the advisory committees, and the manifestly gross inadequacy of the Woburn plan in the face of rising demand for high school courses, finally forced the adoption of the most significant innovation in the school system since the public high school was founded in 1852.

The new English High School was built in 1894 and 1895 on Central Hill next to the city library and the old high school (which became the

Latin High School) (Fig. 5.1). The shared location ensured that curriculum and not different geographical access to neighborhoods would shape its attendance patterns relative to that of the Latin High School. A streetcar line conveniently ran in front of the high schools on Highland Avenue to provide transportation for those who could afford it. When the English High School opened its doors in 1895, an ebullient school committee hailed the institution as the "College of the People."[43] Truth and hyperbole emanated from that epithet: The most imaginative educators looked forward to the coming age when the American college would help young people prepare for the duties of life. However, practical Somerville schoolmen believed that until such time the English High School would serve as the popular form of higher education for the next generation.

An extremely flexible elective system was installed to maximize choice of career-oriented subjects. Students took as many elective as required courses in English, history, mathematics, and civics.[44] Gleaming with the latest apparatuses, the scientific laboratories attracted 197 students to physiology, 59 to botany, 59 to biology, 42 to physics, and 38 to chemistry.[45] Commercial and clerical courses were also popular: forty-two students enrolled in bookkeeping, twenty-four in commercial arithmetic, ninety-four in stenography, and seventy-seven in typewriting. One-hundred-twenty-two students in five classes took turns working in the mechanical-drawing room outfitted with twenty-four drafting tables. Although they did not supply the equivalent of apprenticeship training, a woodshop and a metalshop gave ninety-five students a chance to learn rudimentary carpentry and foundry techniques.[46] The English High School's novel curriculum contrasted vividly with the Latin High School's traditional academic offerings (see Appendix I). Indeed, with such a variety of courses, English High School students had difficulty selecting a set of courses that would provide integrated career training.

The practically oriented offerings of the English High School dramatically increased the popularity of secondary education. The new institution became the growth frontier of the city's secondary schools. From 1896 to 1900, its student body grew from 520 to 747, whereas the Latin High School's declined from 272 to 271.[47] Primarily due to the attraction of the English High School, the ratio of high school students to all 14–17-year-olds in Somerville rose to 30.7 percent by 1905 and the ratio of high-school graduates to 17-year-olds climbed to 20.3 percent (See Table 5.1) The dawn of popular high school attendance issued from the English High School, the institution that prepared students for the tasks of making a living.[48]

Social origins of high school students, 1870–1910

The suburban city of Somerville, a nest for stolid Yankee Republicans, lacked unusual distinctions except that it was a trailblazer for the expansion of the high school. Who were the youths who flocked to the high school in a proportion unexceeded in other large Massachusetts cities? What kind of families did they come from? Who were their parents and their siblings? How did they differ from those who only attended grammar school?

These questions inquire into the social origins of high school attendance, a topic of rising controversy in the local affairs of many urban communities and in educational circles by the 1880s. Promoters of the high school faithfully believed that the high school operated to dissolve class distinctions by bringing together youths of all class backgrounds. In 1883, a Massachusetts educational writer happily reported in the journal *Education* that his study of more than 1,000 high school students in five Massachusetts communities revealed that a quarter of them had parents who paid no property taxes, whereas only a seventh had parents who were assessed taxes on property worth more than $10,000. In 1889, an influential article was published in an issue of *Academy* by the principal of the high school in Erie, Pennsylvania, which reported that 57.6 percent or 200 out of 347 enrolled students had parents who owned less than $500 of property; two years later in the same journal, a principal of the high school in Adrian, Michigan, published a study showing that his students had parents who worked in a very diversified spectrum of occupations.[49]

The validity of these reports remains cloudy, however. Schoolmen were overeager to obtain these findings demonstrating the democratic character of the high school because they were sensitive to the complaint that they operated an institution for the most privileged youngsters. Furthermore, they did not clarify the techniques and data that they used to arrive at their findings. The question of who attended high school during its modernization in the late nineteenth and early twentieth century remains inadequately studied.[50]

The first stage of high school expansion in Somerville from 1870 to 1910, a community that was a pioneer in popularizing secondary education, affords a useful case study for determining more objectively and precisely the social origins of high school students in the period when the modern secondary school emerged. Students were identified by searching high school enrollment records and tracing them to their parents and households as listed in the Somerville *City Directory* and enumerated in the manuscript schedules for Somerville of the

Table 5.4. *Boy and girl entrants enrolling in Somerville's high schools* (%)

Year	Boys	Girls	Total N
1885	39	61	166
1890	41	59	185
1895	48	52	263
1900	43	57	349
1905	42	58	489

Source: Computed from "Reports of the School Committee" in Somerville, *Annual Reports.*

1870, 1880, and 1900 U.S. Census. The unavailability of the 1890 federal census due to accident precluded a manuscript trace for that year.

As in the 1850s and 1860s, and as throughout the nation up to the turn of the century, more girls than boys continued to enroll in the Somerville high schools by a ratio fluctuating around six to four (Table 5.4). This gender differential in enrollment can be more fully understood when it is related to class origins by tracing students to their parents' occupations as listed in the city directory.

This procedure reveals that the gender differential varied according to parent's occupation. White-collar parents showed a preference for sending sons, whereas blue-collar parents sent more daughters (Table 5.5). The proportion of boys among students with white-collar parents was usually higher than the proportion of boys among students with blue-collar parents. Conversely, the proportion of girls among students from workingmen's families was usually higher than the share of girls among students of white-collar background.

Parental occupation affected the gender differential in high school attendance because the opportunity cost of sending a son to high school remained significantly greater than for a daughter, as it had been in mid-nineteenth-century Somerville. The assets and earning of white-collar parents permitted them to absorb the educational opportunity cost of forgoing their sons' earnings. Most were businessmen and clerical workers, familiar in their jobs with the linguistic and numerical skills taught in high school. In contact with managers and employers, they knew that their sons would need clerical-technical training if they were to qualify for future white-collar posts or professional occupations.

Blue-collar parents, more than white-collar parents, needed an employed son's annual earnings of a few hundred dollars to make ends

Table 5.5. *High school entrants by parent's occupation*

Parent's occupation		Boys	Girls
1871–2			
White collar	N	48	34
	%	59	41
Blue collar	N	32	43
	%	43	57
1879–81			
White collar	N	70	50
	%	58	42
Blue collar	N	36	39
	%	48	52
1890–1			
White collar	N	76	127
	%	37	63
Blue collar	N	55	112
	%	33	67
1899 English High School			
White collar	N	60	72
	%	45	55
Blue collar	N	38	53
	%	42	58
1900 Latin High School			
White collar	N	32	30
	%	52	48
Blue collar	N	15	8
	%	65	35

meet. The pinched family budget could not await the deferred rewards of greater income from high school training. A statement from
a high-school principal in nearby Providence, Rhode Island, indicated
a general awareness of the importance of opportunity cost to working-class parents:

> The chief burden of sponsoring secondary schooling is, after all,
> borne by the parents, who feed and clothe the child while he is
> receiving free instruction; and in many a family the loss of the child's
> time and labor is of great importance in the economics of the
> household. The poor man, then, does really pay the larger part of
> the expense of educating his child, even in a free high school, and
> the father therefore values that education, even though the child
> may not.[51]

Table 5.6. *Weekly wages of male and female workers in Massachusetts, selected occupations ($)*

Year	Occupation	Wages of males	Wages of females
1883	Clothing presser	16.00	10.00
1885	Packer	12.00	7.00
1885	Textile reeler	9.00	6.00
1885	Sorter	10.00	5.00
1885	Tailor	14.00	8.00
1885	Cloth trimmer	5.76	4.95
1886	Spinner	6.18	4.26
1886	Sewing machine operator	12.78	8.40
1886	Paper ruler	15.00	6.00
1891	Metal polisher	15.00	7.00

Source: Massachusetts Bureau of Statistics of Labor, *29th Annual Report* (Boston, 1899), pp. 103–412.

Blue-collar parents, therefore, sent a smaller proportion of their sons to high school than white-collar employees. But since females could earn only one-half to two-thirds as much as males in most jobs, the income sacrificed due to high-school attendance of their daughters was substantially smaller (Table 5.6). The prospect of their sons' forgone earnings discouraged blue-collar parents from sending their sons to high school as often as white-collar parents, but blue-collar parents took greater advantage of the comparatively low cost of a daughter's secondary schooling, believing that it was a small price to pay if it would enhance family prestige or improve a daughter's chances of marrying an educated, highly paid husband.

The influence of opportunity cost (and hence parent's occupation) on gender differences in secondary schooling did not remain constant. By the turn of the century, schooling rates by gender were converging: At the English High School, white-collar sons led blue-collar by a slim 45 to 42 percent, and blue-collar daughters led 58 to 55 percent. In the Latin High School, blue-collar sons overtook white-collar, 65 to 52 percent, while blue-collar daughters were eclipsed by white-collar, 48 to 35 percent. To ascertain why this shift occurred, in other words why the link between opportunity cost and gender differences in attendance changed, a finer resolution of family history must be gained by student-record linkage with household information in the manuscript schedules of the U.S. Census. This type of record linkage also helps identify the points in the city's social structure from which high school attendance originated, when the households of high school students are compared with those of individuals who only went to grammar school. (The sample of grammar school leavers was constructed out of all youths 15–16 years old in 1870 and 16 years old in 1900 not listed in high school enrollment records, and residing in families of origin who were recorded in the U.S. Census manuscript schedules of 1870 and 1900.)

Two cohorts of high school and grammar school students are analyzed and compared according to this approach. For purposes of comparison and continuity, students enrolled in the 1870s and 1880s will be considered as the late-nineteenth-century cohort and those who enrolled in the 1890s and 1900s will be the turn-of-the-century cohort. (The cohort of students enrolled in the 1850s and 1860s analyzed in Chapter 3 will be referred to as the mid-nineteenth-century cohort.) The students of the 1870s and 1880s attended on the threshold of high school expansion, while those from the 1890s and 1900s enrolled during the take-off years of high school expansion.

High school and grammar school students of the late nineteenth century: 1870s and 1880s

In the 1870s and 1880s, when the economy of Somerville and the surrounding areas increased its industrial and commercial development, the share of high school students with white-collar fathers grew larger than in the high school of the 1850s and 1860s, because many more children of clerical workers (other white-collar employees) were attending (Table 2, Appendix III). Correspondingly, the representation of students with blue-collar fathers shrank from the levels found in the enrollments of the 1850s and 1860s, but proportionally more were children of semiskilled or unskilled workingmen. A higher percentage of girls than boys had blue-collar or unemployed parents because of the lower opportunity cost of their schooling. As for accumulated wealth, 50 percent of the boys and nearly 40 percent of the girls had parents who owned at least $5,000 in real property. When all these data are combined it appears that high school enrollments of the Gilded Age suburb represented the growing presence of property-owning white-collar families who settled there to capitalize on widening occupational and homeowning opportunities.

The trend toward enrollment by children of migrants to the suburb, visible originally in the high school classes of the 1860s, intensified: Nearly half of all students from 1871 to 1872 and male students from 1879 to 1881 had native parents who migrated from outside Massachusetts. Students with parents from Massachusetts – many from outside Somerville – formed the second largest group. Only a small minority of students had immigrant parents.

High school students of the late-nineteenth-century cohort came from smaller families than those who enrolled at midcentury. Their families tended to have fewer boarders and relatives (Table 1, Appendix IV). Like the mid-nineteenth-century cohort, however, most students were the sole child or the eldest of their gender and as such became the focus of their parents' investment in education.[52] Age priority, however, was not as consistent among girl students as among boys (much like the cohort of the 1850s and 1860s). Also like the earlier cohort, high school girls came from families that sent more daughters to school than boys, while high school boys came from families that sent more boys to school than girls.

In contrast to the mid-nineteenth-century, however, high school boys came from families in which more sons went to school and fewer worked, while fewer daughters went to school and more worked or helped at home (Table 2, Appendix IV). This suggests that daughters who worked or performed domestic duties were more available for family-role exchange to help a sibling attend high school. Indeed, for the first time, a small number of boys and girls were being helped by the employment of an older sister (Table 3, Appendix IV). In addition, the type of instrumentalism characteristic of the mid-nineteenth-century cohort in which only an older brother worked to help a younger sibling attend high school declined in frequency.

In Gilded Age Somerville, the life-cycle pattern that had emerged originally in the 1860s – of migrating to the suburb (from another state or Massachusetts town as well as from the central city), gaining a commercial or clerical job, purchasing a home, rearing a small family, and sponsoring a high school education – grew more prevalent, consistent, and sharply defined. By the 1870s and 1880s, the high school had made the transition from its beginnings as an institution for local commercial and artisan elites, into an institution serving native newcomers seeking mobility and security in the Gilded Age suburb. The high school was dominated by students from smaller, home-owning, white-collar families, whereas the remaining 10 to 20 percent of students came from poorer working-class families.

Why were these youngsters able to go to high school? In other words, what advantages did they hold over their age peers who could not go beyond a grammar school education? An analysis of the family origins of grammar school leavers who were 15 to 16 years old in 1870 shows that they usually came from poorer and larger families than those of high school students, headed by a blue-collar worker who had been born in northwestern Europe or English Canada (Table 2, Appendix III). The age peers who dropped out after grammar school came from families with a tradition of much lower rates of school attendance and much higher rates of adolescent employment than the families of high school students (Table 2, Appendix IV). Small but higher percentages of grammar school leavers had illiterate parents and came from female-headed households (Table 2, Appendix III). The inability to prolong schooling to high school was strongly associated with manual employment, lack of property, foreign parentage, and a preference for employing adolescents rather than sending them to school. To help their parents, the majority of boy grammar school leavers were working in blue-collar jobs at the ages of fifteen and sixteen, while most girls were staying at home doing domestic chores (Table 2, Appendix III). Some families of school leavers also supplemented their income by taking in boarders and relatives (Table 1, Appendix IV).

Because they came from poor families, the great majority of grammar school leavers often joined an older brother or sister in working and providing additional income (Table 3, Appendix IV). Thus when a child dropped out he usually did not work to help an older sibling finish high school. Instead, the exchange of one sibling's work for another's education was often directed from eldest toward younger siblings. Table 3, Appendix IV, suggests that in the families of grammar school leavers older children were employed at a higher rate than younger siblings so the latter could finish an elementary education. Role exchange also occurred across gender lines. Table 2, Appendix IV, shows that boy grammar school leavers who went to work came from families where roughly twice as many daughters attended school than sons and twice as many sons worked than daughters; and girl grammar school leavers who went to work or helped at home came from families where daughters went to school less than half as often as sons. This pattern held for native as well as foreign-born families.

Historian John Modell found a similar pattern of sibling role exchange to permit younger children to finish basic schooling in a sample of families headed by Irish-born workers in 1889. He concluded, "The fact of low wages, then, goes a long way to explain why Irish families took children out of school and put them to work: their families often depended upon these supplemental incomes. But one of the things these families typically spent their incomes on was the further schooling of a younger sibling."[53]

Major differences in household characteristics existed among the grammar students according to ethnicity (Table 3, Appendix III). More Yankee grammar school leavers came from small families and had literate fathers who worked in white-collar or skilled jobs. They were much more likely to be the sole child of their gender. In contrast, more school leavers of foreign parentage, especially those of Irish parents, came from families with at least four children, and had fathers who were blue-collar workers. A third to a half were the children of laborers and semiskilled workers. Irish grammar school leavers most often were the offspring of female-headed families and illiterate parents. Despite some variations, the families of foreign-parentage school leavers had in common a preference for sending their sons less frequently to school and more often to work than Yankee families (Table 2, Appendix IV).

High school and grammar school students of the turn of the century: 1890s and 1900s

To move forward in time to the turn-of-the-century cohort of high school and grammar school students is to reach a complex stage of interplay between educational achievement and the increasingly pluralistic social order of an early-twentieth-century city. By 1900, Somerville was near the tier of the ten most populous cities in Massachusetts. It was the site of several large manufacturing enterprises, a destination of a rising influx of working-class immigrant peoples, and a Republican bastion of Yankee businessmen and white-collar workers.

By 1900, the city had made fully operational the two new secondary institutions created out of the old Somerville High School, the Latin High School and the English High School. Because each offered separate specialized educations, they attracted student populations with sharply contrasting social characteristics. The high opportunity cost of a preparatory and college education kept the enrollment of blue-collar students in the Latin High School proportionately smaller than in the English High School (see Table 4, Appendix III). Over 78 percent of the boys and 86 percent of the girls in the Latin High School had white-collar parents, and of these students most had professional or businessman fathers. A little more than 12 percent of Latin High School students were the sons of artisan fathers, and only a few boys were the children of low-skilled fathers. In contrast, the majority of English High School boys and over 41 percent of the girls came from blue-collar origins. Furthermore, Latin High School students came more frequently from homeowning families than did those in the English High School, although almost half of the latter did so as well. The Latin High School attracted the most affluent student body of any secondary institution in the history of the city, while the English High

School served an unprecedented number of working-class children as a source of advanced education.

The proportion of girls at the Latin High School among both blue-collar and white-collar students was smaller than at the English High School (Table 5.5). For nearly all parents, the exceptional expense of preparatory and college education was a constraint determining that sons more often than daughters be given that chance for schooling – sons who were paid more and thus who would yield sufficient returns to make investment in such extensive schooling worthwhile.

More Latin and English High School students came from small and medium-size families than high school students of the mid- and late-nineteenth century (Table 4, Appendix III). High school enrollment increased at the turn of the century partly because family limitation was more widely practiced, permitting the concentration of family resources on fewer children, which allowed prolongation of schooling.[54] Continuing a trend beginning in the 1870s, the households of high school students were less prone to contain boarders and relatives than those in the mid-nineteenth century (Table 1, Appendix IV). The more affluent families of Latin High School students were about twice as likely to have servants than English High School families.

Family-role instrumentalism to support high school education continued to involve the employment of students' older brothers (Table 3, Appendix IV). In the Latin High School and English High School, over half of the boys and girls with older brothers had an older brother who worked. Role exchange, however, also began to involve many more sisters than before. The exchange of an older sister's work for a younger sibling's secondary schooling reached new heights. Over 22 percent of the boys and 29 percent of the girls with older sisters had one who worked. As in the mid- and late-nineteenth century, high school boys came from families where sons were educated at a higher rate than daughters, and high school girls came from families where the converse pattern developed (Table 2, Appendix IV). The families of turn-of-the-century students, however, showed an unprecedented willingness to employ their adolescent daughters. Indeed, the families of English High School students were more likely to send an older daughter to work than to have her stay at home unemployed.

As in the preceding two cohorts of high school students, the majority of the turn-of-the-century cohort were the sole sons or daughters, or the eldest. Priority of age continued to gain family support for secondary schooling. Parents felt it strategically important to educate the first upcoming male income earner so as to have a family member capitalize as soon as possible on increased earning power.[55] Age priority was slightly weaker among girls in larger families, as in the previous cohorts. Parents often educated the first marriageable daughter in the hopes she might bring an early favorable marital alliance for the family. But due to the probability of older sisters staying home longer than older brothers and the growth of role exchange with older resident sisters, a greater share of girl students in larger families were younger daughters.

The age peers whom Latin and English High School students left behind – those students who never advanced beyond the grammar school grades – resembled the grammar school leavers of the late nineteenth century. In contrast to high school students, a great proportion of these school leavers came from larger families headed by manual workers and immigrants (Table 4, Appendix III). A sizable share of grammar school leavers had unemployed or single parents. About half as many grammar school leavers as high school students had homeowning families. The households of school leavers were simpler in structure than those of high school students because fewer took in relatives and hardly any could hire servants (Table 1, Appendix IV).

Instead, in order to gain additional income, these families had a strong preference for sending both adolescent sons and daughters to work rather than to school. In fact, the families of grammar school leavers in 1900 sent a higher proportion of their adolescent daughters to work than they did in 1870, and for the first time sent more daughters to work than they kept at home (Table 2, Appendix IV). Furthermore, such families were even willing to sacrifice the education of a growing share of 12- to 15-year-old daughters, who were also sent to work (Table 3, Appendix IV).

The strong pressures to enter children early into the labor market in the families of grammar school leavers stemmed in part from the substantial proportion of female-headed households among them. A woman was left in charge of the family usually by the death of her husband. The incidence of widowhood was especially severe among the families of girl grammar school leavers (Tables 4 and 6, Appendix III). Over 27 percent of Yankee girl school leavers, 33 percent of English-Canadian girls, and 20 percent of Irish girls had widowed mothers. The mothers of these girls usually were unemployed, thus intensifying the necessity for daughters to sacrifice their schooling by going to work.

The ethnicity of grammar school leavers was associated with the same family-background differences as in 1870. Yankee school leavers came chiefly from small families, whereas the majority of foreign-parentage school leavers came from medium and large families (see Tables 5 and 6, Appendix III). Foreign-parentage school leavers were more frequently younger brothers or sisters, who, along with older siblings, provided multiple incomes for their households. The practice of pervasive child employment was demanded not only by the needs of large families, but also because immigrant parents were more concentrated in the lowest paying occupations. Fifty-six percent of Irish boy school leavers and 40 percent of Irish girl school leavers had fathers in low manual occupations. Indeed, Irish school leavers were pressured by an added factor to leave school and work: their parents' need for funds to finance homes. More Irish school leavers came from homeowning families than any of their classmates.

The families of grammar school leavers were structurally and functionally so different from the families who sent children to high school that it seems unlikely many developed into the latter at a subsequent stage in their life cycle.

Most grammar-school leavers continued to be the sole son or daughter, or the eldest (Table 4, Appendix III). A grammar school leaver's age or gender priority imposed a different calling from that created for the high school student. For the latter, age or gender priority conferred the privilege of receiving resources to support advanced schooling, but for the former it meant responsibility to find a job to add to the family's slim income. Most of the grammar school leavers of 1900 obtained immediate employment. In fact, they were more likely to be employed and less likely to be at home than their counterparts a generation earlier. Although the largest share took blue-collar jobs, especially semiskilled jobs, 35 percent of the boys and 17 percent of the girls secured white-collar posts, particularly in clerical work.

By early entrance into the labor market, the grammar school leaver provided the margin necessary to help a younger sibling finish school. Table 2, Appendix IV, indicates that role exchange continued to function across gender lines as in 1870: boy school leavers, most of whom were immediately employed, came from families where daughters were twice as likely as sons to go to school, whereas girl school leavers, most of whom also immediately worked, came from families where sons were more likely to go to school. Furthermore, the majority of grammar school leavers had older siblings who worked so that their younger siblings could stay out of the labor market and finish their schooling (Table 3, Appendix IV).

A dramatic new development at the turn of the century, however, was the sharp increase in students of foreign parentage at the high school (Table 4, Appendix III). About a third of the Latin High School students had immigrant fathers, as did a slightly higher share of the

English High School students. The largest number of foreign-parentage students were English Canadian, followed in order by students with Irish and British parents. Another sample of English High School students suggests that the proportion of enrollment by children of immigrants persisted throughout the first decade of the twentieth century.[56]

In both the Latin High School and the English High School, foreign-parentage students were more likely than Yankee students to have a manually employed parent (Tables 7 and 8, Appendix III). An especially large majority of the children of English-Canadian and Irish immigrants in the English High School had blue-collar parents; and Irish children there most frequently had parents in low-manual employment. However, a great social differential separated the foreign-parentage students of the Latin High School from those in the English High School. A minority of the former came from blue-collar origins, as compared to a majority of the latter, who did.

More foreign-parentage students, especially the children of Irish immigrants in the English High School, came from larger families than their Yankee classmates. As a result, comparatively fewer were the only son or daughter, as were many of the Yankee students. Foreign-parentage students came from families in which fewer children went to school and more worked than in the families of Yankee students (Table 2, Appendix IV). Consequently, family-role instrumentalism was a more prominent support for their secondary schooling than it was for Yankee families. More children of foreign parentage with older siblings had working older brothers or sisters (Table 3, Appendix IV). Irish and English-Canadian students were much more likely than Yankee students to have an older brother or sister who worked. Nearly half of the Irish students with an older sister had an older sister who worked. A small number of students with immigrant parents even had a younger sibling who worked.

Immigrant parents who sent their children to high school took in boarders less frequently than Yankees to supplement the family income that was depleted by continued schooling (Table 1. Appendix IV). They decided to rely on sibling role exchanges rather than on taking in a stranger to gain the margin that permitted a child to attend high school.[57]

What advantages did the children of immigrants in high school have over the children of immigrants who dropped out after grammar school? As in the late nineteenth century, the former had access to greater family support and resources than the latter. More children of immigrants, especially those in the English High School, came from small families. A higher share had white-collar or skilled parents and lived in family-owned homes. In contrast, more children of immigrants who dropped out had blue-collar fathers or unemployed widowed mothers, a large number of siblings, and did not live in homes owned by their parents.

How did the families of Somerville high school students compare in their family-member role strategies with families in the general population of other American industrial cities? A comparison with family strategies in Detroit, Michigan, in 1900 suggests what forms of family organization facilitated Somerville's high levels of secondary-school sponsorship (Table 4, Appendix IV). Families of Somerville high school students sent their adolescent children to school at a much higher rate than any ethnic group in Detroit. Correspondingly, a much smaller share of their children were working or helping at home. The contrasts were especially sharp in relation to the family strategies of German and Polish children and Russian-Jewish girls. On the other hand, the families of Somerville grammar school leavers more closely resembled those of the Detroit immigrant population. Indeed, immigrant families with grammar school leavers in Somerville displayed even lower rates of school attendance. It is obviously important to keep in mind that Somerville and Detroit were enormously different: Somerville was a streetcar suburb without the size, ethnic variety, and heavy industrial development of Detroit. These comparisons suggest, nevertheless, that families who sponsored secondary schooling differed from those in the general urban population in what John Modell has called "school proneness" – their willingness to send an exceptionally large majority of their adolescent children "at risk of work" to school.[58]

One of the striking facets in the sponsorship of secondary schooling by immigrant parents was its connection with high rates of home ownership (Tables 7 and 8, Appendix III). Over 60 percent of the foreign-parentage students in the Latin High School, as well as 61 percent of the sons of immigrants and 42 percent of their daughters in the English High School, came from homeowning families. Over a third of English-Canadian students and over two thirds of the Irish students had homeowning parents. Irish students in the English High School exceeded even the most privileged set of Yankee students in the Latin High School in the rate by which they came from homeowning families.

The strong support of secondary education by homeowning Irish workingmen modifies Stephan Thernstrom's hypothesis, derived from his study of Newburyport, Massachusetts, that they consistently decided against sponsorship of advanced schooling in favor of accumulating property.[59] They were able to accomplish both in Somerville, partly because this Boston suburb experienced dynamic real-estate development and the expansion of desirable jobs, whereas Newburyport was comparatively stagnant. Furthermore, the Irish parents who sent their children to Somerville's high schools came to the United States one generation after the "Famine Irish" Thernstrom studied in Newburyport. Perhaps this later generation, which valued education more as a result of the expansion of schooling in Ireland since the famine, which faced an unprecedented demand for white-collar personnel, and which reached middle-class positions in larger numbers, were more willing to support advanced schooling than their predecessors in Newburyport.

The history of the family of James Kenney, a carpenter who arrived in America as a 16-year-old youth in the final year of the Civil War, illustrates how Irish immigrants made secondary schooling part of the cumulative process of intergenerational mobility. Kenney married a young woman who had also migrated from Ireland. They had seven children and saved enough to purchase a home in Somerville. The eldest son, James W. went to work as a book binder; the eldest daughter stayed at home to help her mother with chores; the youngest became a saleslady; and two younger sons worked as a salesman and a machinist's apprentice. As a result of the added income and domestic help provided by the oldest five children, James Kenney could keep up his mortgage payments and afford to send his two youngest boys, Frank and Charles, to the English High School in 1899 and 1901 respectively.[60]

By the turn of the century, a growing number of Irish, English-Canadian, and Northern European immigrant workers were making high school sponsorship an adjunct of preexisting occupational mobility and home ownership. In their method of combining these achievements they exceeded Yankees in their utilization of role instrumentalism – a complex orchestration of exchanges between one child's work and another's advanced education – to balance income and expenditure so that homes could be owned and at the same time adolescents be permitted to attend high school. These developments cast light on a probable answer to the question of the changing relationship between opportunity cost and gender differences in education that began this section on the student household. Because of the unprecedented mobilization of human and material resources by the turn of the century, blue-collar sons were approaching, and even overtaking, to an extent, white-collar sons, in the rate at which sons went to high school relative to daughters (Table 5.5). Simply put, their parents could now afford more often the higher opportunity cost of a son's secondary schooling.

The growing rate at which students prolonged schooling until graduation from grammar school produced the increase of qualified secondary applicants necessary for the expansion of high school enrollment. This process occurred gradually and indirectly. Prolongation resulted from the independent decisions of thousands of families concerning the role of children in the household. The centralization of curriculum and evaluation that increased the rate of promotion was aimed to facilitate universal grammar education. It was not the core of a coherent or farsighted plan to modernize the high school. By 1890, however, these developments produced an important demographic threshold, as more students were graduating from grammar school than were dropping out.

Overcrowding in the high school supplied the impetus to initiate institutional reforms that modernized the high school's coursework. Recognizing the increased popularity of secondary schooling, the city fathers created two high schools out of the original Free High School. The Latin High School specialized in college preparation; the English High School specialized in preparing students for immediate white-collar employment. The high school thus interlinked itself with movement into higher education and the bureaucratic labor market.

Beginning in the 1880s, the high school entered its most important phase of expansion since its establishment. Youths of immigrant and blue-collar backgrounds became a major component of growth. These changes in Somerville appeared to be part of a wider pattern of enrollment diversification and institutional differentiation in the secondary systems of New England urban communities. Historian Joel Perlmann's analysis of high school students in Providence, Rhode Island, in 1880 and 1900 reveals similar increases in the enrollment of children of immigrant and blue-collar families.[61] In both Somerville and Providence, the enrollment of immigrants' children in high school grew from a tiny fraction of students in 1880 to a third or more in 1900. In these cities, the increase in workers' children accompanied the creation of course tracks that differentiated students by social class. High enrollments of blue-collar students centered in the English High School in Somerville after 1895 and in the English and Science Department of the high school in Providence as early as 1880 (Table 5.7).

In general, the Somerville students who climbed up to the secondary level of schooling had many more advantages than those who dropped out after grammar school. Proportionally more high school students came from two-parent families. More had white-collar or skilled parents who owned their homes and who preferred to prolong their children's education instead of sending them to work. Nativity also influenced secondary-school attendance. The children of Yan-

Table 5.7. *High schools students by parent's occupation in Somerville, Massachusetts, and Providence, Rhode Island (%)*

	Boys		Girls	
	Parent's occupation		Parent's occupation	
	White collar	Blue collar	White collar	Blue collar
Somerville[a]				
1879–81 High	63.3	33.3	51.0	36.7
1900–1 Latin High	78.6	20.2	86.0	12.2
1899 English High	43.9	53.0	56.3	41.4
Providence				
1880 High				
Classical Department	77.7	32.3	62.3	37.7
English and Science Department[b]	58.1	41.9		
1900 Classical High[c]	54.8	45.2		
1900 Hope Classical	75.0	25.0		
1900 English High	47.5	52.5		

[a] Percentages for Somerville do not total 100 percent because the percentage of students with unemployed parents is not included.
[b] Enrolled only boys.
[c] Figures for girl students unavailable.
Source: Joel Perlmann, "Curriculum and Tracking in the Transformation of the American High School: Providence, R.I., 1880–1930," *Journal of Social History* 19 (Fall 1985), pp. 29–55.

kees predominated among high school students, whereas the children of immigrants made up the bulk of grammar school leavers. Perlmann found that in late-nineteenth-century Providence middle class and native origins similarly yielded a large advantage in gaining access to secondary schooling. In 1880 in Providence, although one in four middle-class boys reached high school, less than one in twenty working-class boys did; only 4 percent of the children of immigrants reached high school as compared to 25 percent of the children of natives.[62] The Somerville and Providence cases combine to project a picture of opportunity for secondary schooling that was rigorously constrained by advantages of social background. Simply put, in the late nineteenth century children of middle-class and native parents were overrepresented in the high school, whereas the children of working-class and immigrant parents were underrepresented there.

Nevertheless, the balance was tilting more in favor of the children of immigrants and workers by 1900. In the faster growing English High School of Somerville, about half of the students had blue-collar parents and over a third had immigrant parents. High school students whose parents were immigrant workingmen had smaller family incomes and more siblings than their Yankee classmates, so they relied more on role exchange with an employed sibling who provided the family-income margin that allowed them to continue their education. However, when compared to immigrant workers' children who only went to grammar school, more of these students had parents who gained higher occupational rank. Furthermore, they often had parents who saved, purchased homes, limited their family size, and preferred to educate children "at risk of work." These students came from families who operationalized an ideology of mobility through instrumental mutual support in the household.

The grammar school leavers, on the other hand, came from families who employed cultural traditions that might have stressed corporate welfare to the point where education was comparatively undersponsored. Insufficiency of resources could reinforce such traditions, which then dictated role exchanges aimed at providing basic material security. Always, however, the shape of school careers was the product of the collective decisions and capacities of the family, not the individual. Educational opportunity was not equally distributed through the social order. But immigrants who adopted the disciplines needed to accumulate capital and to maximize resources available to their children improved their offspring's chances of going to high school. Historian John Bodnar postulated these preconditions succinctly: "Economic success and mobility actually preceded a commitment to education."[63]

The expansion of high school attendance from 1870 to 1910 played out changing patterns of social inequality. White-collar and skilled property-owning families capitalized on the opportunity to send their sons and daughters to high school. The majority of workers who fell behind in occupational rank and wealth saw their children's chances for going to high school lag correspondingly in an era when a secondary education became a widely desired commodity. The wealthy and middle-income households gained the additional social advantage of equipping their children with a high school education, whereas the impoverished and the foreign-born were rarely able to obtain its benefits. In this way, the turn-of-the-century high school helped to define the experiential boundaries separating the middle class from the industrial working class.[64]

By particularly drawing the support of white-collar natives, the modernized high school furthered an articulation of a complex of experiential components that defined a Yankee middle class. Social theorist Anthony Giddens has produced a model for class formation, based on the convergence of such class-related experiences, called "structuration."[65] Historian Stuart Blumin has explained the empirical variables which control the structuration of the middle class:

> [The] final and most critical question to be raised in any test of the hypothesis of middle-class formation is whether the various dimensions of experience converge in such a way that they constitute a distinct way of life for a distinct subgroup of the population. Put another way, the boundaries that were established between upper, intermediate, and lower strata by changes in work, consumption, the spatial structure of urban neighborhoods, formal and informal group life, the organization and child-rearing strategies of families, and any other definable areas of relevant experience must coincide to such a degree that each type of experience reinforces the distinctiveness of each stratum. This convergence or coincidence of class-relevant experiential boundaries is what Giddens means by "structuration" and represents the point at which one can begin to speak of classes rather than strata.[66]

The growth of the high school overlapped with the structuration of the native middle class. The capacity of Yankee families to become the dominant sponsors of secondary schooling grew out of the interlinked effects of residential concentration in suburban neighborhoods, the culture of voluntary association, family limitation, insulation of prolonged child dependency, home ownership, and the expansion of bureaucratic employment. A major component of investment in secondary schooling in the last decades of the nineteenth century was produced by the convergence of these social developments upon Yankee households to a greater degree than on others. The high school was thus a window on the formation of a native middle class that was itself an integral facet of that process.

6 *The origins of high school youth culture*

At the turn of the century, Somerville's high schools served not only as centers of career and college preparation, but also as institutions where youths were socialized by their peer group, rather than by their families or the workplace. By the 1890s, entering classes were sufficiently large and graduation rates rose to ensure a sizable age cohort would pass all the way through high school together. Reaching this demographic threshold set the stage for the growth of an institutionalized peer-group culture.

By 1900, nearly a thousand boys and girls attended the Latin and English High Schools, and, although they were in different educational courses and institutions, they were able to participate jointly in the social-cultural component of secondary schooling called "the extracurriculum." The extracurriculum consisted of a diverse array of voluntary intellectual, recreational, athletic, and sociable activities. It provided the opportunity for youngsters to express themselves and gain recognition outside of the classroom.

Because extracurricular groups were drawn from both the Latin and English High School they fostered a wider sense of community. Students referred to both schools as a joint institution called "Somerville High School." For example, the interscholastic athletic teams were recruited from both schools and were called the Somerville High School teams. A writer for the student monthly magazine explained, "The two high schools have always been united by the strongest ties, and it is to this union that Somerville owes her high position in athletics."

They were subjected to close supervision by faculty sponsors, but extracurricular groups, not their sponsors, were the reference points by which students judged their self-worth. The values and rituals of high school youth organizations were derived from the adult world, but they were interpreted and applied by adolescents who made them meaningful for their peers as standards for conformity to the group.[1]

The high school institutionalized the peer society, formalizing and legitimizing it at a sensitive period of identity formation.[2] The high school also insulated the peer society, thereby strengthening its ability to discipline its members. Away from parents, away from the church, and away from the workplace, high school students felt pres-

119

sure to conform to the standards of the group. By socializing students through their membership and identity in the peer group, the high school homogenized the diversified student population of the turn-of-the-century high school. The children of immigrants and natives, businessmen and artisans, boys and girls, came to know themselves and know each other by their age-group consciousness and their common social experience as high-school students.[3]

The following analysis of the high school youth culture is based primarily on the student magazine, the *Radiator*. The ideas, behavior, and values it describes were the expressions of the "official" or mainstream culture of the institution. From the turn-of-the-century high school, no other records survive that could distinguish its ethnic, gender, or social-class based subcultures. The names of the majority of students in school organizations were unavailable, preventing a systematic trace to population records that would sort out subcultures within the institution.[4] However, the *Radiator* is helpful in revealing the fabric of the official and normative culture which supplied standards for students to judge and motivate themselves as they matured.

The structure and function of peer-group societies

Educators at the turn of the century saw in peer-group activity an indirect means to inculcate habits and discipline they deemed desirable.[5] The best example of this concept was provided by the introduction of student government, which allowed students to manage the school by the devices and policies dictated by adult administrators. Historian Joseph Kett has observed, "Student self-government conveyed the semblance of power without its substance, for principals kept an absolute veto over anything worth vetoing."[6] The popularization of student government in high schools sprang from the belief of educational and political progressives that it would innoculate the future generation against the plague of boss politics and civic apathy by training in democracy during the formative years.

In the Somerville high schools, the squads of class officers, club leaders, and school-magazine editors comprised the machinery of self-government.[7] These student leaders and the members of their organizations gained practice in writing constitutions and bylaws.[8] Faculty sponsors hoped boys and girls would learn that democracy could operate only through the active participation of citizens in responsible decision making. Boys dominated class offices and the *Radiator* staff. Among class officers, boys monopolized the presidency and girls were often chosen vice president, treasurer, and secretary.[9] On the board of the school magazine, the *Radiator,* the large majority were boys out of whose ranks came the Editor-in-Chief, but a few girls appeared each year who became Associate Editor, Exchange Editor, and Class Editor.[10] An unwritten principle of gender ordering was followed in which boys assumed the highest leadership posts, whereas girls were ritualistically appointed to junior executive positions.

The different classes composed a social hierarchy that disciplined groups according to their age. Upperclassmen bullied freshman as a compulsory initiation rite. A freshmen who entered in 1894 antici-pated the close of a year of persecution, "Our misery as fourth-class 'infants' is almost ended. We should remember our own sad experi-ence and treat the next fourth class with as much respect as possi-ble."[11] A freshman of 1902, in contrast, looked forward to the time when he would reverse roles, "Next year we shall be Sophomores and there will be a class of green Freshman for us to ignore and tyr-annize. We had to take our turn this year."[12]

Symbols were created to mark the passage from one younger, in-ferior class to the next older, superior, class. The selection of rings and the invention of insignia defined class status (Fig. 6.1).[13] The class of 1895 prided itself on choosing "a class pin" instead of a ring. "For-mer classes have had rings," observed some members, "but it was left for enterprising '95 to find something different."[14]

Social clubs grew in prominence in the 1890s. The youths from af-fluent, homeowning families probably had certain advantages in shaping them. They had the facilities and funds to entertain their club friends. Their material assets helped them to set trends for fashion and style. From their parents, they probably learned sophisticated forms of dress and etiquette and the consciousness of status within a peer-group. Youth clubs became small-scale copies of the various so-ciable and charitable societies in Somerville to which middle-class adults belonged.

Fraternities and sororities modeled after their college counterparts sprang up in the 1890s. By 1904, the high school had four fraternities and eleven sororities. These organizations were nakedly dedicated to "unqualified success" in "social intercourse."[15] They took pride in their elite status in the high school. The Phi Alpha sorority cheerfully referred to themselves as "the wealthy, curled darlings of our na-tion."[16] The most socially exclusive clubs, however, were the secret societies, where only members knew each other's intimate identities and activities.[17] For example, the F.H.P. fraternity, connected with the Latin High School, pompously proclaimed its traditions:

> Being synonymous with all that is omnipotent, stately, imposing, and pre-eminent in rank, the F. H. P. stoops to none. We are not the oldest club in the school, but we have a song of our own, a style of our own, and an organization of a peculiar originality characteristic of ourselves. We are no ordinary collection of revelers, but, feeling our superiority to the ordinary societies, we have decided to tread in a path of our own selection. We step aside for nobody, doff our hats to nobody, except the fair sex, and hold nobody in awe. Both in darkness and dawn we have still continued our act of persistently following with the purpose of securing what little fame we have not already attained.[18]

The fraternities and sororities competed with each other to rule the establishment of social leadership. They gave their members a snobbish sense that they were the pacesetters of institutional life. And those who were not admitted to their ranks deferred to the clubs, though they were irritated or depressed by their exclusion.

The high school's official sanctioning of club and class socials established social gender mixing as part of the institutional culture.[19] For the first time, schoolgirls and schoolboys were getting to know each other socially through dances, club socials, and class festivities. "Students will no doubt look back on the social season of '98–'99 with a great deal of pleasure and satisfaction," noted the school magazine, because of the "successful and enjoyable" receptions and dances.[20] Boys and girls even flirted with each other in class. A student joked that an instructor was having "such a hard time trying to keep Harris from talking to the girls" that he "might have a little cage and lock Harris in."[21]

A literary society offered stimulating companionship, while a variety of activity groups attracted students with other cultural interests. The late 1890s was a period when the student body grew large enough to promote several new activity organizations. A Glee Club[22] and a camera club[23] were formed in those years. The Phi Sigma dramatic club of the high school gave budding thespians their chance to become stars before an audience of their peers (Fig. 6.1). The high school sponsored amateur theatricals not only for cultural edification but because it taught youths the useful habits of "careful preparation and attention to business."[24]

The voluntary extracurricular associations made the high school a loose network of competitive peer groups. Competition for popularity in the group and between groups implanted a feeling of insecurity about the approval of others.[25] Even the socialites and sports heroes held leadership only by virtue of their ability to retain command of a popular following.

PHI SIGMA THEATRICALS

Fig. 6.1 The Phi Sigma club of dramatic players. *Radiator*, 1900.

Student journalism and school spirit

The unique sense of community felt by students was expressed by the invocations of "school spirit." It was the analog of boosterism practiced by parents who promoted Somerville's civic virtues. "School spirit," however, developed sluggishly because the primary loyalty of students was to their circle of friends, to their class, or to their club. Student leaders struggled constantly to create a broader, abstract concept of school spirit that though lacking the power of intimacy might embrace all by its common symbolism and ritualism.

The *Radiator* assumed the task of fabricating the image of the high school as an all inclusive civic community. Their goal was to make identification with the high school override ties to the class or peer-group societies by making familiar and attractive the workings of the whole institution. The *Radiator* would accomplish this by publishing student stories, poems, and essays on public affairs. Thus the editors felt their task was to act as "an exponent of our High School life." "While realizing the necessity of maintaining the class spirit, we feel that the strength of our endeavors should be to create loyalty to school as a whole."[26] The *Radiator* would serve as the medium for the public interest of the high school, functioning as "the organ of all societies, clubs, and organizations . . . its voice will be raised in behalf of every worthy object; and it will gladly record every event of interest to its constituents."[27]

School spirit grew by the development of forms of competition between Somerville High School and other secondary institutions. Comparisons with rival high schools that showed Somerville High School in an inferior position were taken as a spur for emulation. "Our respected neighbor, Brookline High," noted the school magazine, "glories in a successful orchestra, and we hope that it will not be many years before Somerville will follow a good example."[28]

The development of the student magazine into a nationally renowned secondary-school publication illustrated how interscholastic competition could crystalize school patriotism. In 1891, the *Radiator*, which had been a newspaper, was turned into a monthly magazine. In the subsequent years, the *Radiator* staff called for the recruitment of the most talented writers so that the student magazine could "maintain a high standard of excellence" whose "results would cause honest pride at home and envy in other schools."[29] Setting their ambitions high, they announced in 1896, "We intend to have the June issue of the RADIATOR the best school paper in the country, and we need the aid of the High School pupils."[30]

The fictional stories written by students that the *Radiator* published dealt with sentimental subjects such as frustrated romance, family problems, orphaned children, and the vicissitudes of athletics. Adventure stories involving boys or young men were also published. A common ingredient of the student literature was the theme of search or struggle to find personal fullment: romantic love, fame, glory (often in sports), and a happy family life. These short stories were generally well-written but quite superficial in plot and philosophical insight. They were designed to entertain and evoke sympathy with the personal affairs of others. But most importantly, they expressed and manipulated youths' expectations about their prospects in adulthood.

By running advertisements the *Radiator* expanded its operations to print a thousand copies each month, to enlarge its physical dimensions, and to install several artistic illustrations and photographs in each issue.[31] The students who edited and managed the magazine were operating a major business enterprise that grew to handle a thousand dollars a month.

The Exchange Editor of the *Radiator* aggressively circulated the magazine in a nationwide "exchange" system in which high schools sent their student publications to one another. The *Radiator* thereby gained recognition as one of the "best school papers in the country" by the early 1900s.[32] The editors of the high school *Spectator* of Johnstown, Pennsylvania, praised the *Radiator* as a "model high school paper," observing that "a school paper which has the literary ability indicated by the stories of this paper need never take a back seat."[33] The high school *Monthly Chronicle* of Alexandria, Virginia, concluded, "the *Radiator* is possibly the most elaborate exchange we have. . . . Its half-tones and general get-up are really wonderful for a school paper." The high school *Recorder* of Poughkeepsie, New York, called the *Radiator* "the best exchange we have this month." The high school *Life* of neighboring Melrose, Massachusetts, concluded that "the January *Radiator* is beyond criticism."[34] The editors found it "exceedingly gratifying to hear the esteem in which the *Radiator* is held by our exchanges." "Many of them say it is unexcelled, and wonder at the the great store of school spirit it reflects," they beamed.[35] The magazine attained such prominence that an issue of the *Radiator* was selected for display in an educational exhibit at the Paris World's Fair of 1900.[36]

The young editors were pleased by the compliments, but they were fascinated by what "exchange" responses revealed about youths in different communities across the nation. Because the magazine "goes to at least twenty-five states in the Union . . . [from] Maine to California," they admitted, "when we stop to realize that every month the *Radiator* is read thousands of miles away, it does seem rather surprising." What particularly struck the editors was that the exchanges showed youths in every region had common interests and values:

> "What a vast difference," some will say, "must there be in those papers from such far-distant states." How different school life must be in Oregon and Texas from that in prosaic Massachusetts. But no, it is not so. Everywhere among high school students the same feeling exists; the American spirit of freedom, of good-fellowship, and of patriotism. Everywhere is the same attention and interest given to athletic sports.

The editors felt that the Somerville High School *Radiator* had been well-received elsewhere because it struck a powerful resonance with the mood of all American youths. Through the development of this student magazine, they believed they were not only expressing their identity, but also discovering the common bonds joining turn-of-the-century high school students in every part of the country. The competition with other high schools in student journalism thus brought

Somerville students to an awareness that their peer-group culture was part of the national evolution of a high school experience uniting a generation.[37]

High school sports and school spirit

High school athletics was the most powerful catalyst of school spirit. Interscholastic sports was treated as a symbol of the quality of a school. A student declared that "a school's athletic teams are a reliable test of its scholastic and social standing."[38]

Unfortunately, Somerville's high school sports teams never established a winning tradition that glorified the institution. In 1895, the *Radiator* proclaimed its aim to turn this dismal situation around, "to take up the seemingly hopeless task of booming athletics in the Somerville High School." In "gallows" humor, the magazine quipped, "It is hardly an exhilarating thought that no athletic championship has come to Somerville high school since pre-historic times. A cup has been dug up near the Y.M.C.A. grounds which bears record of having been won by Somerville in the year 1732 B.C."[39]

The high school's unsuccessful football and baseball teams of the early 1890s had caused school spirit to lag. Before the end of the decade, however, Somerville fielded teams that were perennial champions in both sports. From 1895 to 1904, Somerville's high school football teams won seven league championships.[40] At the same time, the baseball team discovered the taste of victory, winning six championships from 1896 to 1904.[41]

The turning-point year for school sports was 1895, when the high school won its first football league championship (Fig. 6.2). As the football team began a winning streak, the crowds grew larger than ever and formed "a patriotic gathering." That fall among the fans "everywhere have been seen the [school colors] red and blue," which had just been adopted.[42]

During the early years of athletic triumphs, however, it was baseball, not football, that was the focus of popularity. The championship game of 1897, in which Somerville High School defeated Boston English High 12 to 11 to win its first league title, attracted the largest and most enthusiastic crowd ever at a high school sports event:

> Not only S.H.S. students, but almost all Somerville turned out to see the great contest and "root" for the boys. Long before 3 o'clock the bleachers were packed, crowds gathered on the baselines and still they came, until the five stalwart coppers of Somerville's finest had all they could do to keep the surging mass of humanity off the diamond. And this immense crowd not only brought their voices

Fig. 6.2 The first championship football team of Somerville High School. *Radiator*, 1896.

with them, but carried also a complement of torpedoes, bells, horns, rattles and revolvers and, to crown all, three brass cannon, which altogether furnished a pandemoniac din seldom heard at any interscholastic contest.[43]

A huge civic celebration followed that evening to celebrate the baseball team's first Interscholastic League championship. It started with "about 500 enthusiasts, chiefly S. H. S. students, assembled on the school grounds":

Forming a procession, the joyful students proceeded to Headmaster Whitcomb's home, singing and cheering as they went. After listening to an enthusiastic speech by Mr. Whitcomb, in which he congratulated our heroes, the boys marched to Principal Baxter's home, where they heard a second oration. Thence they marched through Union Sq., and as the procession trudged through Summer and Central Sts., it was greeted with storms of applause and displays of brilliant fireworks from citizens as happy as any of the boys. Turning down Highland Ave., amid the booming of cannon crackers, the brilliancy of fireworks and the din of cheerings, a huge bonfire was mysteriously built and set.[44]

Success in high-school sports not only stimulated school spirit, it acted as a generator of local pride in the hometown.

In the football championship year of 1898, football began to rival baseball in popularity. "Enthusiasm of the students has reached every part of the city," reported the *Radiator*, "and businessmen who have hitherto regarded the game with indifference or distaste have been converted into enthusiastic devotees by the clever and sportsmanlike work of this year's senior champions."[45] Parents, students, and ordinary citizens were proud that because of the success of the football team, "Somerville is a synonym for champion."[46]

Competitive team sports had a key place in high school because they were regarded as educational for both the athlete and the spectator. The editors of the *Radiator* declared, "Athletic fame is a good thing for any school. . . . To secure the benefits and to exclude the harms of athletic sport; to raise the standard of our Anglo-Saxon games; to make athletics an end only so far as they can be employed as a means – these desires should be in the heart and brain of every schoolboy as he 'limbers up' a running shoe or laces on a football jacket."[47] They taught youngsters to deal with the vicissitudes of success and failure. During the losing years of Somerville's baseball and football teams, student spokesmen emphasized that classmates should not be depressed by lack of success; losing was an opportunity to exhibit loyalty, patience, and courageous faithfulness:

If we applaud and cheer only when our ball team wins, we show ourselves no better than the common run of the multitude, who never see success in defeat. Let us rather try the harder . . . to retrieve ourselves in the days to be. Don't get discouraged! Come to the games! Don't try to give Teague [the team captain] advice in regard to the best way to win games, but say something which will show him that the school is with him and has faith in him, and remember that in union there is strength.[48]

Thus spectator partisanship as well as team participation built ethical values that would prepare young people for the turns of fortune in "the race for life."

The high school worked hard to expand sports spectatorship. Administrators secured for home games the use of the Tufts College field known as the Oval, where more than 2,000 fans could cheer on the

Red and Blue. Students organized a special concert and theatrical show to raise funds to buy "suits, bats, balls, etc." for the baseball team. "Going to the concert is the way to boom the Somerville athletics – and boom it we must to the skies," cried the *Radiator*.[49]

Students studied cheering like a classroom subject. In 1898, they criticized the high school cheers as "invariably too hurried, so hurried, in fact, that from the field a yell that should have been sharp, decisive and encouraging was no more than an inarticulate rumble." The athlete "stars in the Somerville constellation" suggested that "nothing so helps a team along as spirited, systematic cheering, given slowly and decisively."[50] As the high school students improved their cheering, they believed their teams played better: "Time and time again have you seen the effect of a great ringing cheer. It is like a tonic to those staggering, dizzy, and breathless fellows, and it puts new fire and dash into the next onslaught, possibly for a touchdown."[51]

Girls increasingly attended the baseball and football games where they served a unique role.[52] Male spectators believed that the attendance of girls had a "refining influence" on interscholastic contests. They inspired the athletes to higher levels of effort and made them aware of sportsmanlike conduct. "The presence of the fair sex," it was noted, "has without a question a telling effect upon the character and result of every game played."[53] At the ballgame, girls could throw prudish restraint aside and vociferously exhort their heroes. By 1899, they were leading "organized cheering": the girl spectators were gradually acquiring the role of high school cheerleaders.[54]

The girls' growing interest in team sports competition became sufficiently high to encourage many to form girls' basketball teams. In 1900, eight full uniformed and formally organized intramural girls teams competed against each other. In addition, each class had its own girls' team, as did the Latin and English High Schools (Fig. 6.3). "Spectators from all over the city" gathered to watch the varsity contests with high schools in neighboring towns such as Cambridge, Medford, and Belmont. So "many admiring young men" were attending the games that the girls contemplated restricting the admission of the boys.[55]

Self-conscious identity: ideals, role models, and personality

The turn-of-the-century generation assumed it had to keep apprised of national and world affairs to prepare itself for future citizenship. The *Radiator* ran articles and notes on world events such as the persecution of Armenians and the infamy of the Dreyfuss case.[56] It published an article on global peace because "the school boy, the man of

ENGLISH HIGH BASKET BALL TEAM.   *Freeman Photograph*

Fig. 6.3 The girls' basketball team of the English High School. *Radiator*, 1903.

the future, should be interested in his country's affairs and we are glad to do what we can to aid in promoting research in these things."[57] The magazine editorialized regularly about current events. The student writers derived their views from the adult opinionmakers of the progressive movement. They decried industrial monopolies, called for an end to corruption in municipal government, and backed enlightened imperialism for the benefit of backward regions such as South Africa, where English control would ensure "that the light of civilization will now more quickly reach the dark savages of the interior."[58]

The student journalists believed that the high school audience should be regularly informed about the largest, most consequential issues of the day. They delivered confident, highly serious, and opinionated views on these issues. They prescribed in detail the course that American as well as foreign policymakers should pursue. An editorial on the Russo-Japanese War shows the type of opinions they supplied their classmates:

> But in looking forward what do we see? An overt act by one of the belligerents might draw in another power, say, for instance, the

United States. The cause of Japan is ours. They are fighting for
what we demanded. Then upon our entrance into the arena, Russia by alliance would have France with her for a clause says that
when either party to the alliance is attacked by more than one power
the other party shall fight also in her behalf. Continuing, then, we
have Japan fighting two powers, and a similar clause in the Anglo-
Japanese Treaty would thus draw England into the conflict. So we
see that a misstep by one of the warring powers would force no
less than five nations into war. . . . As to our sympathies, not one
worthy reason can be mustered to support Russia's action, – so
here's to courageous Japan, may she hit hard and often!![59]

The high school students were constantly looking for ideals to guide
them in adulthood. They admired patriotism and self-sacrifice, especially as these were embodied in two heroic generations: the men
who won American independence, and the defenders of the Union
who fought the Civil War. As far as they were concerned, the most
exemplary figures of these generations were George Washington and
Abraham Lincoln.[60]

Students related patriotism to the fabric of middle-class domesticity
and high school culture. To them, Thanksgiving Day best displayed
the blending of home and high school life that exemplified American
patriotism. "Few stop to think when the cycle of the year's events
brings to us Thanksgiving," observed a student, "that beneath the
pleasure of the gathered family at the board, mingling with the football game and kindred festivities, there lies a powerful influence which,
though it cannot be abstractly named, is the forger of a link in the
great chain that binds the hearts of all in common loyalty to this glo-
rious republic." This youth described this forger as the unique American attitude of intense patriotism without militarism. It was "the
enormous force of that quality which makes the United States the
most peaceful, yet one of the most formidable of the world's powers." Thanksgiving Day, with its high school football game and family dinner, expressed the essence of American patriotism.[61]

The many sons of middle-class Republican fathers had their contemporary heroes. One of the most revered was President William
McKinley, "the ideal of an upright American gentleman," whose
"whole public career was marked by kindness, consideration, and
courtesy, and not a tinge of scandal."[62] But by far the most popular
was the rough-rider, "Teddy" Roosevelt, in whom "we have a man
who is the idol of every American boy, one who is fearless to meet
danger, whether it be in the shape of beast or political trickery, and
he generally comes up on top."[63] In classroom discussion, students
searched for the exemplary models of the day. In the "immortal" En-

glish literature class of 1893, girls turned their minds to "the new woman" after a debate over whether "women should do as they please (in some things or in all?)"[64]

Interscholastic sports created a new kind of heroism to be admired: the athlete who won glory and fame for his school. One of the first such heroes was baseball star Billy Macrae, who led Somerville High School to its first championship in 1897:

> The hero of the game was by all odds Billy Macrae, who just now is the most honored gentleman in the school, for he is the one man responsible for the victory. In the eighth inning, when the score was 12 to 11 and English High had two men on base with two out, Walsh made a terrific drive over second base for an apparently safe hit, but Billy knew that if he did not stop it S. H. S. was a goner, so gathering himself together he made a great spring, catching the ball with his right hand and saving the day. This play brought all on the grand stand to their feet in an instant, and Billy received cheer upon cheer.[65]

Billy Macrae was celebrated as the individual who alone supplied the victory. The vision of a talented person singlehandedly defeating opponents helped popularize sports in an urban society. The triumphant sports hero who conquered the odds was a vicarious antidote to the sense that people were cogs in an impersonal environment. Among youngsters struggling to gain recognition of their identity in a large institution, Billy Macrae was admired as a peer who had achieved the ultimate prominence.

The high school transferred emotional ties from the family to the peer group. Students felt compelled to present themselves to win approval from their classmates. The students who voted, worked, played, and set their own goals together in organized activity carved out personalities derived from the role models of their parents and teachers, but infused with unique youthful styles to win popularity or prestige.

Irreverent pranks and humor gained attention (Fig. 6.4). Moreover, they expressed independence from the codes of adults. When Mr. Baxter, the principal, asked a young Irish lad named Flaherty why he was tardy, the boy quipped, "Well – er – I didn't get here in time." A student reported that a classmate named Gilbert "has taken to giving a sort of stereopticon views on the back of his desk cover. The scene changes every time away."[66]

One of the most vivid ways to impress classmates with impertinence was to smoke a cigarette in public. At the turn-of-the-century high school, boys were the chief perpetrators of this obnoxious act. Student spokesmen thought that the girls might discourage smoking

The Sigma Delta Fraternity of the Senior class, Latin School, was organized in the early part of the Sophomore year for "athletic and social purposes." Although the club ran a creditable basket ball team —for in those days basket ball was considered athletic—the first of these two purposes was practically abandoned some time last year, and since then it has devoted itself to taking the lid off, and furthering social intercourse twice a month. The club has enjoyed an unqualified success in this line. In February a dance was given in co-operation with the S. T. D. Club, and on April 6 the third annual ladies' night was held.

The membership now stands: Warren Lawson (president), Oliver Wyman (vice-president), Walter Stevens (treasurer), Ernest Moore (secretary), George Cohen, Charles Getchell, Richard Bell, Alfred Trueman, Herbert Cole, William Phillips, Elmer Osgood, and Gladstone Henderson.

Photo by Purdy

The above is a snapshot of the Opeeche Canoe Club in session. Crosby, in the centre of the picture, took his usual nap while our worthy Commodore Currier, represented by the bunch of hair in the fourth boat from the right, cracked Scott's usual jokes. During the meeting Perry gave us some exhibitions of the best way to hang by one's toes. Bradford had a weak neck, and it doubled up under him just as the exposure was made. Since the club was organized, it has increased its membership to eight sunburned specimens of insanity—Commodore Currier, Vice-Commodore Bradford, Treasurer Scott, Gray, Crosby, Perry, Nangle, Wentworth, and five canoes bearing the Opeeche flag. A fierce discussion was held as to the advisability of going on a cruise, but to the end of the meeting the discussion remained on the fence.

W. L. S. Club, L. '06

This club of L., '06, girls has just finished its second season. The present organization consists of: President, Miss Whitney; secretary, Miss Richardson; and treasurer, Miss Woodman. The other members are: The Misses Eastman, Spinney, Wilson, Sherwood, Stephens, Norton, Symonds, and Lowell.

E. W. L.

The last meeting of the E. W. L. was held at the home of Miss Annie McCoy. The following officers were elected: President, Miss Ethel L. Mulliken; vice-president, Miss Annie McCoy; secretary and treasurer, Miss A. Myrtle Merrill. At the meeting plans were made for a picnic to Plymouth June 25.

Fig. 6.4 This picture and caption for the Canoe Club reveal the competitive use of humor within the peer group. *Radiator*, 1904.

by concerted disapprobation since "in the association of young ladies and young men, the young ladies may hold the balance of power in their hands." Smoking was a naughty act that conflicted with the duty of high school students "by their example [to] elevate the moral tone of the rising generation."[67]

A safer way to gain attention was to affect an unconventional style of dress or behavior that would eventually become popular in the peer group. Those who could start a new trend or mode would gain distinction as sophisticates. In 1902, an English High School student spotted "The latest fad, young men bringing their books to school in a Boston bag."[68] In 1904, some girls began to come to school without hats. Admiring classmates of both genders followed their example. "The 'no hat' fad," remarked a student, "is contagious. Even some of the boys are getting into it."[69]

A curious artifact of irreverent, even subversive, undercurrents in the minds of high school youths was a set of graffiti-like cartoons published in the *Radiator* in 1902 (Fig. 6.5). They are cryptograms impregnated with crude symbolism. Many appear to express deviant ideas that penetrate the wholesome official culture of the high school and society to the gross reality beneath. A cartoon shows a couple embracing as they sit in the dark under a tree; the man cries out "Mother dear? . . . Ahem!" as the face of a bespectacled old woman gazes from below. A cartoon portrays a milkman pouring milk next to a sign with the words "Alger's Pure Milk" while a box of chalk lies at his feet. A portrait of "Prof. Cook" with dotted lines and an arrow diagrams the lateral expansion of his head to suggest that he is fatheaded. Another cartoon shows an adolescent daughter embracing and sweetly addressing her father as "Papa dear," while she dips into his coat pocket for money.

The full meaning of the cartoons remains enigmatic because they are based on ideas and preoccupations of the time, many of an esoteric and subversive nature. Nevertheless, it is apparent that the cartoons were a statement that high school students can see through facades, that youth was wise to the falsehoods of convention and propriety that conceal a baser world. Students wanted their peers and adults to know that they were not foolish innocents: They relished their role as iconoclastic truthsayers, even "smartalecks." It was an important part of their self-conscious identity not to be overconventional, and thus they had to proclaim it.

The *Radiator* installed in its pages a monthly "class notes" section containing gems of irreverent humor in which students asserted their individuality by poking fun at educators and the peer-group culture. The editors hoped that "the classes will continue to be funny enough"

Fig. 6.5 Cartoons in the student magazine expressing the subversive side of adolescent humor. *Radiator*, 1905.

and boasted "we have more class notes than any other school paper in the country." They teased a teacher, Miss Fox, about her lessons in free-hand drawing: "Her 'symmetrical man' was, indeed, fearfully and wonderfully made." Students mocked the principal's vigilant prowling to expose hijinks.[70] And, above all, they needled each other mercilessly in print:

Charlotte A. Percival spent a whole period in chemistry without blushing. Cheer up, Charlotte.

Even "Gabe" is dabbling literature. What next?

So Kelley spent his May vacation "down South," did he? We hope he enjoyed it down there in southern Massachusetts.

Duhig intends to return to school next September to complete his High School course, this making his sixth year. Pretty work, Henry.

M———— is playing ping-pong to reduce his weight. Note the results. A "before using" picture has been taken.[71]

The *Radiator* published a remarkable section, sometimes known as "The Senior Information Bureau," which was the most elaborate expression of the fascination with personality types. It was a gallery of cartoons and personality sketches, in prose and verse, of various notable members of the senior class (Figs 6.6 and 6.7). A cartoon of a pretentious classmate named Sanders whose arms were "piled high with books" included a poem declaring, "We wonder if he studies them, or carries them for looks." Anxieties about romance also surfaced in these character lampoons. A cartoon portrayed a girl wielding an axe above a human heart on a chopping block and in poetry explained, "Alma's a bright little maiden, Who dearly loves a good time, And yet the hearts she has broken, Add up to ninety and nine." If the caricatures were revealing or amusing, they often achieved these results at the expense of open ridicule.

An editorial called "Personality in Class Notes" called for delicacy in criticizing or satirizing others in public. It assigned the Class Editor the task of finding out whether a personal note, one that poked fun at a student by name, "is a serious 'knock,' or merely an amusing allusion to a blunder – furthermore, how this person alluded to will take it." The editor "should carefully consider the nature of the joke submitted to him, and should know or acquaint himself with the temperament of the person mentioned."[72]

Turn-of-the-century high school students were acutely self-conscious about their "personalities." The public ribbing that appeared in the pages of the monthly magazine was a projection of intense preoccupation with their identities and an insecure need for acceptance. Competing for popularity in the peer group, students were anxious about their image and let off steam about classmates who annoyed, fascinated, or amused them. They compulsively searched for the attractive and unattractive qualities in themselves and others. In the process they defined preferred modes of self-presentation and personality distinctive to the high school peer society.

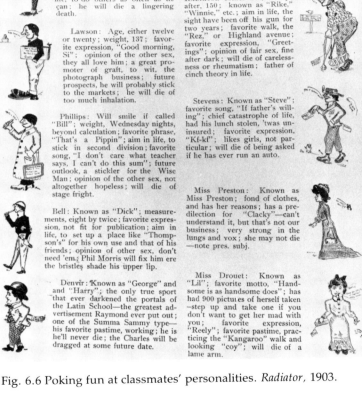

Fig. 6.6 Poking fun at classmates' personalities. *Radiator*, 1903.

Here's to our Chickering, gallant and
    gay,
Who works for our paper by night and by
    day;
And though, as he says, it's not really
    fun,
Yet, wherever the ads are, he gets every-
    one.

Here's to the human paradox,
    He makes the teachers sad,
But just as long as he is Goode,
    He can't be very bad.

Miss Garton has a thoughtful mien,
    Her voice is sweet and clear;
Stop studying, my dearest maid,
    Or for your health we fear.

At the Phi Delta game,
    It's always the same,
        Miss Gow you'll surely find there.
Perhaps there's a reason,
    It may be the season,
        Or,—but why should we care?

There's such a thing
As "short and sweet"
    And Benting's that, you see.
For when he's walking with McCoy
    He comes but to his knee.

Oh, Miss Jones our bright, witty captain,
    A leader of sports of all kinds,
Who excels in tossing the basket,
    And fills her place well at all times,
Who enjoys both walking and riding;
    But just at the present time,
She's busily watching the ball field,
    And our mighty and glorious nine.

Here Sanders comes all breathless in,
    His arms piled high with books;
We wonder if he studies them,
    Or carries them for looks.

Olive Green comes waltzing in,
    So happy and care-free;
When she can sing and dance and whirl,
    She's suited to a tea.

Alma's a bright little maiden,
    Who dearly loves a good time,
And yet the hearts she has broken
    Add up to ninety and nine.

The finest songster of our class,
    How mellow is his voice,
When Harris Howard starts to sing
    We needs must all rejoice.

She is poring o'er her exchanges,
    Looking ever for some new joke;
And yet in spite of her labor
    Miss Carleton finds time for a walk.
And, indeed, she enjoys a concert,
    Or even a basket ball game,
If some one can only entice her
    To forget for a time goodly fame.

Merrifield cares not for tricks,
    Which many others ply;
But asks all puzzling questions,
    And mostly this, just "Why?"

By Marguerite Bertwell.
Frances Frost.
Illustrated by

Fig. 6.7 More lampoons of personalities in verse and picture. *Radiator,* 1904.

Competition and the peer-group culture

The high school students of the turn of the century believed they were growing up in a more brutally competitive world. They assumed it was their duty to equip themselves to rise in this setting. The social competition in the peer-group societies of the high school and the interscholastic competition with other high schools stimulated at an early age a keen sense of rivalry and emulation.

Often, the students expressed a deep ambivalence about the consequences of competition. Those who came from comfortable families, insulated from the struggle of the workplace, were troubled by the aggressive and destructive qualities of competition. They feared that over-ambitious individuals would destroy the harmony of the peer group. Thus they demanded that competition be bounded by the moral code of the gentleman.

The students felt competition was constructive only when it was conducted honorably, in a fair and honest way. The English High School class of 1897 affirmed this belief when it took as its motto, "Honor, Not Honors." In his "Ivy Oration" at commencement, graduating senior William H. Burgess expounded on this theme as he told his classmates "how we will so bear ourselves in life's warfare." The young idealist advised, "In this age of rivalry and competition, when our ambition is so great that in desiring honors honor is sometimes placed in the background or forgotten, let us remember that the only truly great man is the honest man." Burgess pointed out, in fact, that "the object of ambitions in our lives" could only be achieved by honorable acts of "hard work, patience and honesty." The honorable man would be the successful man, "the truly great man."[73]

The notable lack of interest in the Debate Club probably owed to a popular aversion toward sharp, open competition between individuals. The faculty endorsed debate because it developed the mental aptitudes that would give the individual a competitive edge in life. The *Radiator* agreed that "nothing tends to develop the mind, sharpen the wits, and increase the vocabulary like frequent debating." Debating was "of great aid . . . in preparing for after life." The magazine expanded, "A great athlete may receive far greater praise and honor while in school, but the man who can argue a question and win his point is the one who will make the greater success in the world. Which do you think will accomplish more in after life, a great body or a great mind?"[74] The promotion of debate as a supplier of intellectual weaponry useful for success, however, alienated rather than attracted students. Despite unprecedented efforts by faculty and much publicity to encourage debate in 1902, "little interest is shown in it," noted the school magazine.[75] In the spring of 1903, "The Debating Club has withered away like an unwatered flower."[76]

High school sports also expressed an aversion toward individualistic competition and open conflict. The most popular sports were team sports. Football, with its emphasis on teamwork and army-like discipline, appealed especially to parents, students, and educators as the ideal vehicle for instilling an ethic of cooperation within competition. In contrast, track, a sport without a clearly organized team character, struggled vainly to gain a popular following.

The triumphs of the football and baseball teams were valued because they brought the high school community together in a common successful endeavor. The football championship of 1898 was admired because it had been gained by "hard, clean work, the best of coaching and management and enthusiastic support." "Never has a team worked together with greater harmony all along the lines," exulted the student fans.[77] Even the awarding of trophies to individual sportsmen was intended to raise the performance of the group. The Oajaca Club donated a "beautiful cup" as a batting trophy "to stimulate the efforts of the baseball boys to gain high batting averages," not only to honor singular personal achievement.[78]

Students constantly harped on the issue of sportsmanship. Their sharpest criticism of gridiron rivals was that "this team really does not play 'gentlemanly football.' "[79] The *Radiator* periodically praised the Somerville football team for playing "clean games" and carrying themselves as "gentlemen."[80] When Somerville High School's football team won another championship in 1898, they were congratulated as much for the "character of the game put up" as for winning. The *Radiator* proudly noted, "Under the most provoking circumstances they have invariably controlled themselves and played on every occasion a game entirely free from any unpleasant features." The magazine hoped that if this team were remembered in future years, it would be cherished as "as gentlemanly and sportsmanlike an eleven as ever contended for the Senior cup."[81]

The obligation to modulate competition with sportsmanship also extended to the fans. Somerville High School students felt it incumbent to respect the effort of rivals. For example, "the apparent feeling of friendship which existed between the rival schools" made the baseball game between Somerville and Hopkinson High School "so enjoyable." "The Hoppy and Somerville rooters," wrote a student sports reporter, "did not only spend their energy in applauding their own favorites, but applauded and cheered lustily good plays made by their opponents."

These exhibitions of spectator sportsmanship were probably not uncommon or limited in extent. Two out-of-state educators reported a typical occurrence of audience ritual that consecrated the value of gentlemanlike competition in the high school:

> It is also evident that the students of the American high school are coming to appreciate the fact that a team which has exhibited courtesy to the officials and sportsmanship at all times in the game is great in victory or defeat. This ideal of the "square deal" is as much in the thinking of the "rooters" as of the team, who represent the larger group. This fact is exemplified in a situation which occurred in one of the secondary school football games. A young Red Grange was apparently clear of the field and away for a touchdown. He was run to the sidelines and tackled savagely but fairly by the safety of the other team. The fall stunned both players, and the runner allowed the ball to roll from his arms. In full view of both rooting sections, although he did not realize it, the tackler, recovering almost instantly, reached out, recovered the ball, and placed it back in the arms of the opponent, who was still unconscious. There was a tense moment of silence, and then both rooting sections rose and acclaimed this chivalrous action in which a boy who had been playing the game to the limit of his ability for his team and his school refused to take advantage of an incapacitated opponent.[82]

Scholastic achievement also had to be accommodated to the code of genteel sociability. Scholarship remained important at the high schools, especially at the Latin High School, where students had to prepare for college entrance exams. However, intellectual achievement had to be balanced with the extracurricular ethos of the high school. Students felt that scholarliness had to be supplemented by efforts to be socially well-rounded and experienced. The *Radiator* editors advised "all the High School students to work hard and strive with their utmost abilities to master their studies," but they warned, at the same time, "All work and no play makes Jack a dull boy." "Interest yourself in some one of the numerous institutions of high school life," they instructed.[83]

The high school was valued for the experience of the peer-group culture of youth, the effects on character of the extracurriculum, as much as scholastics. Indeed for many parents and students, social life and culture were more important than scholastic achievements. Robert and Helen Lynd also noted this phenomenon in their study of the high school in Middletown. Too much study could ruin the edifying effects of a leisurely and socially fulfilling high school experience. The spirit of intellectual competition in late Victorian schools had to be moderated in order to create an ambience relaxed enough for sociable activity.[84]

Student leaders even argued that the cultivation of social life actually facilitated scholarship:

> We notice with pleasure the marked increase of social matters among the several classes. It is certainly a step in the right direction, for instead of decreasing the interest in the school work, as has been claimed, the result is directly opposite. The scholars become better acquainted with each other, the restraint incident to a mere school-room acquaintance gives place to a good comradeship which is productive of better recitations and consequently better marks. This is only a manifestation of the wave of school patriotism which during the past two years has constantly been increasing.[85]

Social activities also enhanced scholarship by renewing the store of energy. "The pupils want a good time mixed in judiciously, with their studies," observed a student, "and social gatherings will aid greatly the school work."[86] The *Radiator* suggested that an active extracurricular life would "add zest to your studies."[87] It also encouraged students to refresh themselves fully in their midterm vacation and to ignore scholarly pressures or aspirations:

> The time is given you by the school board for vacation, not as time to make up back lessons, not as time to study ahead and prepare lessons for a week or more in advance. No; on the contrary, it is given you for vacation. It is the time to make visits, go shopping, read a good book, go to the theatre, have a new dress made, or anyone of the hundred and one things you want to do at other times in the year, but which you cannot then find time to do. Let the school books be put away on the top shelf, out of sight and reach, and take a vacation in the full sense of the word, and come back at the beginning of the next term with renewed strength and vigor, and make it not only the best in your own lives, but the best in the history of the school as well.[88]

The belief that scholarship adjusted to the social ethic was the most fruitful appeared to be validated by the success of the Latin High School's graduates in gaining admission to college. The entire community prided itself on the seniors' high rate of passing college entrance examinations. From 1896 to 1905, 35 percent of the graduates entered higher institutions, chiefly the most prominent regional schools, such as Harvard, Wellesley, MIT, Dartmouth, Radcliffe, Tufts, Boston University, Boston College, Holy Cross, Northeastern, and the state normal schools.[89] To Somerville High School students, the well-rounded scholar was the successful scholar.

Facing the future

To be high school students at the turn of the century was to be acutely conscious that the era ahead was to be radically different from the one their parents knew. This attitude is shared to some degree by all young people who anticipate the future. But those who came of age in Somerville's Latin and English High Schools entered adulthood at the dawning of a new century, a historical turning point that heightened their sense of momentousness. "The nineteenth century now exists only in history, and the people who have lived and died in it will soon be looked upon as belonging to another time," wrote a student. "Because of inevitable progress," added the young author, "the customs of the nineteenth century would soon be made the subject for much comment as to their imperfection compared with the present, just as we now regard the customs of the country even as late as the Civil War."[90]

The high school students were conscious of their place in historical change. The Civil War had a special meaning to them as a landmark of generational identity. The veterans of the war were of their grandparents' generation, not their parents'. While they knew their fathers as men absorbed in the humdrum world of business, the solid bedrock of burgher Somerville, they romanticized and idealized their grandparents' generation, who appeared as distant figures in legendary times.

In 1901 and 1902 on Memorial Day, the *Radiator* paused to pay tribute to the "brave Grand Army men," whose ranks "are fast thinning." The magazine apotheosized them as men of a heroic age. "The wars of to-day seem slight compared with the war in which you fought," wrote an editor. "You saw real battles," he expanded, "You carried your flag through scenes of heroism whose like may never be known again."[91]

The high school students invoked the achievements of the Civil War generation to show how history had prepared the way for the new generation they were destined to lead. They pictured themselves as future citizens who would culminate the long process of repairing the divisions caused by the calamity. "A new generation is growing up in the South, as we are in the North, and these two sections of our great republic do not feel the hatred for each other as did our fathers." The generation coming of age at the turn of the century would guide a wholly united nation, as "the differences which caused that struggle, have, in a large measure, been obliterated by the elapse of time."[92] Contemplation of Memorial Day and the Civil War it commemorated made high school students aware of their role in the un-folding of their nation's history.

This sense of generational destiny was heightened by the students' belief that they were exemplary representatives of the new genera-tion. They cited the unusual size of their school, its leadership in sports, journalism, and college admissions to prove that they epitomized the special qualities of their generation. Their leadership seemed to be recognized in the selection of Somerville High School as an exhibitor at the Paris World's Fair of 1900, and at the St. Louis World's Fair of 1904. Students fantasized about the global celebrity they would gain by the exhibition of their high school's achievements in Paris:

> Interior and exterior views of the Latin School will adorn the walls and the English High School will be presented in all its cosmopol-itan branches from art to science, from studio to laboratory. And as we might say, last but not least, somewhere in the American collection [,] . . . more than a fair representative of American High School journalism, will be found a copy of last June's *Radiator*, ra-diating memories of the "Hill" [campus], and the "City of Homes," to any stray Somerville sight-seer, drifting perchance upon its wel-coming cover, over the pathless and boundless sea of display.[93]

The self-consciousness of Somerville High School students as lead-ers of a special generation on the brink of a new epoch made them eagerly anticipate the challenges they would face once they left the protective alma mater (Fig. 6.8). The seniors commended the twen-tieth century as a time of unparalleled opportunity for youths. In his Ivy Day Oration, John McMillin quoted Andrew Carnegie, who "re-cently said that the commercial world never offered such opportuni-ties to the ambitious young American as it does to-day."[94]

The *Radiator* in 1904 exhorted seniors, "there is a thrill of delight in the contemplation of new things – the possibilities that are suggested to our minds, no matter whether we go to college or enter the world. There is something exhilarating in the prospective new phase of life we are about to enter."[95]

In spite of this expectant optimism, the seniors who looked ahead to commencement expressed profound regret about being pushed into the outside world. "Nineteen hundred and two at last!" exclaimed the New Year's issue of the *Radiator*. "Once more the great wheel of Time has finished its revolution," editors sighed. "Nineteen hundred and two, Seniors, and just six months before you. Six months, and you will have said 'Good-by' to your first alma mater forever." John M. McMillin, pondering the unknown territory he would enter after his graduation in 1903, advised wistfully, "Undergraduates, rejoice that as yet your High School days are unnumbered; but to the Se-

GRADUATING CLASS ENGLISH HIGH SCHOOL.   *Darby Photographs*

Fig. 6.8 A generation graduating at the turn of the century. *Radiator*, 1899.

niors, alas! we can only say whither, whither, whither?"[96] Carrie M. Frost, a classmate of John McMillin, complained, "Yet fain we would these happy hours prolong, But Time's relentless stream glides swiftly on."[97]

The seniors mourned the irreversible passing of carefree adolescence. "No more we shall enjoy the careless, easy life we have known these last four years," moaned young McMillin. The happy days of youth would soon be engulfed by cares. "The great sea of life will have swallowed us up, some to sink into oblivion, and some to rise to fame." It was fearful for him to contemplate that "the associations of the last four years must soon be broken up for the new and unknown future."

They had all shared the same values and social relationships. Now all that was to change. They could not remain the same as individuals or as a group, and they could not keep in contact with each other. The peer-group society that brought the security of familiarity and shared experience would dissolve forever. A senior *Radiator* editor reflected painfully on this occasion, "No matter how glad we may be that our High School work is ended, the mere fact that we are about to become separated from all our former associations . . . brings an element of sadness into graduation."[98] John McMillin knew, "Another January will see some of us in college and others struggling to make themselves a position in the great commercial world."[99] Another student described what lay ahead as a "voyage in the great world, the hard, practical world." "No more we shall enjoy the careless, easy life we have known these last four years," lamented the graduate, "We shall have a duty to perform – to earn our bread."[100] Another senior echoed, "How soon – alas! too soon – have we become men and women!"

As they peered ahead anxiously into the future, they looked backward fondly upon the institution they were leaving. The verge of separation "from all our former associations" prompted an outpouring of strong sentimental feelings toward the alma mater. May Baker of the Latin High School Class of 1903 rhapsodized about the permanent emotional bond formed between the seniors and their alma mater. "We evermore shall have sweet thoughts of you," she pledged, "We evermore shall feel your presence near, E'en though we be in far-off distant lands, In paths of life that branch away from here. For mem'ries that are cherished never fade; Our tender thoughts of thee shall last for aye."[101]

The seniors proclaimed that the high school youth culture would be treasured as a lifelong object of nostalgia. They believed that the golden years of adolescence were so precious and beautiful that they were meant to be savored forever. The class of 1903 had a song that invoked:

> May youth's bright sunshine
> Transmit a rosy gleam;
> On all our kindred band
> May fortune smile.
> When comes the best of life,
> Time's branches hoary white,
> Memory and retrospect
> Call, "Ne'er forget."[102]

Carrie Frost added poetically:

> "Though future years bring us grief and pain,
> One precious memory we shall e'er retain,
> These happy hours shall be without a peer,
> Oh, joy of youth! Oh, Alma Mater, dear!"[103]

The turn-of-the-century high school was a community with a high degree of social organization and differentiation. Through voluntary choice of course work and extracurricular activities, students sorted themselves into specialized groups. Socialites presided over the fraternites and sororities, the "literary types" edited the school magazine, the scholars flocked to the renowned Latin High School, and the athletes played on championship football and baseball teams. A sense of social hierarchy was produced through the exclusivity of the fraternities and sororities, and the subordination of lower classmen to upper classmen.

Personal identities were molded according to the need to gain acceptance and popularity with their peers. In their clubs and activity organizations students became highly conscious of their personalities and styles of social interaction. A culture of social gender mixing, encouraged by official sponsorship of dances and socials, pressured youngsters early to define what made themselves romantically or sexually attractive. Conformity to the peer group created a high school social ethic that was expressed as good sportsmanship, school spirit, and the well-rounded development of personality.

Somerville High School's prominence in interscholastic athletics, journalism, and scholarship made students believe that they were leaders of a new generation of twentieth-century Americans and that they had unique potentials. A senior described the superior abilities of the high-school educated. "[The] two large schools," he observed, "have turned out men and women prominent in intellectual, literary, and athletic affairs, and we may hazard the opinion that there are still a few in embryo remaining."[104] As youths with the privilege of education, they vowed to lead like true crusading progressives, by living "a life of service to our fellows" on "the world's broad field of battle, in the bivouac of Life."[105]

The high school was a testing ground for the roles of a new generation of women. The institution provided unusual opportunties for self-assertion and accomplishment in the context of competition with boys. Girls occupied prominent positions in student government and journalism, although boys tended to hold the top offices. They represented Somerville High School in interscholastic sports as players on the popular girls' basketball teams. Membership in service organizations supplied an outlet to cultivate female leadership in humanitarian work. Girls wrote a large share of the stories and poems in the literary magazine. In general, their numerical majority in the student population and their scholastic excellence gave them a powerful voice in campus affairs and student organizations. By the senior year, the influence of girls on their classes peaked because their rate of graduation was slightly higher than for boys. Girls shaped the ideals and aspirations of their classes to an extraordinary degree, due to the fact that they were highly represented among the best scholars and writers – the valedictorians, the salutatorians, and class odists who articulated the thoughts and feelings of both male and female classmates.[106] Indeed, the *Radiator* around commencement regularly evoked

Fig. 6.9 The girl graduate as muse on the cover of the June yearbook. *Radiator*, 1899.

the high school experience with an illustration of an idealized female graduate, sometimes in the form of a muse-like or classical figure (Figs. 6.9 and 6.10).

The influence and excellence of girls' achievements in high school also conjured anxious images of modern womanhood. The *Radiator* of February 1895 presented a spoof on "Sweet Girl Graduates" that was a tour through a gallery of lampoons of the intellectual and ambitious woman.[107] "Sweet Girl Graduates" began with a scene in the "home of a private family. Rich and elegant, but in a state of utter neglect." In a rush, Mr. X, the head of the family, frantically searches the house to find a woman to sew a button onto his shirt. He finds his wife in the library "surrounded by important books" and "working on her important monograph." She declines to sew for him announcing "majestically" that she is a "Doctor of Philosophy," "grad-

REVERIES

Now that school is near its close,
  Our thoughts are turned from books,
And wander on to beach and boats,
  To lakes and shady nooks.

And as we in the schoolroom sit,
  We almost feel the breeze,
And hear the flapping of the sails
  Upon inviting seas.

The little Freshman now perceives
  His verdure greener grows,
The Sophomore thinks with aching heart
  Of next year's trials and woes.

The Junior, like a peacock,
  Steps with majestic mien,
For it is not forgotten,
  Next year he reigns supreme.

Lastly comes the Senior,
  Who treads with stately grace,
And now to him both one and all
  Will give the highest place.

To him the world is opening wide,
  With treasures everywhere,
And if his work with honor's done,
  Success will be his share.

And as the sweet girl graduate
  Those four years ponders o'er,
We know she'd give most anything
  To live them all once more.

FRANCES FROST, L., '04.

Fig. 6.10 The "sweet girl graduate" as nostalgic witness to the procession of high school years. *Radiator*, 1903.

uate of Johns Hopkins," "member of several literary societies." Cowed by the imposing Mrs. X, Mr. X retreats to look for the maid. Unfortunately she is that day at the university taking a "B.A. examination." He looks for the cook in the kitchen only to find her conducting a chemical experiment with sophisticated apparatus. Mr. X then approaches the nurse only to find her declaiming poetry. Fit to be tied, Mr. X "leaves the house in a rage, and rushes to the manager of an advertising agency" to request a servant girl who "must be unable to read or write." The manager retorts that no customer will ever get her, for if he could find such a creature he would marry her himself. It is significant that an audience of high school students could relate to the lesson of this anonymously written spoof, that the modern educated woman endangered the traditional privileges of men. It revealed that in the nourishing atmosphere of the high school young ladies became so accomplished and prominent as to prompt classmates to speculate whether the new female generation whose considerable talents bloomed in scholarship and the extracurriculum would revolutionize the American family.

The cultural system of the modern high school emerged in definite form at the turn of the century. In the 1890s, sufficient numbers of students attended and graduated to support a complex matrix of peer-group societies for the first time. Instead of being dispersed in isolated homes and workplaces, youths congregated together in one institution where they developed a common group identity. The distinctive features of modern high school culture were formed in this decade: an extracurriculum of student government, clubs, athletics, and journalism, and the expressions of school spirit such as school colors, cheerleading, and sports spectatorship. And the total high school experience was romanticized as an episode of irreplaceable social and personal discovery. The high school popularized a new image of youth, gaining currency in psychology through G. Stanley Hall, as a creative and progressive life stage that supplanted the Victorian view of adolescence as a perilous, pathological period to be transited as swiftly as possible.[108] The high school's community of youth symbolized to citizens the revitalization of community in the impersonal city. In this milieu, students learned from each other progressive middle-class ideals of popularity, competition, citizenship, leadership, and success that defined their goals in adulthood and supplied the motivation for achieving them.

The turn-of-the-century high school was the cradle of a new regime of transition to adulthood. The institutional culture was an alternative passage for maturation that competed with the Victorian domestic culture of the middle class and the ethnic kin-centered culture of the working class. In the high school, youngsters engaged in role-playing idealized adult models of correct behavior abstracted from an external offical culture. They, and not their parents, controlled their actions in this setting, but their actions were imitative and derivative of an iconography. Social behavior in the high school displayed self-conscious vulnerability to the judgment of peers who possessed the forms but not the experience of maturity. Unsure youths tested these forms before a peer audience by indulging in histrionic and melodramatic posture of their personalities. Ambivalent about their insulation, they basked themselves in sentimental rhetoric revealing the idealism, uniqueness, and fleeting beauty of youth. The preoccupations of high school students suggest that the institution's peer-society culture accentuated the anxieties of "the period of the life cycle," defined by psychologist Erik Erikson, as the time "when each youth must forge for himself some central perspective and direction, some working unity, out of the effective remnants of his childhood and the hopes of his anticipated adulthood."[109]

Adolescent transition in the high school was less "real" than the world of child labor and domestic duties, but it powerfully shaped respect for conformity. In the insecure peer society, students learned to find fulfillment by keeping up with others and acting in groups. They did not innovate or experiment if peer acceptance was jeopardized. In cliques and organizations, they gestured in poses of gentility and in the forms of quality – fair play, loyalty, etiquette, taste in letters and arts, and sophisticated manners – to impress others. In the language of social anthropologist Erving Goffman, they learned "the arts of impression management" – to "give off" the "sign vehicles" that could dramaturgically control "the definition of the situation" to affirm membership in prestige groups. Furthermore, students banded together in peer organizations that functioned as "teams of performers" who depended on reciprocal loyalty and cooperation for performance of ritualized interactions to mark the boundaries of conformity and popularity. The demographic preponderance of students from white-collar Yankee families provided the critical mass that kept the genteel culture dominant in ritualized interaction.[110] Moreover, because they stayed in school longest and predominated in preparatory work, they had the tenure and prestige to control the key institutions defining cultural orthodoxy.[111]

Nevertheless, because the institutional youth culture was peer-centered, generational, and conformist, the high school probably served as a "melting pot" that facilitated cultural exchange and social bonding between students of different ethnic and class backgrounds. In extracurricular clubs, in student government, on sports teams, and in the classroom, popularity and attractiveness among peers counted more than the occupation of one's father. Friendships and even romances blossomed between Protestants and Catholics, Yankees and immigrants, the children of businessmen and the children of workingmen, in an insulated setting that was quasi-independent of the power structure in the surrounding society. The framework of peer-centered, conformist generational culture probably promoted the dispersion of the official culture of gentility and self-improvement to working-class youths. Many sons and daughters of blue-collar parents learned the habits and styles that led to acceptance in different groups and organizations controlled by students from Yankee white-collar families. The youth culture thereby helped create values and social skills in working-class students that enabled them to gain access to middle-class society. Participation in the youth culture was an opportunity to acquire a social advantage independent of inherited status and that might be useful in the competition of adult life.

7 *Educational opportunity and social mobility*

The students of Somerville High School at the turn of the century absorbed new experiences from the classroom and peer group that they knew would affect them for the rest of their lives. For many the high school was a place of self-discovery where they learned about their potentiality for the first time. "Perhaps there in the old school," wondered a graduate of the class of 1904, "the pupil caught the first glimpse of his power, his work in life; possibly there he first realized what he could do." [1]

The coursework pushed students into new terrains of knowledge and habits of thought. The serious scholars learned the study techniques that enabled a majority of the preparatory graduates each year to enter college. They were drilled in class but they had to have the initiative to perform their homework. As George Whipple recalled, "We had received a training in the fundamentals of education and had learned how to study. . . . We were put on our own responsibility; that developed self-reliance."

The scholars also acquired a new sense of educational ambition. Each new class of freshmen was aware that they had a tradition of achievement to uphold when they entered Somerville High School. George Whipple remembered how "From our mathematics room we could look down upon the tower of Harvard Memorial Hall and upon the red roof of Sever Hall, where we were to take examinations the coming June – a view of the gateway to the Promised Land, which kept us 'keyed up' in our efforts to reach it." Whipple reminisced proudly, "Five boys generally entered [Harvard College] from the Somerville High School every year. We passed the admission examinations with honors while holding our own with the Boston Latin School boys."

The strong sense of peer-group membership probably reinforced scholastic motivation in students. They may have felt in order to maintain themselves in their social network, it was necessary to keep up with them in the classroom. Most important of all, students knew they had to get grades good enough for promotion to participate in next year's school activities with their friends and teammates. The bonding of the peer group could even encourage the scholastic am-

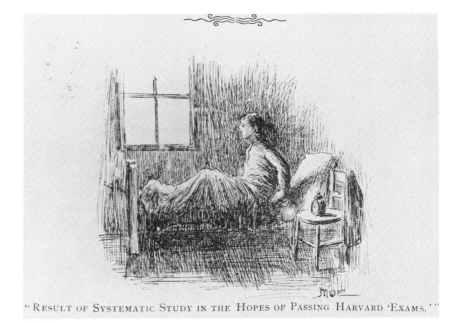

" Result of Systematic Study in the Hopes of Passing Harvard 'Exams.'"

Fig. 7.1 An illustration in the high school magazine of a dismayed student who overslept after a night of study for his Harvard entrance exams. *Radiator,* 1905.

bition to prepare for college. George Whipple fraternized with a "gang" who "were all preparing to take the preliminary examinations for Harvard."[2] Whipple kept his head to the grindstone, for he knew if he fell behind and missed Harvard, he might not share the delights and benefits of college life with his chums. He was probably one of many scholars whose willingness to toil was lampooned by a cartoon in the school magazine, the *Radiator,* in 1896. In that cartoon a young man wakens from his bed to stare in dismay at a sunlit window (Fig. 7.1). Next to him an alarm clock shows that he has overslept until midday. Underneath, a caption sardonically explains, "Result of Systematic Study in the Hopes of Passing Harvard Exams."

A month before commencement in 1905, the *Radiator* carried an advertisement entitled "Success" that took up the whole back cover (Fig. 7.2). An ad for Winter Hill Business College in Somerville, it declared "Success depends upon preparation." It bluntly asked, "Are you prepared to do any one thing well? If you are not, then you are handicapped at the beginning of the race." The advertisement touched the sensitive recognition in turn-of-the-century high school students that

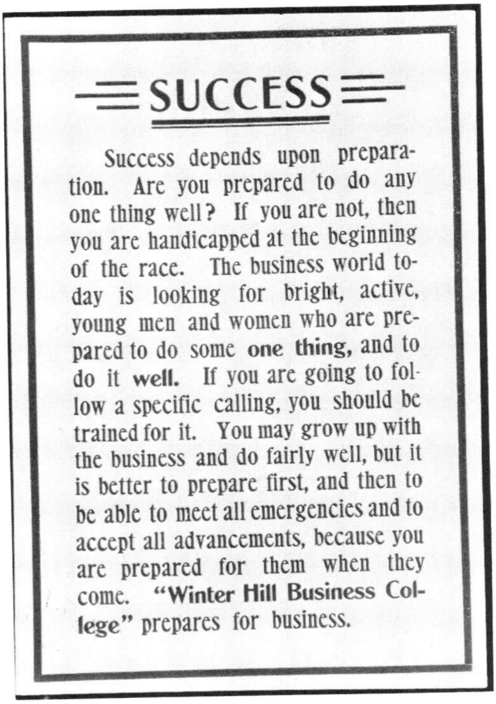

Fig. 7.2 An advertisement in the high school magazine playing on the need for specialized training to achieve success in business. *Radiator,* 1905.

the race to success, in the Darwinian and Algeresque ethos of the middle class, could be won only through proper preparation to capitalize on future opportunities. John McMillin, a graduate of 1903, witnessed that the new century was bringing "increased opportunities, more numerous openings for, and greater need of, the young people who . . . are pouring forth from our high schools to enter life's busy workshop." According to McMillin, "for the best use of these openings," the high school had provided "certain qualifications." The high school had given him and his classmates tools to capitalize on opportunity. The students had acquired knowledge, social graces, good character, a certified record of coursework, even a diploma. "There will be no kind hand to guide us in the stern, practical world," explained the senior. "The youth may well stand abashed in the presence of his opportunities as he recognizes this fact. He may be forgiven if he falteringly asks, 'Have I the necessary qualifications?' "[3]

Indeed, more youths than ever consciously felt the need for the "qualifications" of a high school or college education. In the white-collar labor market of the late nineteenth and early twentieth century, employers relied more and more on the universal school credential to sort out desirable employees from the growing pool of increasingly qualified applicants.[4] They needed an abstract measure of character and skills in an impersonal labor market, where they were not familiar with the applicant, his family, or his references.[5] Historian Joseph F. Kett noted that by the end of the nineteenth century, "education provided a form of certification for young people" and a "diploma could act as a kind of letter of introduction."[6] Educators intensified the concern with credentials by proclaiming that institutions such as the high school supplied to students of humble origins the education to mount the social ladder.[7]

Since employers, educators, youths, and their parents emphasized the utility of a high school or college education, it is logical to ask how advanced schooling affected the prospects of the generations who entered adulthood from the Gilded Age to the Progressive Era. What role did the high school play as a steppingstone to college and to desirable jobs? Oscar and Mary Handlin first presented a sophisticated historiographic formulation of this question in their influential essay, *The Dimensions of Liberty*. Subsequently, Michael B. Katz, Samuel Bowles, and Herbert Gintis argued that the American public high school reinforced inequality by facilitating the transfer of socioeconomic inequality from parents to children. Diane Ravitch has demurred, maintaining that historical research as yet does not permit such definitive conclusions.[8]

An examination of the educational advances and adult life courses of students who attended Somerville High School from 1870 to 1910 provides an empirical and historical focus for further clarification of this issue. It reveals that the process of movement from high school to adult status was subtly structured by occupation, ethnicity, gender, and type of residency. The high school aided the upward mobility of a growing fraction of the adolescent population, but according to limits imposed by these background factors. However, since a large proportion of its students obtained white-collar jobs, the high school helped form a pluralistic, white-collar occupational class in early-twentieth-century Somerville.

Advancing through high school

In what ways did Somerville's high schools affect the adult positions of their students? The mediating effect of schooling upon a child's transition from the status of his family to his adult occupation occurs in two stages: the move from status in the family to a certain level of schooling, and the subsequent application of educational attainment as a means to an adult career.[9] Two successive cohorts of students, those reaching adulthood in the late nineteenth century who went to Somerville High School in the 1870s and 1880s, and those coming of age in the early twentieth century who attended the Latin High School and English High School around 1900, will be examined. Social mobility will be analyzed in terms of occupational mobility, specifically, changes of position in the occupational classification system utilized by Stephan Thernstrom in *The Other Bostonians*.[10] This procedure yields samples that afford a modest assessment of the changing influence of different secondary institutions on the life chances of their matriculants during the first phase of high school expansion. It is important to note here that occupational mobility is only one dimension of social mobility. This limited study does not address other measures such as property ownership and employment of servants.[11] Occupational mobility should not be equated simplistically with movement between social classes, but rather as part of the process of social stratification.[12]

The sons of both white-collar and blue-collar parents entering Somerville High School from 1879 to 1881 had a much smaller chance of either graduating or going to college after graduation than boys attending the Latin or English High School in the 1900s (Table 7.1). In the 1880s, many boys left the high school before securing a diploma because a tenth- or eleventh-grade education was a sufficient qualification for entering most white-collar posts. At the turn of the century, however, more parents were sponsoring longer school careers for their sons. A secondary-school diploma or a college education gave the aspirant to a white-collar job the credentials demanded in a time of rising qualifications and more highly trained personnel.

The effect of parental occupation on the ability of male students to proceed from high school to college shifted in direction. Only a small fraction of boys entering Somerville High School from 1879 to 1881 went to college after graduation, and significant differences in college attendance by social class were visible. Entering white-collar sons were twice as likely as blue-collar sons to advance to college after graduation. The pattern of college attendance, however, dramatically changed in the next generation of students who entered the Latin High School in the 1900s. The percentage of white-collar sons advancing to college nearly doubled and the percentage of blue-collar sons doing so multiplied fivefold. Blue-collar sons were then more likely to proceed to college than white-collar sons.

Girls displayed different graduation patterns from boys. Girls of

Table 7.1. *Graduation rates by parent's occupation for boys entering high school* (%)

Somerville High School entrants, 1879–81			
Parent's occupation	Graduated	Graduated & college	N
White collar	27	16	70
Professional	17	17	12
Other white collar	30	16	58
Blue collar	30	8	36
Skilled	11	0	18
Low manual	50	17	18

Latin High School entrants, 1900–1			
Parent's occupaton	Graduated	Graduated & college	N
White collar	45	28	64
Professional	62	56	16
Other white collar	40	19	48
Blue collar	53	43	30
Skilled	66	52	21
Low manual	22	22	9

English High School entrants, 1899			
Parent's occupation	Graduated	Graduated & college	N
White collar	40	NA	60
Professional	29		7
Other white collar	42		53
Blue collar	26	NA	38
Skilled	21		28
Low manual	40		10

white-collar background had somewhat greater chances than girls of blue-collar origins for obtaining a diploma (Table 7.2). In fact, girls of various occupational backgrounds finished high school more often than boys. As a result, female graduates outnumbered male graduates by almost two to one in the late nineteenth century (Table 7.3). While hustling boys departed from the high school for beckoning jobs, many girls in the late Victorian culture became assiduous scholars. The next generation of boys entering high school at the turn of the century, however, were fast catching up with the girls in graduation rates.

Table 7.2. *Graduation rates by parent's occupation for girls entering high school (%)*

Somerville High School entrants, 1879–81

Parent's occupation	Graduated	Graduated & college	N
White collar	51	10	49
Professional	29	29	7
Other white collar	55	7	42
Blue collar	43	5	39
Skilled	48	7	29
Low manual	30	0	10

Latin High School entrants, 1900–1

Parent's occupation	Graduated	Graduated & college	N
White collar	53	24	55
Professional	50	40	10
Other white collar	53	20	45
Blue collar	42	18	17
Skilled	44	19	16
Low manual	0	0	1

English High School entrants, 1899

Parent's occupation	Graduated	Graduated & college	N
White collar	49	NA	71
Professional	25		4
Other white collar	51		67
Blue collar	47	NA	53
Skilled	56		41
Low manual	17		12

Blue-collar sons who started Somerville High School between 1879 and 1881 and the Latin High School between 1900 and 1901 were as likely as white-collar sons to finish the diploma. In contrast, at the English High School, sons of blue-collar workers had lower graduation rates than sons of white-collar parents. Indeed, this institution attracted boys from poorer families within the working class, who could afford only a few years of technical courses before dropping out to look for work.

Girls graduated more frequently than boys, but they proceeded to college far less often than their male classmates (Table 7.3). Female

Table 7.3. *High school preparatory graduates attending college, male and female*

Year graduated	N graduates		N attended college		% of graduates attended college	
	Male	Female	Male	Female	Male	Female
1879–81	30	66	20	9	67	14
1889–90	43	84	24	11	56	13
1899–1900	38	60	31	34	82	57
1909–10	71	114	42	56	59	49

graduates still lagged behind male graduates in rates of college attendance, but by 1900 the chances for graduating girls to advance to college had greatly improved. Since the 1880s, the proportion of female graduates who moved ahead to college had multiplied over three times (Table 7.3). The proportion of white-collar and blue-collar daughters entering the high school who proceeded all the way to college increased correspondingly (Table 7.2). White-collar daughters, however, had slightly greater chances than blue-collar daughters for entering college.

The growth of college attendance at the turn of the century was affected by family nativity and size, but not by gross real-property ownership (Table 7.4). More students who went to college than those who stopped at high school had native parents and grandparents. This was especially true for boy students who went to college. Native parents were more able than immigrants to prolong their son's schooling beyond a high school diploma to a college education. Family size affected girls' chances for attending college more than it did boys'. Girls who went to college came much more often from small families with one to three children, while those who never went beyond high school were frequently from families with four or more children. It is likely that girls from larger families were needed to take care of their siblings or to go to work. Their parents felt that a high school education for their daughters was a sufficient achievement for a young lady. College was a superfluous and overcostly luxury. Finally, for neither boys nor girls did home ownership per se determine the ability to proceed to college. However, finer measures of different categories of property might very well reveal a connection with college attendance.

Ethnic origin was a factor that determined a student's chances of

Table 7.4. *High school graduates who attended college and all other high school matriculants, by household characteristics* (%)

| | Students who entered Latin High School 1900–1 | | | |
| | Boys | | Girls | |
	Graduated & college $N=28$	Other matriculants $N=56$	Graduated & college $N=17$	Other matriculants $N=40$
Household head				
Native born	85.7	57.2	76.5	67.5
Foreign born	14.3	42.8	23.5	32.5
Father of household head				
Foreign born	32.2	53.6	35.3	47.5
Home status				
Owned	60.7	60.7	52.9	55.0
Rented	39.3	39.3	47.1	45.0
Household head's children				
1–3	60.7	57.1	88.2	57.5
4–6	28.6	35.7	11.8	40.0
7+	7.1	7.1	0	2.5
Head not parent	3.6	0	0	0

graduating. This phenomenon was demonstrated in the English High School, which had the largest enrollment of the children of immigrants. Among sons and daughters of white-collar parents, Yankee students finished diplomas at the highest rate, English-Canadian students were second, and Irish students were last (Tables 7.5 and 7.6).

But among children of blue-collar parents, Irish youths were the pacesetters in graduation. Thirty-one percent of the sons of Irish workingmen graduated as compared to 18 percent of the sons of Canadian workingmen and 22 percent of the sons of Yankee workingmen. Also, 31 percent of the daughters of Irish workingmen gained diplomas, surpassing the graduation rate of the daughters of English-Canadian workingmen, and exceeded only by daughters of Yankee workingmen.

Parent's occupation affected a high school student's chances for graduation in different ways in different ethnic groups. Among Yankee and Canadian students, the children of white-collar parents were

Table 7.5. *Highest level of education by ethnicity and parent's occupation for English High School male entrants, 1896–1905 (percent)*

Parent's occupation	Yankee			Canadian			Irish		
	Attended	Graduated	N	Attended	Graduated	N	Attended	Graduated	N
White collar	60	40	60	68	32	38	76	24	25
Professions	55	45	11	0	100	1	0	100	2
Other white collar	61	39	49	70	30	37	83	17	23
Blue collar	78	22	23	82	18	65	69	31	54
Skilled	72	28	18	85	15	55	63	37	27
Low manual	100	0	5	60	40	10	74	26	27

Table 7.6. *Highest level of education by ethnicity and parent's occupation for English High School female entrants, 1898–1902 (percent)*

Parent's occupation	Yankee			Canadian			Irish		
	Attended	Graduated	N	Attended	Graduated	N	Attended	Graduated	N
White collar									
Professions	35	65	23	67	33	24	81	19	16
	100	0	1	0	0	0	0	0	0
Other white collar	64	36	22	67	33	24	81	19	16
Blue collar	60	40	15	80	20	45	69	31	36
Skilled	62	38	13	82	18	33	61	39	18
Low manual	50	50	2	75	25	12	78	22	18

Table 7.7. *English High School dropouts and graduates of Yankee, English Canadian, and Irish origins, by household characteristics* (%)

	Boys		Girls	
	Graduates	Dropouts	Graduates	Dropouts
Yankee	$N=14$	$N=24$	$N=25$	$N=29$
English Canadian	$N=18$	$N=53$	$N=22$	$N=38$
Irish	$N=16$	$N=39$	$N=25$	$N=16$
Home status				
Yankee				
Owned	42.9	42.3	64.0	17.2
Rented	57.1	57.7	36.0	82.8
Unknown	0	0	0	0
English Canadian				
Owned	50.0	35.8	45.5	28.9
Rented	44.4	64.2	54.5	71.1
Unknown	5.6	0	0	0
Irish				
Owned	87.5	66.7	68.0	68.8
Rented	12.5	30.8	32.0	31.3
Unknown	0	2.6	0	0
Household head's children				
Yankee				
1–3	64.3	73.1	68.0	62.1
4–6	35.7	23.1	28.0	31.0
7+	0	3.8	4.0	6.9
English Canadian				
1–3	61.1	49.1	59.1	55.3
4–6	33.3	45.3	40.9	36.8
7+	5.6	5.7	0	7.9
Irish				
1–3	18.8	35.9	20.0	31.3
4–6	50.0	38.5	52.0	37.5
7+	31.3	25.6	28.0	31.3

more likely to graduate than the children of workingmen. Among Irish students, however, children of workingmen graduated at a higher rate than the children of white-collar parents. Irish blue-collar fathers proved more willing than Irish white-collar fathers to commit family resources for supporting their children in the English High School all the way to the diploma.

The influence of home ownership on high school graduation varied along lines of ethnic origin and gender (Table 7.7). Among Irish and Canadian boys, and among Yankee and Canadian girls, graduates came more often than dropouts from homeowning families. For these students, sponsorship by a homeowning family could be a boost toward graduation.

The ability of a high school student to graduate was not aided consistently by small family size, in any ethnic or gender group. Graduates did not come from small families at a significantly higher rate than dropouts. For example, a larger majority of Irish graduates than among Irish dropouts came from families with four or more children.

The case of Irish graduates indicates that students from families with the burdens of owning a home and providing for a large number of children were not necessarily handicapped in gaining a high school diploma. This accomplishment probably was due primarily to the intensive usage of family-role instrumentalism in Irish households, which allowed a child to finish high school while a sibling worked.

Through the high school, graduation and progress to college was a movement of various figures shaped by class, gender, family, and ethnicity. But by the turn of the century, socioeconomic inequality did not generate all-controlling influence on advancement through the high school. Origin in a Yankee, white-collar family was not an ironclad advantage in prolonging education. Subtle combinations of ethnic and socioeconomic background components that were not uniformly connected with higher social position but variously with a lower one in the external society could confer the advantage for movement to the culminating stages of schooling. The high school, therefore, to a degree, provided opportunity not strictly determined by social origin.

The prolongation of schooling until high school subtly altered the character of family life among the white-collar and skilled parents who sponsored it. Parents in the mid-nineteenth century treated the growth of children as a gradual process of separation, accelerating usually when they went to work at fourteen or fifteen. They encouraged early independence. But by the century's end, many parents supported children who stayed at home until they graduated from high school at seventeen or eighteen. The process of maturation for sons gravitated from acquiring early independence to living out the hopes of parents who sponsored them through high school. And it increasingly involved a sensitive process of negotiation between parents and children about the future of the latter. In some families, ambitious parents pushed reluctant children to prolong their schooling, and in others, eager youngsters pleaded with uncomprehending elders for permission to gain a high-school diploma or to go to college.[13]

Secondary schooling and social mobility

Somerville citizens had created the high school to serve as the principal supplier of skills and certification enabling youngsters to enter white-collar occupations. The transition from high school achievement to an adult career, therefore, was the acid test of the opportunity offered by the city's secondary schools for improving a person's life chances. The transition could occur at one of three switchpoints in the educational track that connected with the network of career tracks radiating into adult life. One group of students emerged at the first switchpoint: They dropped out of high school before finishing the diploma. Another group, emerging at the second switchpoint, obtained a high school diploma; the group leaving at the last switchpoint graduated from high school and attended college before exiting the educational track for the mainline of adult careers. Samples of all three groups were collected from high school records and traced to their last jobs in Somerville.[14]

The large majority of the sons of white-collar parents who went to high school in the 1870s, 1880s, and 1900s became white-collar workers (Table 7.8). Moreover, if they gained a high school diploma or attended college, their chances of persisting in the white-collar occupational class grew progressively higher. In the 1870s and 1880s, the son of a white-collar parent who went to high school or college was almost guaranteed a white-collar job. A generation later, the son of a white-collar parent still had very good prospects to stay in his occupational class, but his chances of persisting fell slightly. A secondary education was still valuable for obtaining white-collar employment in the 1900s, but the increase in secondary-school graduates and rising job qualifications weakened the leverage it afforded.

Sons of working-class parents faced greater difficulty utilizing school achievement as a pathway to white-collar careers. Unlike the sons of white-collar parents, higher levels of schooling did not consistently increase their chances of gaining white-collar employment. Sons of blue-collar workers who graduated from the Somerville High School and the Latin High School actually had lower chances of gaining white-collar jobs than blue-collar sons who had dropped out. Furthermore, sons of blue-collar parents with the same amount of schooling as sons of white-collar parents, first at the Somerville High School and later at the English High School, had substantially lower chances of moving into white-collar jobs. The more limited influence and resources of manually employed parents seems to have hampered their sons' efforts to employ secondary schooling as a step toward white-collar occupations.[15]

Table 7.8. *Education and social mobility of boys entering Somerville High School in 1871–81, the English High School in 1899, 1901, and the Latin High School in 1895–1906*

Highest educational level	Sons of white-collar parents gaining white-collar jobs (%)	Sons of blue-collar parents gaining white-collar jobs (%)	White collar N	Blue collar N
SHS entrants, 1871–81				
Attended	83	63	42	27
Graduated	90	43	10	7
Graduated & college	100	100	11	5
EHS entrants, 1899, 1901				
Attended	75	46	29	24
Graduated[a]	92	71	24	14
LHS entrants, 1895–1906				
Attended	75	88	32	24
Graduated	80	80	10	10
Graduated & college	95	89	21	18

[a] Although the English High School did not record graduates who entered a higher institution, School Committee reports indicated that the vast majority of English High School graduates did not attend college.

For boys from a blue-collar family, how did background factors undercut the advantages afforded by a high school education? In contrast with white-collar sons, many of these youngsters had parents who did not possess financial resources of sufficient size to help them start a business. Most of these lads did not have a position in a family enterprise awaiting their graduation from high school or college. Their parents had fewer personal contacts or family connections that could be utilized to locate a promising clerkship.

Less concrete, but equally difficult impediments also may have blocked advancement to white-collar work. Perhaps some prospective employers discriminated against applicants from working-class backgrounds. Some sons of workingmen probably felt uncomfortable with the character of work in an office and ultimately chose to earn a living by manual employment. The institutional culture of the high school had provided an acquaintance with the rather formal habits

Table 7.9. *White-collar job mobility by ethnicity for English High School entrants, 1896–1905 (%)*

| | White-collar last job | | N white-collar sons | N blue-collar sons |
	Sons of white-collar parents	Sons of blue-collar parents		
Yankee	96	86	25	21
English Canadian	89	86	19	21
Irish	71	66	14	38

expected by office workers, but for some alumni who were the sons of workingmen such demeanor was a superficial veneer intolerably unpleasant to maintain. Only the sons of blue-collar parents who attended the Latin High School were able to match sons of white-collar parents in the rate of gaining white-collar jobs. Perhaps the rigorous Latin High School attracted the boys of blue-collar background who were most determined to enter white-collar ranks and whose parents supplied exceptional support.

Parent's occupation and length of schooling influenced the ability of high school boys to use their education as an avenue to careers. Ethnicity, too, exerted a major influence on the role of education in the process of mobility. The large majority of Yankee, English Canadian, and Irish youths who attended the English High School were able to obtain white-collar jobs (Table 7.9). For all ethnic groups, secondary schooling led to outstanding chances for white-collar work. Students of particular ethnic backgrounds, however, were able to use secondary education to greater advantage. Among both white-collar and blue-collar students, Yankee sons most frequently gained white-collar employment, with English-Canadian sons trailing very slightly behind. Irish graduates were not as successful, but still 71 percent who were sons of white-collar parents and 66 percent who were sons of working-class parents secured white-collar jobs.

In each ethnic group, parental status affected a high school student's chances of entering the white-collar field. In the groups of Yankee, English-Canadian, and Irish boys, the percentage of white-collar parents' sons obtaining white-collar jobs was slightly, but consistently, higher than the percentage of workingmen's sons who climbed into non-manual occupations.

A growing linkage between higher education and professionalization was reflected in the careers of secondary-school students in So-

Table 7.10. *Rate of entry into professions of boys entering Somerville High School in 1871–81, the English High School in 1899, 1901, and the Latin High School in 1895–1906*

Schools	Sons of white-collar parents in professions (%)	Sons of blue-collar parents in professions (%)	White collar N	Blue collar N
Somerville High, 1871–81	6	10	63	39
English High, 1899, 1901	19	11	53	38
Latin High, 1895–1906	19	23	63	52

merville (Table 7.10). Less than one in ten of the high school students from 1871 to 1881 obtained professional employment – became lawyers, ministers, doctors, engineers, dentists, and teachers. By the turn of the century, however, one out of five students who entered the Latin High School entered the professions; about the same proportion of white-collar students at the English High School did so, too. Parent's occupation was not a factor that consistantly restricted access to these jobs. The sons of workingmen who went to the Somerville High School and the Latin High School a generation later entered the professions at a slightly higher rate than the sons of white-collar workers. Although the professions were raising and standardizing training requirements, a number of persons who dropped out of high school or who never went to college entered these fields. No single formal route to the professions had as yet been set.[16]

High school girls, marriage, and careers

The life courses of women in the late nineteenth and early twentieth century were shaped by social expectations considerably different from those confronting men. For men, gainful employment was the primary concern of life; for women, marriage was of paramount significance. The large majority of women thus took husbands and raised children. For them, marriage was the chief vehicle for social mobility, to the extent that they shared their husband's income and status.[17] If a woman found a husband who worked in a secure white-collar job, her position as a comfortable housewife was assured. A much smaller group of women did not marry and worked much of their lives. The

Table 7.11. *Marital and occupational status in adulthood of girls graduating Somerville High School, 1875–85*

Adult status	Number	Percent
Single and employed	17	40
Married and unemployed	16	38
Unmarried and unemployed	9	21
Total	42	

Table 7.12. *Place of residence in 1902 of girls graduating Somerville High School, 1880–4, who married*

Place of residence	Number	Percent
Somerville	23	38
Other Massachusetts town	25	41
Out of state	13	21

remaining women stayed single and unemployed, usually becoming a dependent in a relative's household.

An assessment of the impact of secondary schooling on women's lives must therefore take into account the conventional adult roles available to them. Of all girls who graduated Somerville High School from 1875 to 1885, forty-two were traced to their adult status in the city in 1902 through the *Fiftieth Anniversary* high school commemorative published that year.[18] In 1902, 40 percent were single, fully employed adults; 38 percent were married and unemployed; and the smallest group, 21 percent, were single, unemployed dependents (Table 7.11).

The number of married graduates who could be traced to their adult status in Somerville is disproportionately small. Married women composed the largest percentage of female graduates. For example, of girls graduating between 1880 and 1884 who could be traced to their marital status in 1902, sixty-one were married and thirty were single. However, their numbers in Somerville were reduced because most moved to other towns in Massachusetts or to other states (Table 7.12). Perhaps their high rate of geographic mobility showed that many female graduates were able to marry young men on the rise whose search for better opportunities carried them away from the hometown.[19] That female graduates were able to marry "successful men" is also suggested by the fact that fourteen of sixteen married graduates in Somerville took husbands in white-collar jobs. This inference and others that follow must be regarded as suggestive of lines for further research, because the numbers in the sample are small. All the daughters of white-collar parents in the sample married husbands of that occupational class. Eight of the ten blue-collar daughters also found white-collar spouses. These female graduates were apparently able to use their high-school "finishing" as an attraction to status-conscious husbands seeking culturally sophisticated wives. Also, some girls probably found the high school to be an advantageous place for meeting boys of "good background" who eventually became their husbands.

Although most female graduates fulfilled themselves as housewives and mothers in Gilded Age and turn-of-century Somerville, a substantial minority of girl graduates also sought jobs. In this study's small sample of seventeen "career women," thirteen daughters of white-collar parents moved immediately after graduation into expanding white-collar fields such as teaching and clerical work. Of the four daughters of blue-collar parents, three entered white-collar occupations. Two of the four blue-collar daughters attended college, but none of the white-collar daughters did so. Most of the career women obviously did not need a college education to obtain white-collar employment.

Scholastic achievement and life chances

Educators of the nineteenth century asserted that the public school was a democratic institution where the children of the poor and the children of the wealthy had equal opportunities for scholastic achievement. They did not believe, however, as many twentieth-century educators came to hold, that superior grades were predictors of successful careers.[20]

An inspection of the scholastic ranking of students in the Somerville High School casts doubt upon the notion that the nineteenth-century public high school was a place where students of different social origins were equally able to garner high grades. Among male graduates of the Somerville High School from 1876 to 1885, sons of white-collar parents had a much higher chance than sons of blue-collar parents of finishing in the top half of their class (Table 7.13). And more of the boys ranked in the top half had native fathers and came from propertied families than boys in the bottom half (Table 7.14). Among female graduates, daughters of white-collar parents were also more likely than daughters of blue-collar parents to graduate in

Table 7.13. *Scholastic achievement by parent's occupation of boys and girls graduating Somerville High School, 1876–85*

		Top half of graduating class	Bottom half of graduating class	Total N
Boys[a]				
Parent's occupation				
White collar	N	14	18	32
	%	44	56	
Blue collar	N	4	16	20
	%	20	80	
Girls[b]				
Parent's occupation				
White collar	N	26	29	55
	%	48	53	
Blue collar	N	16	22	38
	%	42	58	

[a]Sample consists of all graduates from 1876–7 and 1880–5 whose parents' occupations could be determined.
[b]Sample consists of all graduates from 1880–5 whose parents' occupations could be determined.

the top half. Seventy-five percent of the girls in the top half came from property-owning families, as compared to only 57 percent of the girls in the bottom half (Table 7.14). Over 70 percent of the students who graduated in the top half had white-collar parents, while about 50 percent of graduates in the bottom half had white-collar parents. In general, parent's occupation and wealth influenced crude scholarship ranking.

White-collar sons had nearly the same chance as the girls of graduating in the top half of their class, but girls nearly monopolized the highest ranking in the graduating classes from 1876 to 1894. In that period, seventeen of eighteen valedictorians were girls; in addition, eight of eighteen salutatorians were girls.[21] The girls consistently performed as the finest scholars in the high school. Outstanding scholarship, it seems, was a manifestation of the "finishing" process, an expression of female refinement in language and arts.

The scholastic ranking of a small group of students graduating from 1875 to 1885 who could be traced to white-collar jobs suggests that in the nineteenth century grades were not viewed as predictors of occupational success. Only six of eighteen sons of white-collar parents

Table 7.14. *Scholarship rank of high school graduates from 1875 to 1885, by household characteristics* (%)

	Boys		Girls	
	$N=7$ Top half	$N=17$ Bottom half	$N=21$ Top half	$N=18$ Bottom half
Household head *occupation*				
White collar	71.5	52.9	80.9	44.5
Skilled	14.3	23.6	14.3	38.9
Low manual	14.3	23.5	4.8	5.6
Unemployed	0	0	0	11.2
Household head *nativity*				
Native born	100.0	88.2	90.5	94.4
Foreign born	0	11.8	9.5	5.6
Real property ($)[a]				
0	0	16.7	25.0	42.8
1–4999	0	33.3	16.7	14.4
5000+	100.0	50.0	58.3	42.8
N children in *family*				
1–3	71.4	52.9	42.9	33.3
4–6	28.6	47.1	57.1	61.1
7+	0	0	0	5.6

[a] Only for students who could be traced to the U.S. Ninth Census 1870 manuscript schedules.

obtaining white-collar occupations whose class ranking was recorded finished in the top half of their class, and none of six blue-collar sons climbing to white-collar jobs did so. The skill standards for white-collar employment were rising, but most employers did not hire people because they had good grades. The qualities employers sought had more to do with character traits such as initiative, cooperativeness, manners, and on-the-job learning ability leavened by a dose of scholastic ability. Many bosses may have felt an aversion toward bookworms; indeed, hardnosed businessmen probably felt they were impractical persons, best suited for teaching.

For career women, however, the small sample assembled suggests scholastic performance played a more prominent role in securing white-collar jobs. Five of eleven daughters of white-collar parents entering white-collar jobs were ranked in the top half of their class, and all three blue-collar daughters attaining white-collar careers also finished in the top half. Their formal learning was instrumental for entering the most important professional field for women: education. Six out of fourteen graduates achieving white-collar employment became schoolteachers.

High school education and the transition of industrial migration regimes

Different periods throughout the long transition from an agrarian to post-industrial economy possessed their characteristic regimes of migration.[22] Stephan Thernstrom, for example, discovered in late-nineteenth- and early-twentieth-century Boston differential rates of residential persistence according to occupational class background. White-collar workers, he found, more frequently persisted as residents of Boston after each decade than blue-collar workers. However, Thernstrom noticed that by the 1930s, the relationship between occupational class and migration began to reverse itself. Blue-collar persistence rates rose to overtake falling white-collar persistence rates.[23] Thernstrom located a turning point from the migration regime of the half-century of post-Civil War industrialization to the migration patterns of the post-Depression era, but the mechanisms that caused the transition remained obscure.

The influence of the high school on the currents of population flowing through Somerville suggests that education was a device causing the shift in migration patterns. The persistence rates of Somerville high school students varied sharply from the persistence rates of students who only attended grammar school (Table 7.15). Among high school students, sons of white-collar parents were more likely to move out of town during the first decade of adulthood than were blue-collar sons. Among grammar school students, the inverse pattern developed, and white-collar sons remained more often than blue-collar sons. Educationally differentiated rates of persistence skewed the tracing procedure toward finding proportionally more high-school educated blue-collar sons than white-collar sons as adults in Somerville, and more grammar-school educated white-collar sons than blue-collar sons.

Moreover, differential levels of schooling affected geographic mobility even within a single occupational class. High school students of white-collar origin had a much lower rate of persistence than white-collar sons who only went to grammar school. Only 27 percent of the white-collar sons entering the Latin High School in 1900–1 remained in Somerville, while 74 percent of grammar-educated white-collar sons in 1900 stayed in town. For white-collar sons, higher levels of education stimulated a higher degree of outward-migration. The universal

Table 7.15. *Rate of residential persistence in Somerville of high school and grammar school male students*

High school students			
Year entered	Parent's occupation	N students	Somerville resident 15 years after entry (%)
1879–81	White collar	70	36
	Blue collar	36	50
	Total	106	41
1899	White collar	60	40
English	Blue collar	38	55
High	Total	98	46
1900–1	White collar	63	27
Latin	Blue collar	30	47
High	Total	93	33
Grammar students			
Census year sample	Parent's occupation	N students	Somerville resident 15 years after census (%)
1870	White collar	28	46
	Blue collar	100	33
	Total	128	36
1900	White collar	69	74
	Blue collar	243	38
	Total	312	46

credential – a high school education – provided access to more distant regional and national labor markets for clerical, professional, and business personnel. And many used the high school diploma to go away to college, where they made new personal connections and found new opportunities requiring geographic mobility to exploit. Among sons of blue-collar workers, the high-school educated tended to stay in town more than those boys who only went to grammar school. The workingmen's educated sons took the local business and office jobs in Somerville left unfilled by white-collar workers' educated sons departing for distant places of employment.

The varying persistence and migration patterns of Somerville's high-school and grammar-school educated young men suggest that the spread of secondary schooling acted as an important stimulus in the transition from the industrial regime of persistent white-collar burghers and "floating" proletariat to the post-industrial regime of mobile white-collar technocrats and stable urban neighborhoods. Between these two migration regimes stood a transitional regime based on the expansion of bureaucratic labor markets and the growth of secondary education. Secondary schooling acted as a new source of supply for highly trained personnel ("human capital" in the language of economists) that also functioned as a sorting device in the machinery of migration, adjusting the distribution of this new labor force according to spatially determined demand in the changing labor market.

The meaning of meritocracy

As Somerville grew into a large, pluralistic urban community, growing social distance and competition complicated parents' efforts to use personal connections for placing their children in jobs. Ambitious parents and children also realized that many attractive white-collar jobs were growing faster in other towns and cities. To compensate for these new conditions an increasing portion of adolescents attended high school. There, they could secure a credential of merit that would serve as a universal recommendation to unfamiliar contacts even in faraway locations. And if they were able to attend college, they could qualify for superior white-collar jobs requiring the highest educational preparation.

Senior John McMillin had expressed his classmates' concern with gaining from a high school education the "necessary qualifications" for success in life. To what extent did attending high school serve as a qualification for desirable careers? A comparison of the career lines of youths of different class origins who were high school students and grammar dropouts indicates some answers.

Students who attended high school from 1870 to 1910 gained a strong advantage over grammar dropouts in securing white-collar jobs. They jumped out to a quick start in life: The majority took white-collar first jobs, while most grammar students had to start out in manual employment (Table 7.16). High school students enjoyed more stable and elevated career trajectories (Table 7.17). About 90 percent persisted in the same occupational class (usually a white-collar job). In contrast, grammar dropouts displayed a higher rate of interclass movement over the span of their careers. And in the end, grammar dropouts' final jobs were more often as manual workers.

Blue-collar parentage reduced the chances for white-collar employment regardless of schooling levels. High school students and grammar dropouts from working-class families displayed lower rates of white-collar employment and higher rates of blue-collar employment than their white-collar counterparts. Workingmen's sons also started more often in manual jobs regardless of schooling level.

Table 7.16. *Influence of family origins upon the career mobility of high school students and grammar dropouts in Somerville and Boston*

	First job				Last job			
	White collar		Blue collar		White collar		Blue collar	
	% of w.c. sons	% of b.c. sons	% of w.c. sons	% of b.c. sons	% of w.c. sons	% of b.c. sons	% of w.c. sons	% of b.c. sons
Somerville								
High school 1871–81								
N = 102	86	66	14	34	87	64	13	36
Grammar 1870								
N = 79	43	24	57	76	76	32	24	68
High school 1895–1906								
N = 206	83	73	17	27	82	75	18	25
Grammar 1900								
N = 130	62	34	38	66	66	50	34	50
Boston								
Birth cohorts[a]								
1850–9								
N = 164	79	28	21	72	87	40	13	60
1860–79								
N = 653	81	42	19	58	84	43	16	57
1880–9								
N = 157	67	35	33	65	76	46	24	54

[a]Stephan Thernstrom, *The Other Bostonians: Poverty and Progress in the American Metropolis, 1880–1970* (Cambridge, Mass., 1973), p. 96, Table 5.4.

Nevertheless, sons of manual workers who went to high school had much greater chances of climbing to white-collar posts than blue-collar grammar dropouts. A high school education indeed helped the son of a workingman increase his opportunities for obtaining white-collar work. High school students from workingmen's families had a ratio of intergenerational upward mobility to downward mobility three times as great as their age peers who only went to grammar school (Table 7.18).

The advantages of a high school education and upbringing in the suburb can be roughly estimated by comparing the careers of high school students in Somerville to those of Boston youths studied by

Table 7.17. *Career mobility across occupational class boundaries from first job to last job* (%)

	Somerville				Boston birth cohorts[a]		
	High school 1871–81	Grammar 1870	High school 1895–1906	Grammar 1900	1840–59	1860–79	1870–89
Same class	89	70	90	65	80	81	76
Different class	11	30	10	35	20	19	24
Blue collar to white collar	6	22	5	26	27	23	28
White collar to blue collar	6	9	5	9	12	17	16
Ratio of upward to downward mobility	1.0	2.4	1.0	2.9	2.3	1.4	1.8
N	102	79	206	130	310	663	443

[a]Stephan Thernstrom, *The Other Bostonians: Poverty and Progress in the American Metropolis, 1880–1970* (Cambridge, Mass., 1973), p. 65, Table 4.9.

Stephan Thernstrom, with randomly diverse schooling levels, or an average amount of education. Because the boys from Somerville and Boston competed in the same metropolitan job market, differences in their career patterns probably reflected, among a host of factors, the differences in schooling between the two groups.

Sons of white-collar parents who went to high school in Somerville did not enjoy better chances for white-collar employment than white-collar sons in Boston with average levels of education. The percentage of white-collar sons attending high school in Somerville from 1870 to 1910 who obtained white-collar jobs was about the same as the proportion for white-collar sons born in Boston between 1850 and 1889 of all schooling levels (Table 7.16). Also, Yankee, English-Canadian, and Irish high school students of white-collar origin displayed about the same rate of class persistence as white-collar central-city co-ethnics of average schooling levels (Table 7.19). Therefore, a suburban white-collar son who gained a high school education did not necessarily enjoy an advantage in finding jobs over a central-city white-collar son who did not go to high school. The latter may have exploited better parental connections and proximity to employment opportunities to gain a desirable job. For a white-collar son without such advantages,

Table 7.18. *Intergenerational occupational inheritance and mobility across occupational class boundaries* (%)

	Somerville				Boston birth cohorts[a]		
	High school 1871–81	Grammar 1870	High school 1895–1906	Grammar 1900	1840–59	1860–79	1870–89
Same class as parent	68	70	56	54	80	81	76
Different class from parent	32	30	44	46	20	19	24
Sons of blue-collar parents moving to white-collar jobs	64	32	75	50	41	41	43
Sons of white-collar parents moving to blue-collar jobs	13	25	18	34	20	17	24
Ratio of upward to downward mobility	4.9	1.3	4.2	1.5	2.1	2.4	1.8
N	102	87	206	147	208	784	193

[a] Stephan Thernstrom, *The Other Bostonians: Poverty and Progress in the American Metropolis, 1880–1970* (Cambridge, Mass., 1973), p. 86, Table 5.2.

however, a high school education may have served as a credential of good social and scholastic training that afforded the means to compete equally.

The blue-collar son who was raised in the suburb and obtained the high school credential had powerful advantages over the average blue-collar son in Boston in obtaining white-collar employment. Blue-collar sons who went to high school in Somerville achieved a higher and faster rate of entry into the white-collar field than blue-collar sons in Boston of all levels of schooling (Table 7.16).

The significant advantages of a high school education and residency in the suburb were most evident in the careers of blue-collar sons of particular ethnic backgrounds – Yankee, English-Canadian, and Irish youths. Blue-collar students of these ethnic origins who went to high school had almost double the chances for white-collar employment as their central-city co-ethnics of average educational levels (Table 7.19).

But it is extremely important to note that the chances for Boston workingmen's sons with average schooling to gain white-collar jobs

Table 7.19. *Upward intergenerational mobility of high school students and persons of all schooling levels, by ethnicity* (%)

	White-collar last job		N white-collar sons	N blue-collar sons
	Sons of white-collar parents	Sons of blue-collar parents		
Somerville English High 1896–1905				
Yankee	96	86	25	21
English-Canadian	89	86	19	21
Irish	71	66	14	38
Boston Cohort born 1860–79[a] All schooling levels				
Yankee	99	53	144	114
British (Including Canadian)	80	45	20	71
Irish	77	35	24	223

[a]Stephan Thernstrom, *The Other Bostonians: Poverty and Progress in the American Metropolis, 1880–1970* (Cambridge, Mass., 1973), p. 134, Table 6.11.

actually grew from the late nineteenth to the early twentieth century. While only 13 percent of the cohort born between 1850 and 1859 obtained white-collar employment, 24 percent of the cohort born between 1880 and 1889 were able to do so. Although suburban upbringing and secondary schooling offered to manual workers' sons definite advantages in climbing up the social ladder, access to white-collar occupations also widened for central-city boys with an average education as the industrial economy matured (Table 7.16).

That high school graduates enjoyed an advantage in entering white-collar occupations was not contingent upon a decline of economic opportunity for grammar-school-educated lads to rise to white-collar employment. As the economy of Somerville and metropolitan Boston diversified and expanded from 1870 to 1920, opportunities for career mobility increased for workers who had only gone to grammar school. The rate at which they moved upward to white-collar jobs in the span of their careers rose gradually (Table 7.17). While the grammar dropouts of 1870 had a rate of upward mobility 2.4 times greater than downward mobility, the grammar dropouts of 1900 were climbing 2.9 times more often than they were falling. Moreover, the proportion of blue-collar grammar dropouts who climbed to white-collar jobs increased from 32 percent in the late nineteenth century to 50 percent in the twentieth century (Table 7.18).

Although high school education served as a faster and more secure pathway to white-collar jobs for a growing number of workingmen's sons, it was clearly not the only route or even the main route to nonmanual employment. Many others with only a grammar education were able to gain white-collar employment by working their way up from blue-collar jobs to managerial posts, by learning clerical skills on the job, or by becoming small proprietors. It was precisely the viability of these traditional avenues of upward mobility that dissuaded many workingmen's sons from sacrificing income for secondary schooling.

The role of higher education in the intergenerational mobility of manual workers in the industrializing Somerville-Boston region from 1870 to 1920 resembled that described by John Goldthorpe in twentieth-century England. Goldthorpe has shown that British skilled workers increasingly capitalized upon schooling to promote their sons into white-collar jobs, even though opportunities remained favorable to rise to the white-collar class through initial manual employment. A similar situation evolved in Somerville, where secondary schooling expanded as an effective route to white-collar occupations, although opportunities to rise also remained strong for grammar-school-educated boys who started out in blue-collar jobs. The evolution of mobility patterns in Somerville confirmed Stephan Thernstrom's observation that it "is quite mistaken to assume that the sons of the threatened artisan were commonly driven down into the ranks of factory operatives; they typically found a place either in the expanding skilled trades or in the even more rapidly expanding white-collar occupations."[24]

In his study, Goldthorpe describes two major theories of the role of education in the social mobility of the workers, the "tightening bond" thesis and the "counterbalance" thesis, as fundamentally opposed in their implications for policies to reduce inequality:

> [The] counterbalance thesis becomes differentiated from that . . . of a "tightening bond" between education and occupational attainment. For while adherents of the latter view have tended to see this development as likely to promote greater mobility, on account of educational expansion and reforms aimed at reducing inequality of opportunity, the counterbalance thesis maintains that any increase in upward mobility achieved in recent decades via educational channels will have been offset by the decrease in chances of advancement in the course of working life. The self-sustaining

> properties of the class structure – as one of differential power and
> advantage – will be little altered by reforms which do not touch
> basic inequalities of *condition;* and since these inequalities have re-
> mained little altered in recent decades, change in the dominant
> modes of "social selection" will simply affect the channels of mo-
> bility without increasing its extent, and without the lines of class
> division being made any less definite.[25]

Goldthorpe, however, discovered through an intricate statistical
analysis of two cohorts of workers in early twentieth-century Britain
that, in the modern industrial context where education mediated
worker mobility, the linkage between schooling and upward mobility
strengthened (the "tightening bond" thesis), whereas the closing off
of other avenues of ascent (the "counterbalance" thesis) failed to occur:

> In sum, then, while our findings could perhaps be taken as lending
> support to the claim that mobility chances are becoming increas-
> ingly influenced by educational attainments, they go contrary to
> the counterbalance thesis in indicating that, over recent decades,
> an increase in direct entry [through education] to the higher levels
> of the class structure has occurred without there being any appar-
> ent decline in the chances of access via indirect routes [through a
> working-class occupation].[26]

To the extent that it complements Goldthorpe's findings and his
theoretical interpretations of the function of education in social stratification, this study suggests that the expansion of secondary schooling in American industrial society from the late nineteenth to the early
twentieth century added a new channel of upward mobility for workers that sustained fluidity as a property of social structure. Indeed, a
global comparison of blue-collar high school students in Somerville
with the sons of workers with average schooling in Canada and Europe suggests that the modern American high school was raising
workingmen's sons into white-collar jobs at a speed much greater
than the upward mobility rate of the general blue-collar population of
workingmen's sons in the industrializing communities of the trans-
atlantic world (Table 7.20). Workers' sons who went to high school
experienced a rate of entry into white-collar occupations 1.6 to 3.4
times higher than that for workers' sons with average schooling in
other North American industrial cities and 1.4 to 5.3 times higher
than that for workers' sons in European industrial cities. Even youths
from the most disadvantaged backgrounds, the sons of semiskilled
and unskilled workers (including those of immigrant parentage), were
able to use a high school education to gain a much greater rate of
white-collar employment than grammar-school-educated low-manual

Table 7.20. *Intergenerational occupational mobility for workers' sons in North American and European cities, 1870–1920 (%)*

City		Sons of blue-collar workers gaining white-collar jobs	Contemporaneous cohorts	
			Sons of blue-collar workers divided into (A)	Sons of blue-collar workers divided into (B)
Somerville Students				
High school	c.1886–96	64 (A)		
High school	c.1910–21	75 (B)		
Grammar	c.1885	32	2.0	—
Grammar	c.1915	50	—	1.5
Other North American cities[a]				
Hamilton, Canada	1871	21	3.0	—
Poughkeepsie	1880	26	2.5	—
Boston	c.1890	41	1.6	—
Boston	c.1910	41	—	1.8
Indianapolis	1910	22	—	3.4
Boston	c.1920	43	—	1.7
European cities[a]				
Cologne, Germany	1870	15	4.3	—
Euskirchen, Germany	1870	18	3.6	—
Esslingen, Germany	1870	45	1.4	—
Vasteras, Sweden	1890	26	2.5	—
Bochum, Germany	1900	12	5.3	—
Cologne, Germany	1910	18	—	4.2
Euskirchen, Germany	1910	17	—	4.4
Esslingen, Germany	1910	39	—	1.9

[a] Stephan Thernstrom, *The Other Bostonians: Poverty and Progress in the American Metropolis, 1880–1970* (Cambridge, Mass., 1973), p. 244, Table 9.7; Michael B. Katz, Michael J. Doucet, and Mark J. Stern, *The Social Organization of Early Industrial Capitalism* (Cambridge, Mass., 1982), p. 194, Table 5.10; Hartmut Kaelble, *Historical Research on Social Mobility: Western Europe and the U.S.A. in the Nineteenth and Twentieth Centuries* (New York, 1977), p. 36, Table 3.1.

sons in Somerville and those in other American cities (Table 7.21). The higher rates of occupational mobility for workers' sons who went to high school suggest that entry into better jobs grew increasingly related to prolonged school careers and was made more difficult by early school leaving. The modernization of the high school that im-

Table 7.21. *Low-manual sons gaining white-collar occupations*

City		Low-manual sons in white-collar last job	
		Percent	Number
Somerville			
Students			
High school	c.1886–96	67	15
High school	c.1910–21	72	32
HS Irish & Canadian	c.1910–21	72	32
Grammar	c.1885	24	37
Grammar	c.1915	49	57
Grammar foreign parentage	c.1915	43	35
Other North American cities[a]			
Hamilton, Canada	1871	22	192
Newburyport	c.1880	10	245
Poughkeepsie	c.1880	22	121
Boston	c.1890	43	63
Boston	c.1910	39	261
Indianapolis	1910	22	278
Boston	c.1920	46	73

[a]Stephan Thernstrom, *The Other Bostonians: Poverty and Progress in the American Metropolis, 1880–1970* (Cambridge, Mass., 1973), p. 246, Table 9.8; Michael B. Katz, Michael J. Doucet, and Mark J. Stern, *The Social Organization of Early Industrial Capitalism* (Cambridge, Mass., 1982), p. 194, Table 5.10.

pinged upon a rising enrollment of workers' and immigrants' sons distributed a new form of economic opportunity in the lower orders of society, thereby keeping the boundaries between social strata permeable.

In the final analysis, it is important to keep in mind that, although the sons of immigrants and workers composed a growing subgroup of the high school, access to secondary schooling, and, therefore, to enhancement of opportunities to gain white-collar employment, remained directly proportional to the occupational rank and nativity of parents, as well as to their propensity to own homes and to limit the number of children. Boys from immigrant workingmen's families who lacked these background advantages were limited most frequently to a grammar education and compelled to enter the labor market early; thus they had comparatively smaller chances for moving up to non-manual occupations.[27] And workingmen's sons with a high school education had smaller chances for gaining non-manual employment than the high-school educated sons of white-collar employees. The principal beneficiaries of a high school education and the mobility it enhanced were the children of Yankee white-collar and skilled employees who comprised the majority of secondary students.

These patterns lend substance to the general thesis of Samuel Bowles and Herbert Gintis that the institutional structure of public schools reflected and reproduced inequalities of the social-economic structure.[28] But the Somerville findings also indicate that the general relationship between schooling and social structure was more subtle and complex. By the turn of the century, a growing minority of workers' sons, many of immigrant origin, were able to attend high school through the industry of parents and family strategies of role exchange. Workers' sons who went to high school gained a significant advantage over those who did not that led to higher rates of occupational mobility. Something important happened to them in high school: By the turn of the century, this institution was an arena for competition that was semi-detached from the influences of unequal social origin. Blue-collar or immigrant parentage did not necessarily dictate lower rates of graduation or college entry. The high school's curriculum and extracurriculum equipped students with meritocratic qualities and their credentials. These were the results of academic performance and constituted a social advantage derived independently of parental occupation.[29] The extent that workers' sons who went to high school lagged behind their middle-class colleagues in white-collar employment probably stemmed from the latter's external social advantages coming from parental status and influence that outweighed the effects of advantage gained from prolonged education. The high school supplied certain meritocratic qualifications affecting the distribution of social position in the rising turn-of-the-century generation, but their influence was modulated by the powerful constraints of social structure.

8   The birth of progressive reform and the junior high school

On the threshold of the twentieth century, Somerville Yankees looked ahead to a continuing partnership between Republican supremacy and business prosperity. The Yankee regime's municipal policies had galvanized population growth and economic expansion, but these became the very forces that eroded the foundations of Republican power. As the decades of the new century unfolded, the old-stock elite discovered that the relentless movement of mobile newcomers to Somerville was turning their Yankee Republican suburb into an immigrant Democratic city that resembled the ethnic neighborhoods of Boston.

Somerville Republicanism and nativism retreated before the flood-tide of immigrants and workers unleashed by the maturation of the industrial economy, the affordable suburban housing market, and rapid transit. In 1926, the Republican-controlled city government gerrymandered ward two to concentrate the Irish into one voting bloc. This maneuver brought only a brief interval of safety. In 1929, "The Banner Temperance City of the Commonwealth" fell to the invaders, when for the first time in history, a Democratic mayor and a Democrat-controlled board of aldermen were elected.[1]

A growing zone of emergence

In the early twentieth century, Somerville's role as a "zone of emergence" in the social geography of the Boston metropolitan region reached new magnitude. This inner-suburban area attracted upper-working-class and low-white-collar employees with its cross town rapid transit and inexpensive housing conditions. Second-generation northern European, Canadian, and Irish immigrants on the rise had filtered into the Somerville "zone" since the late nineteenth century, but their flow speeded up and was infused by new arrivals from southern and eastern Europe. These newcomers gradually displaced the Yankees, and in the process, they transformed the housing market. Double- and triple-unit houses and single-family cottages jammed tightly into small rezoned and resubdivided lots replaced the larger homes of the Yankees.[2]

The influx of foreign workers and second-generation immigrants

186

Table 8.1. *Foreign white stock by country of origin, 1930*

Country of origin	N
French Canada	2,373
English Canada	18,253
England	3,639
Scotland	2,406
Ireland	16,654
Sweden	1,358
Italy	12,848
Portugal	2,550
Other	12,153
Total	72,234

Source: U.S. Census *Reports* 1930, Vol. II, p. 333.

turned Somerville from a spacious suburb into one of the most densely populated cities in the Commonwealth. Its population swelled from 61,643 in 1900 to 103,908 in 1930, which produced an increase in the number of wards from four to seven (Fig. 8.1).[3] Each year, new rows of two- and three-family houses lined the hillsides. Twenty-five thousand people lived on every square mile of land by 1930. The city had reached the limits of its physical capacity.

The resurgent tide of immigrants that poured into the Boston metropolitan area diversified its population.[4] New waves of Irish, English-Canadians, British, Germans, and Swedes flocked to the colonies that predecessors had established in the nineteenth century (Table 8.1). Now strange newcomers were settling the suburb. From neighboring Quebec came French-Canadian workers. The southern Italian settlement grew until it became the third largest immigrant group in Somerville, after the English-Canadians and the Irish. The Portuguese also became a prominent new element in the city's growing Catholic population.

The foreign-born Irish continued to huddle around the large meatpacking plants and the railyard known as the "Patch." These neighborhoods contained the cheapest housing in the shadows of the plants, factories, and stationhouses where immigrants found low-skilled, low-paying jobs. The Italians, Portuguese, and French-Canadians gathered in the interstices of the Irish quarters and socialized with their conationals in adjoining Cambridge.[5]

Nativist Protestants, derisively called "APAs" by Catholic immi-

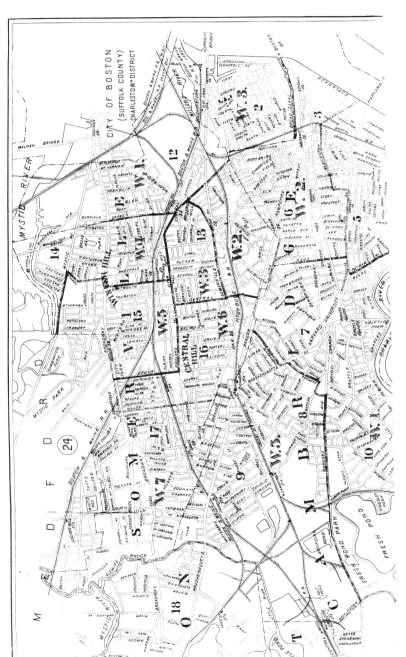

Fig. 8.1 Map of Somerville and its neighborhoods with its new system of seven wards, 1900. *Atlas of Middlesex County, Massachusetts, Volume I.*

grants in reference to the American Protective Association, were alarmed by the growing ranks of "papists." Three parishes and three parochial schools had been opened in the years before 1900. Three more parishes were founded between 1900 and 1920 – one in Yankee West Somerville.[6] A veteran wardleader observed that "Somerville was about 40 percent Catholic in 1920."[7] By 1930, it was probably almost 60 percent Catholic.[8]

The momentum of upward mobility impelled Irishmen into every neighborhood of the city. Many middle-class Irish families crossed over from East Boston, Charlestown, and the West End of Boston.[9] Others were workingmen who were gradually ascending the occupational ladder. Escaping from the railyards and meatpacking palaces in wards one and two, the Irish shouldered their way "up the Hill" (a local colloquialism for social ascent) into ward three, a more affluent residential section.[10] During the economic upswing of the World War I years, the Irish living in the Patch dispersed throughout Somerville, settling heavily in westernmost wards four, six, and seven, where many English-Canadians and Yankees resided.[11] They were reinforced by other Irish families who filtered into these districts from neighboring North Cambridge.[12]

The Italian community was also split into a prosperous middle-class group and a working-class segment. They arrived in substantial numbers after 1900. The economic boom years of wartime and the 1920s propelled the migration of middle-class Italians from Boston and East Boston into Somerville. By 1920, sizable numbers of Italians – many second-generation and Republican – lived in every ward. Many joined the G.O.P. out of resentment over Irish domination of the Democratic Party.[13] "Naturally, with all this success," observed one contemporary, "the old North End was not fit to live in although quite suitable to do business in. From 1925 to 1935, practically every large house for sale in Somerville was purchased by North End Italians."[14] On the other side of the tracks, poor Italian immigrants congregated in their settlements and worked in the warehouses, factories, and packing plants. The population of these immigrants grew from 590 in 1900 to 5,039 in 1930. They replaced the Irish workers who were moved "up the Hill."[15]

In the first quarter of the century, Somerville's labor force was about 45 percent white collar and 55 percent blue collar.[16] Patterns of property ownership displayed large disparities that marked the gap between the middle class and the working class (Table 8.2). Ward one, ward two, and part of ward six had large populations of working-class Irish and Italians. There, the average property valuation per family ranged from 55 percent to 90 percent of the middle-class wards three,

Table 8.2. *Average real estate valuation per family, ($)*

Wards	1905	1910	1915	1920
1	2,728	2,430	2,604	2,683
2	1,858	2,262	2,074	1,883
3	3,189	3,205	3,198	3,268
4	3,073	2,979	3,029	3,039
5	3,206	3,194	3,162	3,174
6	2,719	2,563	2,602	2,759
7	3,662	3,321	3,268	3,411

Source: Somerville *Journal*, Tax Valuation Lists: August 4, 1905; July 15, 1910; July 30, 1915; September 4, 1920.

four, five, and seven, where their more successful countrymen had moved.

Economic gains promoted residential mobility. As immigrants and their children climbed economically, they sought to differentiate themselves through residential mobility from poorer newcomers, even though they might be fellow countrymen. Economic advancement stimulated the spatial dispersion of different class elements in the immigrant community.

Great extremes in the cost of housing and rent did not exist in Somerville, as property values and rents clustered in the middle bracket of prices (Table 8.3). Seventy percent of all Somerville homes had values from $3,000 to $9,999. In addition, Somerville had the highest proportion of homes in the middle-price rent bracket – thirty dollars to forty-nine dollars per month – of any city in the country with a population over 100,000. Housing expenses indicated that Somerville was an attractive residency for low-white-collar and high-blue-collar workers of the medium income range.

The availability of housing functioned as an internal accelerator that reinforced the dispersion of ethnic groups. Following the commuter lines to cheap homes and apartments, the Irish, Italians, English, Swedes, Canadians, Portuguese, and Scots spread residentially throughout all seven wards of the city (Table 8.4). By 1920, Somerville residents of immigrant background had become numerically dominant; they had formed large settlements in every ward (Tables 8.5 and 8.6). The intermingling of ethnic groups at work and on the street made people conscious of their separate identities and competing interests.

As population rocketed upwards, pressure on crowded facilities and resources in the community made social tension run high. Moreover,

Table 8.3. *Value of homes and cost of rent, 1930 ($)*

Value of homes	N	%	Rent paid per month per rental unit	N	%
0–999	3	—	0–9	33	0.2
1,000–1,499	52	0.6	10–14	209	1.2
1,500–1,999	80	1.0	15–19	738	4.3
2,000–2,999	286	3.4	20–29	3,302	19.3
3,000–4,999	1,301	15.5	30–49	10,496	61.5
5,000–7,499	2,498	29.8	50–74	2,122	12.4
7,500–9,999	2,099	25.1	75–99	111	0.7
10,000–14,999	1,754	20.9	100–149	20	0.1
15,000–19,999	193	2.3	150–199	1	—
20,000–	65	0.8	200–	0	—
Not reported	42	0.5	Not reported	37	0.2
Total	8,373	100.0		17,069	100.0

Source: U.S. Census *Reports* 1930, Vol. VI, pp. 60–3.

Table 8.4. *Percentage of foreign-born whites by country of origin in each ward, 1910, 1920*

Country	Year	N	Ward 1	Ward 2	Ward 3	Ward 4	Ward 5	Ward 6	Ward 7	%
Ireland	1910	5,320	17	35	9	5	13	15	6	100
	1920	5,741	16	29	11	6	12	17	9	100
Italy	1910	1,777	6	42	2	4	6	31	9	100
	1920	3,463	13	25	4	9	13	29	7	100
Canada	1910	7,493	13	11	11	11	12	21	21	100
(English)	1920	7,679	14	7	10	12	13	19	25	100
England	1910	1,538	10	15	10	9	15	22	19	100
	1920	1,335	13	10	9	11	11	22	24	100
Scotland	1910	704	12	11	12	8	17	25	15	100
	1920	899	9	8	12	8	14	25	24	100
Sweden	1910	710	7	19	6	5	13	30	20	100
	1920	754	6	8	5	6	15	26	34	100
Portugal	1910	335	7	45	5	9	12	17	5	100
	1920	686	7	53	10	4	7	9	10	100

Sources: U.S. Census *Reports* 1910, Vol. II, p. 895; U.S. Census *Reports* 1920, Vol. III, p. 468.

Table 8.5. *Native and foreign-born white, by ward,*[a] *1900–30*[b]

	Year	Ward 1	Ward 2	Ward 3	Ward 4	Ward 5	Ward 6	Ward 7
N native- and foreign-born white in each ward	1900	10,018	12,041	7,078	6,801	9,001	8,897	7,599
	1910	10,378	12,994	7,630	7,505	11,212	14,428	12,709
	1920	12,322	13,969	8,824	9,206	12,630	16,527	19,247
	1930	14,793	19,537	12,581	15,877	15,508	11,968	13,321
Percentage of native white of native parents	1900	40	16	51	56	41	40	53
	1910	34	15	46	50	41	39	51
	1920	33	18	37	41	37	33	45
	1930	30	19	31	35	27	41	35
Percentage of native white of foreign or mixed parents	1900	33	46	26	23	33	30	24
	1910	38	47	30	28	35	32	27
	1920	40	49	38	37	39	39	33
	1930	41	47	41	40	44	35	38
Percentage of foreign-born white	1900	27	38	23	21	26	30	24
	1910	28	38	24	22	24	29	22
	1920	27	33	25	22	24	28	22
	1930	29	34	28	25	29	24	27

[a]"Mixed" means one parent is foreign born.
[b]In 1926 ward boundaries were changed.

Sources: U.S. Census *Reports* 1900, Vol. I, pt. 1, p. 664; U.S. Census *Reports* 1910, Vol. II, p. 895; U.S. Census *Reports* 1920, Vol. III, p. 468; U.S. Census *Reports* 1930, Vol. III, pt. 1, p. 1111.

Table 8.6. *Native and foreign-born white, the city as a whole, 1900–30*

	1900		1910		1920		1930	
	N	%	N	%	N	%	N	%
Native white of native parents	24,657	40	29,573	38	32,289	35	31,351	30
Native white of foreign or mixed parents	19,618	32	26,632	35	36,254	39	42,689	41
Foreign-born white	17,160	28	20,741	27	24,182	26	29,545	29
	61,435	100	76,946	100	92,725	100	103,585	100

Source: U.S. Census *Reports* 1900, Vol. I, pt. 1, p. 660; U.S. Census *Reports* 1920, Vol. II, p. 895; U.S. Census *Reports* 1930, Vol. III, pt. 1, p. 1111.

two basic conditions intensified the strain caused by the rising tide of population: first, the cleavage between the middle class and the working class; second, ethnic-group rivalry and intolerance. The mixing and flowing of population expressed these conditions. Well-to-do Irish and Italians sought residence further away from their working-class neighbors, only to be ostracized by old-stock citizens, who in turn moved away from unwanted new neighbors who were "papist" and "foreign." Economic mobility and ethnic discord churned up the existing spatial groupings of Somerville residents. Neighborhoods cut from one ethnic cloth unraveled under the impact of these forces. The shifting, growing population of Somerville in the early twentieth century transformed the Yankee city into a community dominated demographically by immigrants. The proportion of Somerville residents who were native-born of native parentage declined to 30 percent by 1930, while the proportion of foreign-stock persons rose to 70 percent (Table 8.6).

As a "zone of emergence," Somerville housed an increasing proportion of people who were advancing in economic welfare and moving along the path of assimilation. But these newly established people felt themselves to be perched precariously between the poverty of working-class, tenement life and middle-class status. Their transitional position encouraged a sense of insecurity. As a result, the newcomers who had climbed halfway up toward assimilation became politically and civically active to protect their interests. As one historian has written about "zone" communities such as Somerville, their state of transition provoked "a defensive posture that expressed itself in a passion for organizational affiliation":

> This section of the city, as one reporter put it, housed the "so-called middle class . . . ," a class in which "there are many organizations, societies, associations, fraternities and clubs that bring together people who are striving upward, trying to uplift themselves." Many belonged to building associations, savings institutions that catered especially to those of modest means who aspired to home ownership. Unions also garnered most of their members from among the residents of the Zone, but singing societies, rifle clubs, bowling leagues, mutual-benefit associations, charity organizations, and groups devoted to educational uplift also flourished in this region. . . . The conflicts of loyalties and the economic vulnerability and social insecurity, which motivated the joiner spirit in this area, made the Zone the most politically unpredictable section of the city.[17]

The seeds of organizational potential in the new pluralistic middle class of the Somerville "zone" were sown at the turn of the century, and grew into a full-scale revolt against Republican rule that expanded Democratic power through an educational reform movement.

Seeds of revolt against the Republican establishment

The adoption of a new city charter in 1899 revealed the interplay of forces that underlay the emergence of Democratic political power. Furthermore, it established the institutional conditions for an eventual life-and-death contest between the Republicans and the Democrats for control of Somerville.

Since 1897, the city government had discussed proposals for a new municipal charter. The aldermen and common councilmen all agreed the growth of the city dictated an increase in the number of wards.[18] Many advocated the subdivision of the four wards of the city into nine wards. Strong differences in opinion were expressed, however, over the structure of the new city government. The wheelhorses of the G.O.P. machine endorsed a one-chamber government composed of twenty-one aldermen from seven wards.[19] Two aldermen from each ward would be selected by the voters of that ward, and one would be elected at large. They also wanted a strong executive. In their plan, the mayor would make all appointments to administrative posts.

The Republican plans troubled "good government" reformers who wanted to curb the power of the long-reigning G.O.P. machine. Their voice of opposition was the citizens' Municipal League, which was formed to promote non-partisanship in city government and to elect the best qualified men to public office.[20] Most of the League's members were "reform" or independent Republicans. James W. Kenney, an artisan who joined the Municipal League and later became one of the first Irish aldermen in the city, objected to the proviso for at-large election of aldermen, rather than by the "voters of the respective wards."[21] The Somerville Irish were beginning to flex political strength in East Somerville's working-class wards; they saw the proposal for a single chamber, a third of whose members would be elected at large, as an attack aimed at their local power base. On the eve of a referendum to approve the charter, James J. O'Brien, a clergyman and prominent spokesman of the Irish community, stated he "regretted that the new charter did not provide for minority representation."[22]

Vehement opposition came from other sources as well. John W. Converse, a reform alderman from the 1880s, defended the current charter as "the people's charter." "The proposed one is the politician's charter," he warned. Converse charged that the appointment power of the mayor and the single chamber comprised a formula for extending the control of the Republican machine. Criticizing "bossism" and "one-man power," Converse foresaw for the mayor "a great opportunity . . . to build a strong personal political machine to retain himself and friends in office."[23] Dr. Albert E. Winship, editor of the *Journal of Education* and a long-time friend of reform, attacked the proposed charter for undercutting minority representation.[24] He further criticized the charter advocates for proposing explicitly to model the municipal government after a business corporation.

Despite these opposing views, on September 29, 1899, a small turnout of voters approved the new charter in every ward of the city (Table 8.7). Both parties in the controversy were surprised that it passed smoothly in ward one, where many Irish voters were expected to oppose it.[25] The charter encountered greatest opposition in ward two, the constituency of James W. Kenney. The G.O.P. machine obtained the mandate they needed to remain in command of the city. They looked forward to the next decade as a time of reinvigorated Republican hegemony. Nevertheless, the unprecedented attack on the G.O.P. machine had brought together for the first time the political forces of reform Republicanism and Irish Democracy. That political alliance would resurface again in an educational reform movement to establish the junior high school.

New safety valves for rising enrollments

As Somerville entered the twentieth century, it seemed destined to maintain its reputation as a showcase of the middle-class ethos. The family unit, the building block of the social order, was small and sta-

Table 8.7. *Referendum for new city charter, 1899*

| | Vote | | Registered |
	Yes	No	voters
Ward 1	171	117	1,266
Ward 2	397	279	2,408
Ward 3	398	96	2,394
Ward 4	366	109	2,273
Total vote	1,332	601	8,341

Source: Somerville *Journal*, September 29, 1899, p. 1.

ble. The average family numbered slightly over four members and lived in a dwelling with over six rooms.[26] Men and women usually married well into their twenties. One out of four Somerville residents 15 to 20 years old was married, but three out of four persons over 25 were married.[27] Since men and women married relatively late, families were not formed until a wage-earning capacity had been established. Also, births came within a shorter span of years, allowing parents more time to concentrate on the rearing of individual children. The small number of children, maturity of marriage partners, and the small fraction of employed wives shaped a household conducive to sponsorship of schooling and to encouraging the mobility of the next generation.[28]

The sponsorship of schooling by Somerville parents combined with a 66 percent increase of the city's population from 1900 to 1930 to boost school enrollments far beyond the previous base of support. In 1900, Somerville still ranked 52 out of 353 municipalities in per-pupil spending, but it plummeted to 109 out of 354 in 1910.[29] Rampant growth of the student population outstripped the ability of the town to maintain previous levels of per-capita school funding. From 1900 to 1924, public-school enrollment swelled from 8,792 to 12,964, an increase of 47 percent. Nearly a third of the native white population was in the school-age years of 5 to 19 in 1920 and 1930 (Table 8.8). Helping to ease the pressure on the public schools were parochial elementary schools, whose enrollment more than doubled from 1,351 in 1900 to 3,295 in 1924.[30]

The rise in attendance was heightened by stricter enforcement of the compulsory schooling age of 15 years and tighter control of truancy. Also, foreign-born males, brought by the resurgence of immigration, filled factory jobs native youths would have taken, thus keeping older children in school.[31] Complaints of overcrowding in school depart-

Table 8.8. *Distribution of native white population by age; 1920, 1930*

	1920		1930	
	Native white of native parents	Native white of foreign or mixed parents	Native white of native parents	Native white of foreign or mixed parents
Over 65	1,205	542	2,389	1,093
45–64	6,265	3,764	5,479	4,665
35–44	4,461	3,455	3,576	4,489
25–34	4,927	5,755	4,233	7,298
20–24	2,661	4,072	2,622	4,810
15–19	2,219	4,130	2,483	5,032
10–14	2,529	4,538	2,919	5,241
5–9	2,920	4,792	3,523	5,040
Under 5	3,766	5,206	4,127	5,022
Total	30,953	36,254	31,351	42,690

Sources: U.S. Census *Reports* 1920, Vol. II, p. 327; U.S. Census *Reports* 1930, Vol. II, p. 768.

ment, superintendents', and headmasters' reports were commonplace. In this atmosphere of urgency, Somerville educators erected new institutional structures to handle the students pouring into the school system.

In 1911, the school committee decided to reunite the English High School and the Latin High School. It was an attempt to maximize facilities and staff in the face of overloaded classrooms. In the reunited high school, classes doing parallel work were combined; classes were distributed between the two plants to utilize all available space; teaching loads were reassigned to gain the widest coverage of subjects.

The reunification of the high school also seemed logical because the Latin High School and the English High School had grown closer in function. The N.E.A.'s *Report of the Committee of Ten* on secondary-school studies had spurred a nationwide movement to broaden college admissions standards by making acceptable English, modern languages, and scientific courses.[32] By the second decade of the century, the English High School was able to place a small but increasing number of its graduates in college. With the work of the English High School and the Latin High School converging, reunification would produce a complementation of college preparatory offerings.

The reunified high school was called the "comprehensive high school."[33] It offered a wide selection of preparatory as well as practical courses and supplied a common curriculum with flexible options for individual specialization. A framework for a modified form of the common-school tradition had been restored at the secondary level of the system. A comprehensive high school promised to be the most functional institution for the approaching age of mass high school attendance.

The new Somerville High School enrolled an increasing share of all high-school-age youths. Adaptation to overcrowding had produced an innovative institution that further stimulated the popularity of a high school education. The enrollment at Somerville High School was 42 percent of the city's high-school-age population in 1915, outdistancing that of secondary schools in Boston, Lynn, Lawrence, Lowell, and Cambridge.[34] Nationally, as late as 1920, only 32 percent of high-school-age youths were enrolled in secondary schools.[35] From 1915 to 1930, Somerville High School grew modestly from 2,258 to 2,500, an increase of 11 percent. The number of graduates, however, increased by 81 percent in that period, from 311 to 564.[36] The comprehensive high school greatly enhanced a student's chances of securing a diploma.

Other valves for releasing the pressure of overcrowding were installed when Somerville educators established a boys' vocational school in 1910 and a girls' vocational school in 1911.[37] As the English High School had, they broke with the traditional view that educational opportunity meant equal access to a common schooling. They, too, were created on the principle that educational opportunity meant the special training of students determined by differentiated talents and needs. A statewide movement for separate industrial training had been strengthened by the election of David Snedden to Commissioner of Education, a zealous positivist who urged increased usage of schools as a sorting system for channeling different students into a stratified array of careers. Somerville's vocational schools were founded in the years from 1909 to 1915, when the number of industrial schools in the Bay State grew from fifteen to fifty-nine.[38]

The boys' vocational school offered two years of training in metalwork and woodwork in preparation for apprenticeship. The girls' vocational school furnished its students with millinery and dressmaking skills.[39] Vocational schools supplied a completely different set of courses from the manual training of the last century, which had been subservient to cognitive development. Instead, the vocational program was a practical end in itself, a simple and plain preparation for industrial work.

The school committee explained that these schools were useful for students with "mediocre" records in academic courses. Their training in the "three Rs" would have carried them further in life in "former days," noted the committee members, but currently they were little in demand because of the ample supply of people with superior literacy and numeracy skills. The school committee studied a group of these students who dropped out to work in 1909.[40] Many entered low-skilled, low-paying jobs with dim prospects for future advancement, especially since they faced increasing competition from foreign-born adults. The study's conclusion corresponded to the findings of the noted 1906 "Kingsbury" report on child labor that drew attention to victims of "wasted years" who entered "the grades of industry" at "the lowest order."[41]

Somerville educators concluded that the brightest opportunities for these youths lay in vocational training for skilled industrial work. They cited the complaints of employers about the scarcity of skilled labor; they noted apprenticeship conditions were "rapidly growing worse."[42] They believed the vocational school would help replenish the supply of well-trained, reliable workingmen. Despite its putative advantages to lagging students, the vocational schools failed to grow. In 1913, they enrolled 103 students, and in 1920 they contained only 112 students.[43] For secondary education, Somerville parents and youths preferred the comprehensive high school over the vocational school.

A new institution that became the main safety valve for overcrowding was the junior high school. Like the English High School and the comprehensive high school, it was a secondary-school innovation made urgent by a peak in the periodic cycle of overcrowding. It was installed at the height of demographic pressure in the grammar classrooms. It became a high-volume pipeline conveying more students to secondary grade levels and made possible the development of mass high school attendance.

Proponents of the junior high school argued in educational journals and scholarly monographs that this intermediate school would supply the special education needed by students making the difficult transition from childhood to adolescence.[44] It would earlier provide, they contended, "high-school type courses" and equip students with clerical and technical skills increasingly demanded by the gradually expanding white-collar class of the Boston area labor force.[45] These two features – a more mature school setting and technical courses – would make the junior high school an effective device for keeping students in school longer. Moreover, it would encourage them to continue on to high school to complete a sequence of related courses.

Social reformers embraced the junior high school because it promised a prolonged education, a better informed citizenry, and improved vocational preparation. The proponents of these progressive goals, who established the junior high school in Somerville, were middle-class Democrats of immigrant stock. Their growing political strength in the city was the decisive force that produced this signal addition to the school system.

Somerville was one of the first eastern cities to establish permanent junior high schools. From 1916 to 1920, visitors from school systems in eighty American and two Japanese cities inspected the Somerville junior high schools and acclaimed them as prototypes of progressive secondary schooling.[46]

The phase of experimentation

Responding to agitation in the previous few years from citizens' groups seeking better school accommodations,[47] the school committee drafted an experimental plan in 1913 called the "intermediate school," which was based on proposals for junior high schools expounded in educational journals and educational societies.[48] Somerville had set the stage for the junior high school by replacing the old primary and grammar school with a single elementary school. Beginning in September 1914, moreover, the seventh and eighth grades of Forster Elementary School were separated from the school and given "high school type" courses.

Although he was cautious about the new plan, Superintendent of Schools Charles S. Clark called attention to the special needs and capacities of the early adolescent years from twelve to fifteen. The "Forster Intermediate School," he felt, would provide an institutional setting better equipped to develop fully the potentials of this pivotal age, "an interesting, vital, formative time" that educators had to midwife into adulthood.[49]

The Forster Intermediate School operated its first year satisfactorily in 1914. The school committee decided to upgrade its program in the following year, and ordered that four separate "courses" or tracks – preparatory, commercial, manual arts, and household arts – be created, "all of which courses shall devote approximately two-thirds to the differentiated courses." Pupils and their parents were to decide at the beginning of the seventh grade what courses to pursue.[50] Of the students in the first class at Forster Intermediate to select courses, 115 took preparatory, 104 commercial, 23 household arts, and 19 manual arts. The preference for white-collar careers communicated by parents to children was evidenced by these choices: 219 out of 261 pupils chose a preparatory or business course.[51] In this way, before intelligence testing and tracking were introduced to steer younger students, the Somerville junior high school developed an easily administered system of ability grouping.

The junior high school was the most practicable means for managing the growing mass of students and organizing their behavior into constructive, social activity. It established interest and aptitude grouping at an earlier switchpoint in the pathway taken by the student through the school system. It thrust into what were formerly the higher grammar grades secondary-style subjects that interlinked with high school courses to form a continuous, longer secondary curricular track for more students. It separated young adolescents from the distracting company of elementary-age and high-school-age pupils. It therefore appealed as a more specialized instrument for socialization. Civic leaders, educators, and citizens, aware of the demographic pressures turning Somerville into one of the state's most densely populated cities,[52] looked to the junior high school to sort and to assimilate the throngs of children brought in by the influx of newcomers.

The junior high school would keep children in school longer and give them useful skills earlier. If they dropped out, they would be better trained to take jobs. It repaired the Achilles heel of the school system – the 12 to 15 age bracket – where the highest drop-out, truancy, and absentee rates occurred (Table 8.9).[53]

After two years of the Forster Intermediate School experiment, the school committee voted unanimously in April 1916 to establish a system of four junior high schools.[54] Support for this decision came vigorously from community associations in West Somerville (ward seven), where colonies of Yankees, English-Canadians, and Swedes lived. The West Somerville Civic Association and the West Somerville Board of Trade immediately convened a public meeting that filled every seat in West Somerville's Columbian Hall, at which the school committee's plan was endorsed.[55]

Pursuant to the new city charter of 1900, two school committee members were chosen from each ward and held office in staggered terms of two years. In 1913, four Democrats, two progressive Republicans, and one progressive Democrat held seats on the school committee. In 1914, there were also four Democrats, two progressive Republicans, and one progressive Democrat; and in 1915, two Democrats, two progressive Republicans, and two progressive Democrats. As many as three women in a single year served on the school committee and all Democratic members were Irish. From 1913 to 1916, the Democrats and progressives held at least half of the fourteen seats on the school committee. Between 1910 and 1920, that body reflected the growing power of Democrats and progressives in Somerville more than the

Table 8.9. *Grammar school promotions, 1910–18*

Year	Graduated 8th grade N	Entered 9th grade N	% 8th grade	Graduated 9th grade N	Entered 10th grade N	% 9th grade
1910	743	521	70			
1911	805	609	76			
1912	781	538	69	718[a]	637	89
1913	691	533	77	764[a]	628	82
1914	741	587	79	837[a]	606	72
1915	789	619	78	844[a]	700	83
1916	781	599	77	812[a]	528	65
1917	528	357	68			
1918	207	139	67			
Junior high school promotions, 1918–24						
1918	1,001	863	86	373	325	87
1919				595	492	83
1920	897	880	98	700	624	89
1921	932	912	98	860	767	90
1922	1,028	923	90	946[a]	808	85
1923	989	895	90	985[a]	829	84
1924	1,035	943	91	1,047[a]	904	86

[a] A larger number graduated from class than entered due to parochial transfers. Note smaller number of parochial transfers into 9th grade under "Junior high promotions." Parochial students transferred into the public schools one or two grades earlier – in the 7th or 8th grade – under the 6-3-3 system than they did under the 8-4 plan.
Source: Somerville, *Annual Reports:* "School Department" – Statistics.

board of aldermen (85 percent Republican from 1912 to 1920) which the G.O.P. machine controlled until 1929.[56]

A coalition of Democrats and progressives gained a political presence in the school committee. Their geographic base was composed of wards one and two, the neighborhoods closest to Boston and Charlestown, twin strongholds of Irish Democracy that elected all but one of the Democratic school committee members from 1912 to 1920. These were the only wards in the city that gave an electoral majority to the progressive gubernatorial candidate Eugene N. Foss in the 1910 and 1911 elections (Table 8.10). They also threw heavy support to David I. Walsh, the Irish progressive who ran for Lieutenant Governor in 1911.

Table 8.10. *Votes for governor and lieutenant governor in 1910 and 1911*

1910	Ward 1	Ward 2	Ward 3	Ward 4	Ward 5	Ward 6	Ward 7
Governor							
Eugene N. Foss (Democratic Progressive)	578	825	451	380	647	748	688
Eben S. Draper (Republican)	497	234	661	683	869	981	1,122
1911							
Governor							
Eugene N. Foss (Democratic Progressive)	620	939	473	346	672	730	542
Louis A. Frothingham (Republican)	538	253	759	731	960	1,129	1,445
Lieutenant Governor							
David I. Walsh (Democratic Progressive)	559	900	422	294	562	656	499
Robert Luce (Republican)	563	247	792	778	999	1,156	1,463

Sources: Somerville, *Annual Reports*, 1910, p. 447; *Annual Reports*, 1911, p. 466.

Irish politicians of the Democratic and progressive camp assumed a guiding role in the planning and enactment of the junior high school. In 1913, Thomas M. Clancy, Martin P. Hogan, Charles A. Kirkpatrick, and Herbert A. MacDonald sat on the all-important subcommittee on school accommodations that conducted the first serious discussions of overcrowding. In 1914, Thomas A. Kelley, Martin P. Hogan, Guy Healey, Herbert A. MacDonald, and David Fulton sat on the subcommittee (five Irish members out of eight subcommittee members) that launched the intermediate school at Forster. In 1913, eight out of fourteen school committee members were of Irish origin; in 1914, seven out of fourteen members. Without the active support of these Irish members, the experimental phase of the junior high school would have foundered.

Irish politicians spearheaded the drive for that institution because they saw the public schools as a steppingstone to higher social status for their children. Support for the junior high school was part of a complex of adaptation and compromise made by the Somerville Irish. Their leaders were not averse to donning the Republican label if they could thereby gain concessions for their constituents.[57] Though sponsoring a parochial elementary system, the Irish probably believed that public schools supplied superior vocational preparation and useful contact with children of the upper classes. Consequently, many, if not the majority, of Irish parents sent their children to the public schools for at least some time. John J. Murphy, the first Democratic mayor of Somerville, remarked that the "fatal mistake" made by natives was to admit the immigrant Irish into the public schools, where they learned to feel themselves the equals of Yankee children.[58]

Immigrant groups composing 64 percent of the city in 1920 and 70 percent in 1930 sent growing numbers of children through the public schools. In 1915, about 4,000 children of foreign parentage were enrolled in the public-school grades; in 1920, around 5,000. This increase occurred partly because foreign parents had nearly twice as many children 5 to 19 years old as native parents from 1920 to 1930 (Table 8.8). Growing numbers of the children of immigrants graduated from the various exit points of the school system from 1913 to 1930.[59]

Somerville residents knew that the junior high school was an important influence upon the changing patterns of school achievement. The Somerville *Journal* hailed its "progressive plan" with a series of feature articles,[60] and civic groups held special meetings to discuss the progress of the junior high schools.

Wartime and the junior high school controversy

From 1917 to 1919, Somerville experienced an economic surge from the wartime growth in manufacturing and commerce. Although the city had more children of school age than ever, attendance rates shrank due to the draining effect of the wartime job market, which attracted young people to work in factories and businesses. Average daily attendance had steadily risen to 12,323 in 1916, but slumped suddenly to 11,933 in 1917, 11,798 in 1918, and 11,609 in 1919 despite the growth of the school-age cohort.[61] Simultaneously, the number of work certificates issued to students leaving school soared from 323 in 1915 to 1,289 in 1920.[62]

The economic upswing hampered the efforts of educators to keep older students in the schools. Not only were drop-out rates climbing, but the percentage of pupils truant or absentee from the fifth to the tenth grade reached peak levels from 1917 to 1920.[63] There also was an alarming concurrent phenomenon: The proportion of criminal cases involving juvenile delinquents climbed to 32 percent in 1919 and 27 percent in 1920.[64]

The war years delivered a shock that unsettled the operation of the public schools. By 1919, the growing immigrant population, the return of youths to the schools as the economy contracted, the maneuvers of Yankees to stay astride of city government, and the rising rates of juvenile misbehavior portended a time of troubles for Somerville. In this agitated atmosphere, concerned parents, civic fathers, and educators looked again to the junior high school to help restore social order.

The postwar resurgence of attendance revived public clamor for expansion of the junior high school facilities. In May 1919, the education committee of the West Somerville Civic Association made a public announcement urging "a comprehensive plan for the enlargement of the Junior High Schools of the city. . . . The members of the school board were told by the committee that the responsibility was on them to make a recommendation; that there had never been any opposition by the public to expense incurred for educational purposes and that the public realizes that relief in the present [overcrowded] condition cannot be had without cost."[65] One month later, in June, the school committee submitted "a comprehensive plan" for enlargement of the junior high school plants requiring an expenditure of $1,000,000.[66]

The school committee recommendation was a flare igniting a two-year controversy over whether the junior high schools would be expanded or dismanteled. The turbulent public debate unravelled the community to reveal the cross section of support for the junior high school by middle-class immigrant-stock activists, and the opposition by Yankee political and business leaders.

On January 26, 1920, 100 members of the Parent-Teacher Association of Southern Junior High School unanimously passed a resolution to urge the school authorities to expand junior high school facilities. The leadership and membership of this P.T.A. reflected the heavy concentration of Irish families in ward two, where Southern Junior High School was located.[67]

Two days later, a "mass meeting for increased junior high school accommodations" in West Somerville's Hobb's Auditorium unanimously adopted a resolution favoring "the mayor, board of aldermen, and the school board, in securing the appropriation of a sum of money sufficiently large to relieve the burdensome lack of accommodation in the Junior High School section of our school system." Every civic group and P.T.A. sent delegates to this meeting of hundreds of concerned citizens. The P.T.A.s had large female memberships and several women officers. James W. Kenney, ex-alderman from ward two – the father figure of Irish progressive Democrats – was the principal speaker of the evening. "With characteristic definiteness and energy," he emphasized that "the interest of the children overshadows all other considerations" and called for popular backing of the junior high school.[68]

On May 12, a meeting of the Western Junior High School P.T.A. voted unanimously to call for the immediate enlargement of the junior high schools to combat overcrowding. A petition of 1,000 signatures was obtained in support of this resolution.[69]

The impetus of popular support from the neighborhoods, however, soon encountered resistance. The Winter Hill Improvement Association, an important chamber-of-commerce-style organization in the wealthiest part of Somerville, bluntly rejected the proposal for expansion. They were unimpressed by the arguments of school committeemen supporting the junior high school, who spoke at an association meeting on March 10 to endorse the enlargement plans. The businessmen recommended that all building be delayed at least one year, and, if undertaken, be restricted to minimal expenditure and improvements.[70]

The hardest blow fell on May 13, 1920, when the board of aldermen approved the recommendation of its public-property committee to abolish "the present junior high school system . . . and in its place to substitute a centrally located vocational school and to convert the present Western Junior High School for use as a high school system."[71] Real-estate and streetcar magnate John Locatelli, the wealthiest Italian-American in Somerville and Republican alderman from ward six, delivered an impassioned speech, published in the Somerville *Journal*,[72] against continuance of the current system. Locatelli had made a fortune as a contractor for the development of large courtyard apartment buildings.[73]

Only two aldermen, Irish Democrats William F. Burns from ward one and Joseph Haley from ward two, opposed the motion for termination. They requested that the school committee be allowed to appeal to the aldermen with further evidence of its proposal. Burns' and Haley's request was voted down decisively fourteen to two.[74] Thus businessmen and the powerful chieftains of the Republican city government began a determined campaign to root out the established system of junior high schools.

The growth of opposition that climaxed in the decisive action of the board of aldermen owed to a number of factors. First, an underlying conservative educational philosophy induced a strong distrust of the junior high school. Its high-school-type courses, increased autonomy for pupils, and departmental divisions requiring students to move from class to class appeared inappropriate for the youngsters. From this viewpoint, the junior high school was a dangerously unsettling influence on the minds and personalities of children too young to handle the "high school experience" and the freedom it afforded.[75] Thus the junior high school damaged the educational setting rather than improved it. The vaunted progressivism of the junior high school was equated with mere permissiveness, evidenced by higher tardiness rates and reports of unruly behavior.[76]

Another charge hurled at the junior high school was financial inefficiency. Locatelli complained that "$1,250,000 plus was asked . . . to increase the seating capacity by 3200, which number is equal to eighty schoolrooms . . . [although] at the present time we have approximately 4000 excess seating capacity."[77] The Winter Hill Improvement Association also balked at the contemplated expenses. Postwar interest rates were steep. The board of aldermen pointed out that a building program would entail abnormally high construction costs due to the inflated prices of building materials and labor. The Somerville board of trade favored the establishment of a "first-class vocational school" because it was more economical and would supply the industrial manpower needs of the city.[78]

The announcement of the aldermen to abolish the junior high school triggered a popular civic campaign against their high-handed action. As in the experimental period of the junior high school, the leaders of Somerville Irish Democracy were its most aggressive supporters.

William T. McCarthy, school committeeman from ward one, one of the most nationalistic Irish leaders, denounced the abolition motion of the aldermen as an "insulting communication." Later in the 1920–21 school year, McCarthy vehemently opposed the adoption of a history textbook he and two other Irish politicians, Francis Fitzpatrick and Christopher Muldoon, labeled "pro-British"; early in 1921 he successfully opposed a move to introduce citizenship classes into night school on the grounds that "partisanship might be brought into the lessons of some of the speakers."[79]

One of the most successful Irish lawyers in Somerville, McCarthy envisaged the junior high school as a progressive milestone for the city-at-large as well as for his Irish constituency.[80] In an angry outburst, he "spoke in vindication of the School Board and in derision of the board of aldermen, a large proportion of which he maintained did not know what they are doing." He charged that the public-property committee of the board of aldermen was "not fit" and accused it of "functioning unconstitutionally and unfairly."[81]

Christopher Muldoon, school committeeman from ward two and a Somerville High School graduate who went to Harvard, acted on the special committee of four to plan retaliation against the aldermen. He helped compose a public rebuttal to the board that won additional popular support for expansion. Urged on by McCarthy and Muldoon, the school committee voted eleven to zero to oppose the aldermen's motion to abolish.[82]

On May 25, a "big parents meeting" was held in Somerville High School Hall to promote the "Stay-in-School" campaign. The meeting "proved a great success in terms of numbers, the floor of the hall being filled and the audience overflowed into the balconies where several hundred people were seated." An orchestra of sixty pieces from the four junior high schools played for half an hour and the glee club of Northern Junior High School sang, accompanied on the piano by headmaster Frank Seabury. The theme of the meeting was "the importance of having . . . children remain in school as long as possible to fit them for the part they are to play as citizens." Professor John M. Brewer of Harvard's Educational Department delivered an address urging the retention of the junior high school in defiance of the aldermen. "Somerville," he warned, "would be taking a backward step if the city that was one of the first to establish the system should now abolish it."[83]

In early June, a tumultuous public meeting was convened in West Somerville's Lewis Hall to discuss the question, "Shall the present Junior High School system be retained and developed?" According to the Somerville *Journal*, the overflow audience engaged in "the liveliest meeting ever in West Somerville." They heard school committee members and former state representative William H. Dolben chastise the board of aldermen. Dolben received tremendous applause when he lashed the board of aldermen for knowing "practically nothing about the educational needs of the children of the city . . . [and] willfully ignor[ing] the wishes of their constituents."[84] At the conclusion of the gathering the motion "that the Junior High Schools be retained and developed" was unanimously approved.

That evening, Dr. Herbert Cholerton, chairman of the school committee, delivered that body's reply to the aldermen at a public meeting in Somerville High School Hall. The 200 people who attended were entertained by a junior high school orchestra. They listened to Frank Irving Cooper of the National Education Association, who presented a "picture lecture" on the relation of school buildings to the artistic sense of the community. Cholerton eloquently marshalled data to prove that the junior high school had not incurred great additional expenses for the city. "Somerville's expenditures for education," he pointed out, "have not increased proportionately to its increase in wealth. . . . [During] the last ten years Somerville's valuation per pupil has increased over 30 percent and its expenditure per pupil has increased only 16 percent."

Furthermore, Cholerton explained that Locatelli's complaint about thousands of existing empty seats was based on the absurd assumption that schoolrooms had capacities of forty-eight or forty-nine pupils. Smaller classes and, hence, more classrooms were needed. Cholerton asserted, "large classes increase failure of promotion. Every failure of promotion increases the cost of instruction. The reduction of the size of classes is, therefore, not only in the interest of the children themselves, but also in the interest of economy."

Finally, Cholerton argued that the junior high school's enriched curriculum and "more mature" way of handling students would upgrade learning and increase educational opportunity. Building a high school might not be as expensive as enlarging four junior high schools, but in the long run it would cost more in student dropouts and lower achievement levels. The junior high school would stem these problems with its individualized program suited for the special capacities of early adolescence.[85]

A month later in July, Dr. Richard L. Rice, president of the board of aldermen, delivered a rebuttal to Cholerton to demonstrate the fiscal impracticality of junior high school expansion. Building costs, Rice maintained, were "more than three hundred percent in excess of prewar prices," and borrowing rates on loans were 1 percent to $1\frac{1}{2}$ percent higher than usual. Municipal spending had to be dampened down by lowering tax rates and restricting loans. Rice enunciated the familiar Republican program of economic health through low expenditures, balanced budgets, and reduced tax rates. The junior high school would have to be sacrificed for the sake of Somerville's fiscal well-being. He concluded by repeating John Locatelli's recommendation that school space be conserved by increasing the number of students in each classroom.[86] And so the board of aldermen and the school committee deadlocked in bitter strife at the highest level of municipal politics. Neither side showed indications of yielding. But the school committee was far more adept at mobilizing popular support for its cause. They and their supporters disseminated their ideas in public meetings; they employed the news media to greater advantage with timely, provocative position statements. They had engaged junior high school bands, a glee club, and rousing speakers in stagey productions normally found in a political campaign, which captured enthusiastic audiences. The issue smoldered for a half year. Meanwhile, the four junior high schools ran without disturbance in the fall and winter of 1920–21.

At last, in February 1921, the first major step was taken toward reconciliation and a compromise agreement. The school committee extended an invitation to the public property committee of the board of aldermen to join them in a conference on accommodations.[87] The two committees toured the junior high school buildings together and mutually agreed they were badly overcrowded. The conference ended on a hopeful note that a final decision would be forthcoming.

The intense public pressure had cracked the glacier of aldermanic opposition. On the night of June 9, 1921, after a year of civic activism had worn down their resistance, the board of aldermen unanimously agreed to construct two new junior high school plants, which would accommodate three of the four existing junior highs, and to enlarge the fourth. By 1924, three larger consolidated junior high schools – Western, Northeastern, and Southern – were built and in operation.

John Locatelli, the enemy of expansion, addressed a face-saving speech to the board, saying although he had become "unpopular," he had saved the city $250,000. He claimed his resistance delayed the date of construction so that costs had declined from $1,250,000 to $1,000,000. Locatelli resentfully complained that he was not appointed to "the Public Property committee this year which fact is . . . a decided slight and rebuke for one who performed his duty too well."[88]

Fiscally conservative Republican businessmen did not easily accept their defeat. On June 13, the West Somerville Board of Trade squashed a motion to endorse the public property committee's proposal to expand the junior high schools. "This proposition was not warmly received, and after it had been opposed by Messrs. Musgrave, Richardson, and others, the resolution was referred to the Board of Directors with the understanding that the board was not to meet before September."[89]

The expanded junior high school plan was finally approved by the board of aldermen in late June. John Locatelli introduced an unsuccessful motion to delay construction once more in order to cut expenditures. It was a futile gesture against the wave of educational reform activated by a seismic shift in the social basis of city politics.

The political and social significance of the junior high school

A school committee with a diverse membership of educators, professionals, Irish Democrats, progressives, and women orchestrated public support for the junior high school. This pluralistic coalition capsized a Republican holding effort, which feared educational innovation for its release of new social forces and its imposition of a heavier financial burden on the city.

In order to understand the political and social factors that shaped the junior high school controversy, it is necessary to inspect the characteristics of the school committee and the board of aldermen. Consistent with the structure of nineteenth-century city government, few individuals moved back and forth between the school committee and the board of aldermen in the early twentieth century. From 1912 to 1921, only two men acquired seats in both organizations. The school committee and the board of aldermen were, for all purposes, sealed off from one another.[90]

In addition to having separate memberships, the school committee and the board of aldermen reflected different patterns of partisan alignment (Table 8.11). Republicans annually composed from 76 percent to 90 percent of the board of aldermen; the number of Democrats never exceeded 24 percent of the board, and for three years (1917 to 1919) was only 10 percent. The school committee, however, had as many as 29 percent Democrats (1913 to 1914) during the formative years of the junior high school. Moreover, the school committee had as many as 29 percent progressives in 1915 and 1916, whereas the board of aldermen had one from 1912 to 1920. From 1912 to 1920, the school committee frequently contained a large bloc of Democrats and progressives, while the board of aldermen was monolithically Republican. During the years 1913 to 1916, when the school committee was most active in planning the junior high school, Democrats and progressives together annually composed 50 percent, 50 percent, 43 percent, and 43 percent of the committee.

Table 8.11. *Party affiliation of the Board of Aldermen and the School Committee, 1912–20*

		Republican		Democrat		Progressive Republican or Progressive Democrat	
		N	%	N	%	N	%
1912	SC	10	71	2	14	2	14
	BA	16	76	5	24	0	0
1913	SC	7	50	4	29	3	21
	BA	17	81	4	19	0	0
1914	SC	7	50	4	29	3	21
	BA	17	81	4	19	0	0
1915	SC	8	57	2	14	4	29
	BA	18	86	3	14	0	0
1916	SC	8	57	2	14	4	29
	BA	18	86	3	14	0	0
1917	SC	10	71	1	7	3	21
	BA	19	90	2	10	0	0
1918	SC	11	79	1	7	2	14
	BA	19	80	2	10	0	0
1919	SC	12	86	1	7	1	7
	BA	19	90	2	10	0	0
1920	SC	10	71	3	21	1	7
	BA	18	86	2	10	1	5
Total	SC	83	66	20	16	23	18
	BA	161	85	27	14	1	0

Source: Somerville, *Annual Reports.*

The school committee and the board of aldermen also differed in occupational distribution (Table 8.12).[91] The board of aldermen had a high proportion of businessmen – averaging 54 percent of the board from 1912 to 1920 – whereas the school committee averaged only 15 percent businessmen in the same period. The average proportion of professionals on the school committee, however, was four times higher than the proportion on the board of aldermen (44 percent to 11 percent). The school committee also included five housewives and six educators, whereas the board of aldermen had none of either. Over 80 percent of the school committee and the board of aldermen were white-collar workers. But on the board, the prominence of businessmen in 1919 and 1920 (67 percent and 62 percent) was crucial for the growth of conservative fiscal opposition to the junior high school. In

Table 8.12. *Occupations of members of Board of Aldermen and the School Committee, 1912–20*

| | | Business[a] | | Professionals | | | | Other white collar | | Other and unknown | |
| | | | | Educators[b] | | Other[c] | | | | | |
		N	%	N	%	N	%	N	%	N	%
1912	SC	4	29	1	7	4	29	2	14	3	21
	BA	9	43	0	0	2	10	4	19	6	29
1913	SC	2	14	1	7	4	29	5	36	2	14
	BA	10	48	0	0	3	14	4	19	4	19
1914	SC	2	14	0	0	5	36	5	36	2	14
	BA	12	57	0	0	3	14	3	14	3	14
1915	SC	2	14	0	0	6	43	3	21	3	21
	BA	10	43	0	0	1	5	5	24	5	24
1916	SC	3	21	0	0	5	36	4	29	1	7
	BA	10	43	0	0	2	10	4	19	5	24
1917	SC	2	14	0	0	7	50	4	29	1	7
	BA	10	43	0	0	3	14	5	24	3	14
1918	SC	1	7	0	0	7	50	5	36	1	7
	BA	13	62	0	0	2	10	4	19	2	10
1919	SC	2	14	0	0	6	43	5	36	1	7
	BA	14	67	0	0	2	10	2	10	3	14
1920	SC	1	7	4	29	5	36	4	29	0	0
	BA	13	62	0	0	2	10	2	10	4	19
Total	SC	19	15	6	5	49	39	37	29	15	12
	BA	101	54	0	0	20	11	33	17	35	19

[a] Includes manufacturers, proprietors, managers, merchants, dealers, salesmen.
[b] Includes teachers, headmasters, submasters.
[c] Includes doctors, dentists, lawyers, engineers, pharmacists.
Sources: Somerville, *Annual Reports* and *City Directory.*

contrast, the large number of professionals on the school committee in those critical years (43 percent in 1919 and 65 percent in 1920) ensured that the most educated members of the community would work for improvements in the school system. The housewives and, of course, the educators on the school committee also shared strong educational concerns. The professionals, educators, and housewives, who formed a large bloc on the school committee, constituted a major source of support for the junior high school.

The school committee and the board of aldermen also differed in

Table 8.13. *Ethnic origins of the Board of Aldermen and the School Committee, 1912–20*

		Irish		Old stock		Other	
		N	%	N	%	N	%
1912	SC	6	43	8	57	0	0
	BA	4	24	17	76	0	0
1913	SC	8	57	6	43	0	0
	BA	5	24	16	76	0	0
1914	SC	7	50	7	50	0	0
	BA	6	29	15	71	0	0
1915	SC	5	36	9	44	0	0
	BA	4	19	17	81	0	0
1916	SC	4	29	10	71	0	0
	BA	4	19	17	81	0	0
1917	SC	3	27	11	73	0	0
	BA	2	10	19	89	0	0
1918	SC	3	27	11	73	0	0
	BA	3	14	18	83	0	0
1919	SC	3	27	11	73	0	0
	BA	3	14	17	81	1[a]	5
1920	SC	4	29	10	71	0	0
	BA	5	19	15	76	1[a]	5
Total	SC	43	34	83	66	0	0
	BA	36	19	151	80	2	1

[a] Alderman John Locatelli was Italian.
Sources: Somerville, *Annual Reports,* Ethnic identification determined by surname. Also helpful were H. R. Taylor, "Somerville Politics, 1921–1929," Thesis, Harvard University, 1939 and manuscript schedules of the U.S. Census.

ethnic composition (Table 8.13). Irish members comprised more than one third of the school committee from 1912 to 1920; they numbered as much as 43 percent, 57 percent, and 50 percent of the committee from 1912 to 1914, the planning and founding years of the junior high school. The board of aldermen, however, averaged 80 percent old-stock members from 1912 to 1920. Those considered to be old-stock Americans in the early twentieth century were Yankees and the descendants of Protestant British and Northern European peoples who had assimilated with comparative speed. Thus, descendants of English-Canadians were also included as old stock.[92] Irish leaders infiltrated more widely into the school committee than the board of aldermen; they occupied key subcommittee posts, and were a decisive force in shaping policy. On the board of aldermen, they were a smaller and much less influential group. The highest percentages of Irish members on the board of aldermen occurred from 1912 to 1916 when the board was most favorably disposed toward the junior high school.

Only fragmentary evidence is available from tax lists on the relative wealth of school committee members and aldermen, but it is nonetheless suggestive. Nine aldermen were reported as "big tax payers" (persons whose taxes exceeded $200) from 1913 to 1919, whereas only two members of the school committee (one of whom had been an alderman) were so designated. For the nine aldermen, the range of payments was $208.98 to $597.06, and the average payment was $325.91. The two school committeemen paid $276.06 and $206.15, which averaged to $241.10.[93] These data, combined with the pattern of occupational distribution, suggest that a sizable number of aldermen were businessmen who were wealthier and owned more property than school committee members.

The school committee and the board of aldermen reflected different social elements competing for control of Somerville. The school committee contained the leaders of a pluralistic new middle class, who were second- and third-generation Catholics, who were Democrats and progressives, and who included a growing number of professionals. The board of aldermen held many more Republicans drawn from the Yankee middle class and big businessmen.

Yankee Republican aldermen saw the junior high school as an objective of immigrant politicians who would use educational reform to expand their influence. A victory for the junior high school would be a striking symbol of Democratic strength. The reform also would jeopardize a school system they felt was operating efficiently. The Somerville Board of Trade, Winter Hill Improvement Association, and the business-oriented board of aldermen opposed the junior high school, fearing its fiscal burden and its experimentalism. Instead they hoped to bolster the established system by expanding the vocational schools and enlarging Western Junior High School into another high school.

The English-Canadians, British immigrants, and Swedes who moved into ward seven turned West Somerville into a hotbed of public agitation for reform. Active in the West Somerville Civic Association and P.T.A.s, these groups embraced the junior high school to improve opportunities for their children.[94] Their support helped to overwhelm Locatelli and the aldermen in unpopularity and defeat.

The junior high school had the strongest appeal to those Irish, Canadians, Italians, and other immigrants who were white-collar employees or edging toward white-collar jobs. Francis Fitzpatrick, Christopher Muldoon, Martin P. Hogan, Charles Kirkpatrick, Harry M.

Stoodley, George C. Mahoney, William McCarthy, Thomas Clancy, Guy Healey, Herbert MacDonald, Thomas Kelley, Daniel Bradley – members of the school committee that established the junior high school – were professionals and white-collar employees, not workingmen.[95] They were the leading citizens and success models of Somerville's immigrant Americans. Christopher Muldoon, a glassblower's son, graduated from Somerville Latin High School, attended Harvard College, and became a lawyer. Herbert MacDonald, a tailor's son, also graduated from the Latin High School; he went to Harvard Dental School, but found his calling as a clerk.

Seven of these eleven men (Fitzpatrick, Muldoon, Clancy, Kelley, Bradley, Healey, and McCarthy, the most vehement critic of the board of aldermen) represented on the school committee wards one, two, and six – three of the poorest, immigrant districts of the city (see Tables 8.2, 8.4, 8.5, and 8.6). These white-collar school committeemen banked on the junior high school to help spread their ideology of mobility and assimilation to their constituents.

But they also reflected their constituents' interest in the schools. Charles and Frank Kenney, the high-school educated brothers of ex-alderman James W. Kenney who had championed the junior high school, were typical of the mobile second-generation immigrants represented by school committee members. They and others who had gone to high school were most likely to support improvements in public secondary education.

Furthermore, many immigrant workers in early twentieth-century Somerville were likely to support educational opportunities that would help their children obtain white-collar jobs. They might have resembled the factory workers of Manchester, New Hampshire, studied by historian Tamara Hareven, who "viewed themselves as being in a transitional stage . . . to an urban middle-class life-style."[96] From the perspective of workingmen seeking educational advancement for their children, the junior high school may have seemed preferable to another high school or a bigger vocational school. The latter would have consisted of branch reforms that would not have solved the existing seventh- or eighth-grade drop-out root problem prevalent among working-class children. Why should blue-collar parents support another high school, which many of their children would not attend? A larger vocational school would reinforce existing patterns of stratification by funneling more working-class students into manual trades.

The junior high school, however, offered the chance for working-class youths to prepare earlier for life's competition and more effectively for entry to higher grade levels. It would offer clerical-technical courses that would train students in the rudiments of skills needed in low white-collar jobs, so those who did not proceed to high school could have some preparation for non-manual work. Furthermore, the junior high school promised to reduce the drop-out and low-achievement rates where they were especially acute, in the seventh and eighth grade. The junior high school did indeed produce a promotion rate to the ninth and tenth grades 20 to 30 percent higher than the elementary school, a fact that may have been satisfyingly evident to many parents (Table 8.9).

For Catholic parents, the junior high school eased their children's transition from parochial school to public school. The changeover to the strange new world of the public school would be gradualized and made less traumatic. Routine promotion through junior high school to the high school was an attractive way of circumventing the tough high school entrance exam for parochial transfers.[97] A junior high school in the neighborhood also gave Catholic groups more local control over an important branch of the school system that was often the highest educational rung their children mounted. A powerful point in favor of the junior high school was its economy. To many Catholic parishioners, it was perhaps cheaper and more cost effective to support a public secondary school than to pay on their own for the establishment of a parochial secondary school and its tuition.

The social and economic advantages of the junior high school induced Catholics to sponsor this form of public secondary school instead of a parochial institution. Although the high school and the junior high schools grew to enroll 5,000 students by 1924, no parochial secondary school was opened. In Somerville, Catholics decided to support parochial elementary schools and to rely symbiotically on the public systems for secondary education. Since parochial schools were valued chiefly for religious indoctrination, perhaps Catholics felt that their elementary schools were quite adequate for that purpose. The installation of the junior high school thus retarded development of parochial secondary education in Somerville. Not until 1926 did the first Catholic high school open in the city.[98]

Irish politicians seized the junior high school as an issue to attack Republican supremacy and to coalesce a broader based Democratic party. By engineering the movement for the junior high school, they established a common ground for the political mobilization of immigrant groups. In its aftermath, they knitted together a political alliance between the Italians and Irish in Somerville.[99] From the orchestration of a popular campaign they learned lessons in concerted leadership and grass-roots organizing that were later applied in ousting the Republican city machine. The rise of the Democratic party in Somerville was one impulse in the political movement that transformed Republican Massachusetts into a Democratic state by 1933.[100]

As with the founding of the English High School, demographic pressure was the triggering mechanism of the reform movement that created the junior high school. If overcrowding had not reached dire proportions, Irish Democrats and progressives on the school committee may not have proposed the junior high school, and Republican aldermen would have seen little reason to reconsider the traditional grammar and high school system.

Since new facilities were unavoidable, it was only logical for Somerville residents to select the one that optimally increased educational functionalism and opportunities in a community where rampant population growth intensified competition for resources. The junior high school epitomized the progressives' ideal of social efficiency. It would speed educational progress, by instructing and socializing students in the mature style of a secondary school. Its vocationally related courses would create options for early career preparation. And its curriculum would expose younger students at risk of dropping out to advanced subjects.

Disagreement over the junior high school between the board of aldermen and the school committee mirrored the escalating tension between the Yankee, Republican middle class, on the one hand, and an ethnic Democratic middle class on the other. The former group looked backward to familiar institutions like the high school and elementary school. They wished to keep the cost of public education securely balanced against the city budget. They dreaded institutional changes that would heighten the dynamism of the city's social order, which was growing harder to control through political devices. Yankee leaders instinctively feared the junior high school because so many Irish Democrats favored it. They suspected what these people espoused could only augment their growing power. They also saw that it was supported by Canadian and Swedish immigrants who were making speedy social and economic advances in ward seven. Progressive natives, however, joined immigrant groups in a pluralistic coalition, recognizing the latter were a force that was here to stay. They conceded these people an influential position and were willing to take a place beside them in the changing social order. A diversified non-partisan progressive coaltion coalesced similar to the political alliance forged in New York State by Democrats like Al Smith.[101]

The campaign for the junior high school was a political expression of the mobility that the descendants of immigrants had gained through

Table 8.14. *Males entering the English High School, 1896–1905, by ethnic group, who remained in Somerville until last job*

	Yankees		Canadians		Irish	
	N	%	N	%	N	%
Remaining in city at last job	46	31	43	37	52	65
Departed from city before last job	102	69	73	63	28	35

secondary schooling. The turn-of-the-century high school was the channel through which a new contingent of white-collar men emerged from the progeny of immigrant workers. And this assimilated cohort was fast replacing the old-stock middle class in Somerville. The large majority of Irish alumni of the English High School forged their careers in Somerville, but the majority of Yankee and Canadian alumni moved out of the city (Table 8.14). The most educated members of the new generation of Irish-Americans remained in Somerville adding to the size and vigor of the Catholic middle class, whereas the exodus of the young generation of educated Yankees and Canadians depleted the ranks of the old-stock middle class. The Irish high school alumni articulated the new white-collar employee's consciousness of the instrumentality of advanced education.

The junior high school campaign mobilized the new middle class as a political force. They supported the Irish school committeemen and aldermen who fought Yankee businessmen, united with progressive natives, and attempted to attract working-class social elements to their ideology of self-improvement through education. Irish Democrats used the junior high school to launch a drive for political power that culminated in the election of a Democratic mayor and board of aldermen in Somerville in 1929. In the streetcar suburb, the volatile "zone of emergence," progressive politics and school reform expressed the mobility of groups rising from below, not the anti-democratic rule of a native elite.[102] The children of immigrants, given advanced schooling by the sacrifices of their families, seized political power from the Yankees to reshape the public life of the streetcar suburb.

Conclusion: The high school in the light of history

The origins of the American high school lodged in two great ramifications of the industrial revolution: the process of urban growth and the ethos to direct it through public education. The expansion of the high school sprang from the recurrent cycle of migration, social mobility, and assimilation that propelled urban growth and restructured the social relationships of wealth and power. The transformation of the high school into a multiprogram, functionalist institution at the turn of the century rested on its ability to attract a pluralistic, numerous student clientele from successive waves of newcomer families. Increasing investment in high school education stimulated and participated in a tightly woven complex of social processes – residential segregation, expansion of bureaucratic employment, voluntary and religious association, family limitation, prolonged and insulated child dependency, home ownership, and strategic intergenerational mobility – that were the behavioral components of Yankee households in the late-nineteenth-century suburb. In this way, high school attendance facilitated and reflected the formation of a Yankee middle class emerging out of these interconnected social changes in this period. Conversely, it helped to articulate the behavioral and strategic dimensions of lower-class experience by excluding families without the prerequisite components for sponsorship of secondary schooling.

The opportunity for a high school education was apportioned according to the structure of social and economic inequality in industrial society. The chances for youths to gain secondary schooling remained directly related to the household's capacity to accumulate and invest resources in them. The Yankee middle class capitalized more than any other social group on high school training. High school students from immigrant and workingmen's families had an edge over grammar dropouts. Their parents had gained better blue-collar jobs and pursued strategies of home investment, family-size limitation, and instrumental role exchange to prolong schooling. For blue-collar families, a degree of social mobility and strategic deployment of family resources were vital prerequisites for investment in advanced schooling.

The high school was a flexible nexus with a changing labor market and shifting patterns of occupational mobility in an advanced industrial economy. Employers increasingly demanded office workers with the educational credentials, the linguistic and mathematical skills, and the socially correct comportment purveyed by the high school. It helped revolutionize the universe of occupations by producing a new white-collar occupational class of professional and bureaucratic technicians. It brought, as the sociologist C. Wright Mills described, the "white-collar people" who "slipped quietly into modern society" and "upset the nineteenth-century expectation that society would be divided between entrepreneurs and wage workers."[1]

The high school stabilized the social structure by facilitating the intergenerational maintenance of families in the middle class. The great majority of Yankee middle-class children who went to high school secured white-collar jobs. The high school supplied the meritocratic credential that substituted for personal references and family connections, which had been outmoded by the spatial and skill expansion of labor markets. The educational degree became the new link for the reproduction of middle-class status.

The high school, nevertheless, served as a small window of opportunity for those farther down the social pyramid. The expansion of secondary schooling at the turn of the century became a pathway to the professions and the bureaucracy for workers' sons in addition to the still viable routes upward, through artisanship and small entrepreneurship, that afforded vertical circulation to the social structure of the industrial city. The high school assumed a new role as an assimilator of a small but growing share of the children of immigrants. They were immersed in a middle-class, Anglo-conformist and peer-centered institutional culture which inculcated values, conduct, and knowledge instrumental for qualifying for white-collar occupations.

The high school provided the meritocratic opportunities to its working-class students that counteracted the determinants of inherited social position and external social structure, and enabled them to prolong schooling and to enter white-collar jobs more frequently than their grammar-schooled counterparts. As historian Joel Perlmann has hypothesized, "schooling's role in creating the social order of the next generation involved an important element of creating advantage, not merely of transmitting position in the social structure."[2] In adulthood, the children of immigrant workers who went to high school rose to the vanguard of a pluralistic new middle class, challenging the Yankee middle class for dominance in the post-Victorian city that was turning into a twentieth-century immigrant city. The high school educated the new social leadership of the Progressive Era that eventually took control of educational and political institutions.

The rise of the new white-collar men was the latest stage of a communal evolution in which sponsorship of advanced schooling correlated with control of the public life of the industrial city. When Yankee children dominated the high school, native middle-class families led the community through the Republican Party and the culture of voluntary association. As children of immigrant workers increased in the high school and junior high school, new white-collar employees based in ethnic neighborhoods launched a progressive reform movement that swept Yankees from the halls of government. The history of the high school revealed that a synchronization of increased schooling, occupational mobility, and political mobilization promoted the process of group mobility in industrial society. The investigation of the high school in Somerville has yielded the kind of history described by Oscar and Mary Handlin as "not only a study of mobility as a general phenomenon, but also an examination of particular aspects of the relation between occupations, opportunity, and wealth, on the one hand, and the political and cultural components of power and freedom, on the other."[3]

It cannot be overlooked that the advantages for occupational mobility gained by a high school education derived from the comparative rarity of achieving such schooling in the early twentieth century. As Michael B. Katz has suggested, "the economic and occupational benefits that school provides came primarily from the *differential*, rather than the *absolute*, amount received. It is, very simply, an advantage to receive more schooling than someone else."[4] While a high school education was the possession of a small portion of labor-market entrants, as it was in the early twentieth century, it had the potential to enhance job prospects.

Ultimately, however, the effectiveness of the early modern high school as a socializing device and facilitator of occupational mobility stemmed from the unique and specific historical conditions surrounding its emergence. The streetcar suburb gathered the middling sector of society devoted to the mobility ideology, provided insulation from the city, offered homeowning investments, and focalized an ethos of Republican, Victorian values.[5] The student population, though not homogeneous, was an unusual sector of the community's youth, absorbing and sharing the benefits of these circumstances. The turn-of-the-century high school was an institution for the children of the middle class and the workers who hovered on its periphery. Thus to trace the modernization of the high school is to confront its location in the matrix of generation and urban community. The institutional peer environment "housed" adolescence, nurturing a generational culture that bridged social class, ethnic, and gender ties. The flowering student culture at the turn of the century inculcated symbolic rites and prestige values of bourgeois community that complemented local boosterism and voluntarism. Through the extracurriculum, the high school solidified the sense of generation and intensified civic patriotism. Moreover, the tightening articulation of public high school graduation with college admissions, the expanding economy's growing demand for office workers, and the rise of meritocratic standards of job qualification enhanced the high school's capacity to place its matriculants in desirable subsequent positions. By contrast, the high school that developed into a mass-attendance institution after the 1920s served a student population from the whole community so diverse that its socializing function grew vastly more complicated. As high school education became nearly universal after World War II, as meritocratic qualifications underwent inflation, and as the white-collar labor-market was restructured,[6] a high school education became insufficient for acquiring attractive jobs or college placement. Every new expert who would refer to the operation and achievements of the early high school as precedents for the contemporary high school must realize that the historical milieu governed irresistibly its impact upon the lives of students.[7]

In the final perspective, the Somerville study raises more questions about secondary schooling than it answers. Its modest answers are based on small sample sizes and on the social dynamics of a single suburban community. Other studies of secondary schooling in different communities have thrown into relief the findings reported here. Still, a host of issues require comparative analysis. Suburbanization played only one role in the development of the social function of high school attendance. The complex neighborhood ecology and diversified social structure of the central city comprised a different arena of secondary school expansion. Alternate institutional forms – parochial high schools and private academies – affected secondary recruitment and prolongation patterns, curricular and extracurricular experience, and social mobility and marriage. The transition of the high school in the 1920s and 1930s to a universal, mass institution changed the distribution of meritocratic advantages in complex ways. The avenues to adulthood through the high school will be charted in history as the variegated field of context is illuminated.

Appendix I: Courses of study

Course of study – English High School 1901

First year	Second year	Third year	Fourth year
Required studies	**Required studies**	**Required studies**	**Required studies**
English 4	English 4	English 4	English 4
Ancient History 2	Mediaeval History 3	English and Modern European History 3	United States History and Civics 3
Algebra 4	Geometry 4	Elocution 1	Elocution 1
Elocution 1	Elocution 1	Ethics 1	Ethics 1
Ethics 1	Ethics 1	Music 1	Music 1
Freehand Drawing 2	Music 1	Physical Training 1	Physical Training 1
Music 1	Physical Training 1	Physiology 1	Physiology 1
Physical Training 1			
Elective studies	**Elective studies**	**Elective studies**	**Elective studies**
French 5	French 4	French 4	French 4
German 5	German 4	German 4	German 4
Latin 5	Latin 4	Latin 4	Latin 4
Botany 5[a]	Physics 5	Chemistry 5	Advanced Botany 5[a]
Zoology 5[a]			Advanced Chemistry 5
			Advanced Physics 5
			Advanced Zoology 5[a]
			Astronomy 5[a]
			Geology 5[a]
			Physical Geography 2
Manual Training 6	Manual Training 6	Manual Training 6	Manual Training 6
Mechanical Drawing 3	Freehand Drawing 2	Freehand Drawing 2	Freehand Drawing 2
	Mechanical Drawing 3	Mechanical Drawing 3	Mechanical Drawing 3
	Domestic Science	Domestic Science	Domestic Science

Advanced Algebra 5^a
Advanced Geometry 5^a

Bookkeeping 5
Commercial Arithmetic 2
Penmanship 2
Stenography 5
Typewriting 3

Analytic Geometry 2
Solid Geometry 5^a
Trigonometry 5^a
Bookkeeping 5
Commercial Law 2
Stenography 5
Typewriting 3

^{a} Half year.
The figures at the right of subjects in the course of study indicate the number of recitation periods each week.

Course of study in the Latin High School 1901

First year – Class I
Latin – First lessons, with translation of easy Latin prose, and introduction to Caesar.
Mathematics – Elementary algebra through quadratic equations.
History – Ancient history, with historical geography.
English – Introduction to English literature, with special study of works of American authors. Rhetoric and English com-
position.

Elective Drawing.

Second year – Class II
Latin – Easy Latin prose, with four books or less of Caesar's Gallic War. Latin prose composition.
Mathematics – Plane geometry.
English – English literature, including part of the works prescribed in the requirements for admission to college. Rhetoric
and English composition.
  One of the three following languages:
1. *Greek* – First lessons, with translation to easy Greek prose and introduction to Anabasis.

Course of study in the Latin High School 1901

2. *German* – First lessons, with translation of easy German. German conversation and written composition.
3. *French* – First lessons, with translation of easy French. French conversation and written composition.
   One of these languages may also be *elective*.
Elective Drawing

Third year – Class III
Latin – Selections from Sallust, Nepos, Caesar, and Ovid. Aeneid, four books. Cicero, three orations.
Mathematics – Algebra reviewed and completed to satisfy the requirements for admission to college.
History – History of Greece and Rome. Ancient geography.
English – English literature, including part of the works prescribed in the requirements for admission to college. Rhetoric and English composition.
Elective Physics – Elementary principles, with experiments and a course of laboratory exercises Friday afternoons during the year.

One of the three following languages:
1. *Greek* – Selections from Anabasis, Hellenica, and other Greek prose. Greek prose composition.
2. *German* – Translation of German prose and poetry, with conversation and written composition. Grammar.
3. *French* – Translation of French prose and poetry, with conversation and written composition. Grammar.
   One of these languages may also be *elective*.
Elective Chemistry
Elective Drawing

Fourth year – Class IV
Latin – Aeneid, five books. Ovid, 2,000 lines. Cicero, six orations. Latin prose composition.
Mathematics – Review of plane geometry, with original demonstrations and solutions of problems. *Elective* solid geometry.
English – English literature, including the remainder of the works prescribed in the requirements for admission to college. Rhetoric and English composition.

Two of the three following languages:
1. *Greek* – Seven books of Iliad and Odyssey. Selections from more difficult Greek prose. Greek prose composition.

2. *German* – Elementary German for beginners. Advanced German for those who have studied the language earlier in the course.

3. *French* – Elementary for beginners. Translation of simple prose and poetry, with conversation and written composition as a preparation for translation at sight of easy French into English and English into French. Grammar. Advanced French for those who have studied the language earlier in the course.

Elective Chemistry
Elective Drawing

Advanced French, advanced German, advanced mathematics, and chemistry may be substituted for a part of the Latin, a part or a whole of the Greek.

Source: Somerville, *Annual Reports*, 1901, pp. 211–14.

Appendix II: Sources and methods

Samples of the student population in high school constitute the backbone of this study. They were constructed out of two series of student records. The first series was composed of student enrollment lists and graduation lists of the Somerville High School and Latin High School. The enrollment lists recorded the date of enrollment, the student's name, home address, date of birth, age, previous school attended, and the name of the parent. The graduation lists listed graduates by name; they recorded the colleges entered; in the 1870s and 1880s they ranked graduates by class standing. The second series, running from 1895 to 1905, listed students in the English High School and came from two sources. One was the high school yearbook which listed entrants and graduates by name and home address; the other was a file of student career records that contained information on family background and coursework.

The primary data on family characteristics of students was derived by linking student records with the manuscript schedules of the U. S. census for Somerville. Students entering high school in the years clustering around the decadal census years 1850, 1860, 1870, 1880, and 1900 were traced to the manuscript schedules. Matches between students and households listed in the census schedules were made according to the name and age of a student, the name of the parent, and household address when available in the 1880 and 1900 schedules. The task of record linkage was performed through simple manual inspection. The availability of the Soundex indexing system for the 1880 and 1900 schedules eased the tedium of this job.

Student records were also linked with the Somerville *City Directory*. This procedure provided additional tabulations on parent's occupation – for example, in 1890, a year for which census manuscripts are unavailable. The *City Directory* was instrumental for the reconstruction of career mobility patterns. Students were traced to the *City Directory* as close to fifteen years after they attended high school to locate their occupation as adults.

Control samples of students who only attended grammar school were constructed out of the schedule data and high school enrollment lists. First, samples were gathered of all 15- and 16-year olds not in school in families of origin listed in the census schedules of 1870 and all 16-year olds not in school in 1900. These individuals were then traced to the enrollment lists from 1865 to 1875 and from 1895 to 1905. Those who did not appear in these lists were classified as students whose highest level of education was grammar school, which they left by the time they were 15 or 16 years old. This simple procedure yielded two cohorts of "grammar school leavers," one for 1870 and another for 1900. Some of these grammar school leavers had possibly attended high school or an academy at a younger age in another town or returned to

230

school at a much older age. This study assumes that those individuals constituted at most an insignificant minority. The purpose of these 1870 and 1900 samples was to serve as controls for high school attenders.

Two other control samples of grammar school leavers were created to compensate for sample attrition due to tracing in the mobility study. The first included all males in the aforementioned 1870 sample, as well as all 14-, 17-, and 18-year-old males determined to be grammar school leavers, drawn from the 1870 census schedules. The second included all males in the aforementioned 1900 sample and all 17-year-old sons of blue-collar workers located in the 1900 census schedules, who were determined to be grammar school leavers.

Appendix III: Students and households

Table 1. *High school students by their household characteristics, entered 1852–3, 1859–61 (%)*

	1852–3		1859–61	
	N = 23	N = 47	N = 27	N = 51
	Boys	Girls	Boys	Girls
Household head gender				
Male	100.0	91.5	100.0	94.1
Female	0	8.5	0	5.9
Household head occupation				
Professional	0	0	3.7	2.0
Business	43.5	42.6	29.6	31.4
Other	4.4	4.3	7.4	11.8
Total nonmanual	47.8	46.8	40.8	45.1
Skilled (building)	17.4	21.3	26.0	9.8
Skilled (other)	26.1	6.4	18.5	21.6
Semiskilled	0	10.6	3.7	11.8
Unskilled	8.7	6.4	0	2.0
Total manual	52.2	44.7	48.1	45.1
Unemployed	0	8.5	11.1	9.8
Spouse employed (student's mother)	0	0	0	0
Household head birthplace				
Native born	91.3	91.5	77.8	100.0
Massachusetts	52.2	38.3	25.9	64.7
Other New England	39.1	51.1	48.1	31.4
Other states	0	2.1	3.7	3.9
Foreign born	8.7	8.5	22.2	0
Great Britain	8.7	8.5	18.5	0
Germany	0	0	3.7	0
Age entered High School				
10	0	0	0	0
11	4.3	6.4	3.7	2.0
12	8.7	19.1	11.1	7.8
13	30.4	19.1	18.5	9.8
14	21.7	6.4	18.5	27.5

Table 1. (*cont.*)

	1852–3		1859–61	
	$N = 23$ Boys	$N = 47$ Girls	$N = 27$ Boys	$N = 51$ Girls
15	8.7	19.1	33.3	39.2
16	21.7	17.0	14.8	13.8
17	0	10.6	0	0
18	0	0	0	0
19	4.3	2.1	0	0
Household head children				
1–3	17.4	31.9	33.3	39.2
4–6	69.6	48.9	48.1	54.9
7 or more	13.0	19.1	18.5	5.9
Household head real *property*				
$0	13.0	17.0	44.4	41.2
1–4,999	34.8	51.0	29.6	21.6
5,000 or more	52.2	31.9	25.9	37.3
Birth order				
Family with 1 boy	26.1		22.2	
Family with 2 boys				
1st born boy	4.3		14.8	
2nd born boy	4.3		14.8	
Family with 3 or more boys				
1st born boy	30.4		25.9	
Middle-born boy	26.1		18.5	
Last-born boy	8.7		3.7	
Family with 1 girl		12.8		23.5
Family with 2 girls				
1st born girl		10.7		21.6
2nd born girl		21.3		17.6
Family with 3 or more girls				
1st born girl		21.3		11.8
Middle-born girl		27.7		19.6
Last-born girl		6.4		5.9

Table 2. *High school students (entered 1871–2 and 1879–81) and 15–16-year-old persons in 1870 who only attended grammar school, by household characteristics (%)*

	Somerville High School 1871–2		Somerville High School 1879–81		Grammar	
	$N=40$ Boys	$N=43$ Girls	$N=60$ Boys	$N=49$ Girls	$N=128$ Boys	$N=109$ Girls
Household head gender						
Male	100.0	95.4	96.7	93.9	89.8	88.1
Female	0	4.6	3.3	6.1	10.2	11.9
Household head occupation						
Professional	5.0	0	8.3	8.2	1.6	0.9
Business	30.0	37.2	28.3	30.6	14.8	13.8
Other white collar	22.5	7.0	26.7	12.2	5.5	2.8
Total white collar	57.5	44.2	63.3	51.0	21.9	17.4
Skilled (building)	15.0	11.6	10.0	4.1	18.0	21.1
Skilled (other)	12.5	14.0	6.7	18.4	23.4	20.2
Semiskilled	7.5	20.9	15.0	12.2	10.2	9.2
Unskilled	2.5	2.3	1.7	2.0	18.0	19.3
Total blue collar	37.5	48.9	33.3	36.7	69.5	69.8
Unemployed	5.0	7.0	3.3	12.2	8.6	12.8
Spouse employed	0	0	0	0	0	0
Household head birthplace						
Native born	87.5	86.1	76.7	93.9	33.6	27.6
Massachusetts	40.0	37.2	28.3	65.3	10.9	15.6
Other New England	42.5	44.2	41.7	22.5	20.3	12.0
Other states	5.0	4.7	6.7	6.1	2.3	0
Foreign born	10.0	11.6	23.3	6.1	62.4	70.6
Ireland	2.5	4.7	13.3	4.0	41.4	51.4
Great Britain	2.5	0	3.3	0	7.0	6.4
Sweden, Nor., Den.	2.5	0	0	0	0	0.9
Germany	0	0	1.7	0	2.3	1.8
Other Europe	0	2.3	0	0	0	0
English Canada	2.5	4.7	5.0	0	10.9	10.1
Other foreign	0	0	0	2.1	0.8	0
Unknown	2.5	2.3	0	0	4.0	2.8
Household head literacy						
Can't read	2.5	0	0	0	5.5	6.4
Can't write	2.5	0	0	0	5.5	6.4
Spouse literacy						
Can't read	0	0	0	0	7.0	3.7
Can't write	0	0	0	0	7.8	4.6

Table 2. (*cont.*)

	Somerville High School 1871–2		Somerville High School 1879–81		Grammar	
	$N=40$ Boys	$N=43$ Girls	$N=60$ Boys	$N=49$ Girls	$N=128$ Boys	$N=109$ Girls
Household head children						
1–3	65.0	41.9	45.0	51.0	35.2	44.0
4–6	32.5	51.2	51.7	38.8	51.6	38.5
7 or more	2.5	2.3	3.3	10.2	10.2	13.8
Head not parent	0	4.6	0	0	3.0	3.7
Household head real property						
$0	35.0	39.5	NA	NA	63.3	54.1
1–4,999	15.0	18.6	NA	NA	23.4	37.6
5,000 or more	50.0	39.5	NA	NA	13.3	8.3
Unknown	0	2.4			0	0
Birth order of students						
Family with 1 boy	32.5		20.0		24.2	
Family with 2 boys						
1st born boy	22.5		21.7		21.9	
2nd born boy	12.5		6.7		8.6	
Family with 3 or more boys						
1st born boy	10.0		23.3		22.7	
Middle-born boy	15.0		25.0		21.1	
Last-born boy	7.5		3.3		1.6	
Family with 1 girl		27.9		26.5		29.3
Family with 2 girls						
1st born girl		16.3		32.7		24.8
2nd born girl		18.6		8.2		9.2
Family with 3 or more girls						
1st born girl		11.6		16.3		19.3
Middle-born girl		16.3		16.3		12.8
Last-born girl		9.3		0		4.6
Status in 1870						
Professional					0.8	0
Business					1.6	0.9
Other white collar					16.4	0
Total white collar					18.8	0.9
Skilled (building)					5.5	1.8
Skilled (other)					8.6	7.3
Semiskilled					39.1	14.7

Table 2. (*cont.*)

	Somerville High School 1871–2		Somerville High School 1879–81		Grammar	
	$N = 40$ Boys	$N = 43$ Girls	$N = 60$ Boys	$N = 49$ Girls	$N = 128$ Boys	$N = 109$ Girls
Unskilled					5.5	0
Total blue collar					58.6	23.9
Unemployed					22.7	75.2

Table 3. *15–16-year-old persons in 1870 who only attended grammar school, of Yankee, foreign born, and Irish household heads, by household characteristics* (%)

	Yankees		Foreign born head		Irish	
	$N = 45$ Boys	$N = 30$ Girls	$N = 82$ Boys	$N = 79$ Girls	$N = 53$ Boys	$N = 56$ Girls
Household head gender						
Male	91.1	90.0	89.0	87.3	84.9	82.1
Female	8.9	10.0	11.0	12.7	15.1	17.9
Household head occupation						
Professional	2.2	0	1.2	1.3	1.9	0
Business	22.2	26.7	11.0	8.9	11.3	7.1
Other white collar	11.1	10.0	2.4	0	0	0
Total white collar	35.6	36.7	14.6	10.1	13.2	7.1
Skilled (building)	17.8	16.7	18.3	22.8	9.4	14.3
Skilled (other)	26.7	26.7	20.7	17.8	22.6	10.7
Semiskilled	6.7	6.7	12.2	10.1	17.0	12.5
Unskilled	2.2	3.3	26.8	25.3	28.3	35.7
Total blue collar	53.3	53.3	78.0	75.9	77.4	73.2
Unemployed	11.1	10.0	7.4	14.0	9.4	19.7
Spouse employed	0	0	0	0	0	0
Household head literacy						
Can't read	0	0	8.5	8.9	7.5	8.9
Can't write	0	0	8.5	8.9	7.5	8.9
Spouse literacy						
Can't read	0	0	11.0	5.1	13.2	7.1
Can't write	0	0	12.2	6.3	15.1	8.9

Table 3. (*cont.*)

	Yankees		Foreign born head		Irish	
	N = 45 Boys	N = 30 Girls	N = 82 Boys	N = 79 Girls	N = 53 Boys	N = 56 Girls
Household head children						
1–3	44.4	50.0	29.3	41.8	22.6	42.9
4–6	46.7	33.3	54.9	40.5	60.4	37.5
7 or more	4.4	3.3	13.4	17.7	13.2	19.6
Head not parent	4.5	13.3	2.4	0	3.8	0
Household head real property						
$0	60.0	50.0	64.6	55.7	58.5	60.7
1–4,999	15.6	36.7	28.0	38.0	34.0	39.3
5,000 or more	24.4	13.3	7.3	6.3	7.5	0
Unknown	0	0	0	0	0	0
Birth order						
Family with 1 boy	37.8		15.9		18.9	
Family with 2 boys						
1st born boy	28.9		18.3		15.1	
2nd born boy	6.7		9.8		13.2	
Family with 3 or more boys						
1st born boy	11.1		29.3		35.9	
Middle-born boy	15.6		24.4		17.0	
Last-born boy	0		2.4		0	
Family with 1 girl		40.0		25.3		23.2
Family with 2 girls						
1st born girl		20.0		26.6		28.6
2nd born girl		13.3		7.6		8.9
Family with 3 or more girls						
1st born girl		10.0		22.8		26.8
Middle-born girl		3.3		16.5		12.5
Last-born girl		13.3		1.3		0
Status in 1870						
Professional	2.2	0	0	0	0	0
Business	0	0	2.4	1.3	1.9	0
Other white collar	26.7	0	11.0	0	5.7	0
Total white collar	28.9	0	13.4	1.3	7.5	0
Skilled (building)	2.2	0	7.3	2.5	7.5	3.6
Skilled (other)	6.7	3.3	8.5	8.9	7.5	8.9
Semiskilled	28.9	3.3	45.1	19.0	52.8	26.8

Table 3. (*cont.*)

	Yankees		Foreign born head		Irish	
	N = 45 Boys	N = 30 Girls	N = 82 Boys	N = 79 Girls	N = 53 Boys	N = 56 Girls
Unskilled	0	0	8.5	0	5.7	0
Total blue collar	37.8	6.7	69.5	30.4	73.6	39.3
Unemployed	33.3	93.3	17.1	68.4	18.9	60.7

Table 4. *Latin High School students; English High School students; 16-year-old persons in 1900, who only attended grammar school, by household characteristics* (%)

	Latin High 1900–1		English High 1899		Grammar	
	N = 84 Boys	N = 57 Girls	N = 65 Boys	N = 87 Girls	N = 152 Boys	N = 112 Girls
Household head gender						
Male	100.0	100.0	100.0	98.9	83.5	76.8
Female	0	0	0	1.1	16.5	23.2
Household head marital status						
Married	98.8	96.5	100.0	95.4	82.9	76.8
Widow/er	1.2	3.5	0	3.4	16.4	23.2
Single	0	0	0	1.1	0.7	0
Household head occupation						
Professional	22.6	17.5	1.5	3.4	0.7	0
Business	40.5	38.6	24.2	34.5	14.6	8.9
Other white collar	15.5	29.8	18.2	18.4	4.6	2.7
Total white collar	78.6	86.0	43.9	56.3	19.8	11.6
Skilled (building)	3.6	3.5	10.6	10.3	15.1	16.1
Skilled (other)	9.5	8.8	30.3	16.1	21.1	18.8
Semiskilled	6.0	0	7.6	10.3	15.1	18.8
Unskilled	1.2	0	4.5	4.6	15.1	13.4
Total blue collar	20.2	12.2	53.0	41.4	66.4	67.0
Unemployed	1.2	1.8	3.0	2.3	13.8	21.4
Spouse employed	1.2	1.8	0	0	0.7	1.8
Household head birthplace						
Native-born	66.7	70.2	60.6	62.0	29.0	35.7
Massachusetts	38.1	33.3	31.8	35.6	17.8	19.6

Table 4. (*cont.*)

	Latin High 1900–1		English High 1899		Grammar	
	$N=84$ Boys	$N=57$ Girls	$N=65$ Boys	$N=87$ Girls	$N=152$ Boys	$N=112$ Girls
Other New England	23.8	31.6	19.7	24.1	8.6	10.7
Other States	4.8	5.3	9.1	2.3	2.6	5.4
Foreign-born	33.3	29.9	39.4	37.8	70.9	64.3
Ireland	10.7	5.3	9.1	8.0	27.0	22.3
Great Britain	6.0	7.0	7.6	10.3	7.2	8.0
Sweden, Nor., Den.	0	1.8	1.5	0	3.3	3.6
Germany	2.4	0	3.0	0	3.3	3.6
Other Europe	6.0	3.5	1.5	1.1	5.9	8.0
English Canada	7.1	10.5	12.1	17.2	21.1	16.1
Other foreign	1.1	1.8	4.5	1.1	3.3	1.8
Unknown	0	0	0	0	0	.9
Household head literacy						
Can't read	1.2	0	0	2.3	5.3	3.6
Can't write	0	0	1.5	2.3	5.9	5.4
Spouse literacy						
Can't read	1.2	0	0	1.1	7.9	4.5
Can't write	1.2	0	0	1.1	8.6	4.5
Household head children						
1–3	58.3	66.7	59.1	59.8	36.1	44.6
4–6	33.3	31.6	33.3	31.0	50.0	40.2
7 or more	7.1	1.8	7.6	9.2	12.5	15.2
Head not parent	1.2	0	0	0	1.3	0
Household head home status						
Home owned	60.7	54.4	50.0	40.2	27.6	23.2
Home rented	39.3	45.6	50.0	59.8	70.4	75.0
Unknown	0	0	0	0	2.0	1.8
Birth order						
Family with 1 boy	32.1		39.4		23.7	
Family with 2 boys						
1st born boy	21.4		19.7		16.5	
2nd born boy	11.9		12.1		13.2	
Family with 3 or more boys						
1st born boy	13.1		15.2		19.8	
Middle-born boy	13.1		6.1		21.1	
Last-born boy	8.3		7.6		5.9	
Family with 1 girl		38.6		28.8		30.4

Table 4. (*cont.*)

	Latin High 1900–1		English High 1899		Grammar	
	N = 84 Boys	N = 57 Girls	N = 65 Boys	N = 87 Girls	N = 152 Boys	N = 112 Girls
Family with 2 girls						
1st born girl		12.3		14.9		15.2
2nd born girl		15.8		12.6		8.9
Family with 3 or more girls						
1st born girl		10.5		16.1		18.8
Middle-born girl		17.5		19.5		23.2
Last-born girl		5.3		8.0		3.6
Status in 1900						
Professional					0	0
Business					7.2	2.7
Other white collar					27.6	14.3
Total white collar					34.9	17.0
Skilled (building)					5.3	0
Skilled (other)					6.6	5.4
Semiskilled					30.9	35.7
Unskilled					6.6	0.9
Total blue collar					49.3	42.0
Unemployed					15.8	41.1

Table 5. *Boys 16 years old in 1900 who only attended grammar school, of Yankee, foreign-born, English-Canadian, and Irish household heads, by household characteristics (%)*

	N = 44 Yankee boys	N = 108 Foreign boys	N = 32 Eng. Can. boys	N = 41 Irish boys
Household head gender				
Male	79.5	85.2	81.2	82.7
Female	20.5	14.8	18.8	17.3
Household head marital status				
Married	79.5	84.2	81.2	75.6
Widow/er	18.1	14.8	18.7	22.0
Single	2.3	1.0	0	2.4

Table 5. (*cont.*)

	N = 44 Yankee boys	N = 108 Foreign boys	N = 32 Eng. Can. boys	N = 41 Irish boys
Household head occupation				
Professional	2.3	0	0	0
Business	15.9	13.9	15.6	9.8
Other white collar	9.1	2.8	6.2	0
Total white collar	27.3	16.7	21.9	9.8
Skilled (building)	18.2	13.9	21.9	9.8
Skilled (other)	25.0	19.4	21.9	4.9
Semiskilled	15.9	14.8	12.5	19.5
Unskilled	2.3	20.4	6.2	36.6
Total blue collar	61.4	68.5	62.5	70.7
Unemployed	11.3	14.8	15.7	19.5
Spouse employed	2.3	0	0	0
Household head literacy				
Can't read	0	7.4	0	9.8
Can't write	0	8.3	0	12.2
Spouse literacy				
Can't read	0	11.1	0	14.6
Can't write	0	12.1	0	14.6
Household head children				
1–3	61.4	25.9	21.9	29.3
4–6	31.8	57.4	50.0	58.5
7 or more	4.5	15.7	25.0	12.2
Head not parent	2.3	0.9	3.1	0
Home status				
Home owned	27.3	28.7	18.7	41.4
Home rented	72.7	69.4	78.1	58.5
Unknown	0	1.8	3.1	0
Birth order				
Family with 1 boy	36.4	18.5	18.7	9.8
Family with 2 boys				
1st born boy	18.2	15.7	15.6	17.1
2nd born boy	15.9	12.0	9.4	17.1
Family with 3 or more boys				
1st born boy	15.9	21.3	25.0	22.0
Middle-born boy	9.1	25.9	25.0	24.4
Last-born boy	4.5	6.5	6.2	9.8
Status in 1900				
Professional	0	0	0	0
Business	6.8	6.5	9.4	4.9

Table 5. (*cont.*)

	N = 44 Yankee boys	N = 108 Foreign boys	N = 32 Eng. Can. boys	N = 41 Irish boys
Other white collar	40.9	22.2	37.5	17.1
Total white collar	47.7	28.7	46.9	22.0
Skilled (building)	2.3	6.5	9.4	4.9
Skilled (other)	0	9.3	3.1	14.6
Semiskilled	22.8	34.3	21.9	43.9
Unskilled	9.1	5.6	0	7.3
Total blue collar	34.1	55.6	34.4	70.7
Unemployed	18.2	15.7	18.7	7.3

Table 6. *Girls 16-years old in 1900, who only attended grammar school, of Yankee, foreign-born, English-Canadian, and Irish household heads, by household characteristics* (%)

	N = 40 Yankee girls	N = 71 Foreign girls	N = 18 Eng. Can. girls	N = 25 Irish girls
Household head gender				
Male	67.5	81.7	77.8	76.0
Female	32.5	18.3	22.2	24.0
Household head marital status				
Married	70.0	81.7	66.7	80.0
Widow/er	27.5	18.3	33.3	20.0
Single	2.5	0	0	0
Household head occupation				
Professional	0	0	0	0
Business	10.0	8.4	5.6	4.0
Other white collar	2.5	2.8	5.6	4.0
Total white collar	12.5	11.3	11.1	8.0
Skilled (building)	10.0	18.3	11.1	16.0
Skilled (other)	12.5	22.5	33.3	16.0
Semiskilled	27.5	14.1	11.1	12.0
Unskilled	10.0	15.5	11.1	28.0
Total blue collar	60.0	70.4	66.7	72.0
Unemployed	27.5	18.3	22.2	20.0
Spouse employed	2.5	1.4	0	4.0

Table 6. (*cont.*)

	$N=40$ Yankee girls	$N=71$ Foreign girls	$N=18$ Eng. Can. girls	$N=25$ Irish girls
Household head literacy				
Can't read	0	5.6	0	12.0
Can't write	2.5	7.0	0	16.0
Spouse literacy				
Can't read	2.5	5.6	0	8.0
Can't write	2.5	5.6	0	8.0
Household head children				
1–3	67.5	31.0	27.8	24.0
4–6	25.0	49.3	66.7	40.0
7 or more	7.5	19.7	5.6	36.0
Head not parent	0	0	0	0
Home status				
Home owned	15.0	28.2	11.1	44.0
Home rented	85.0	69.0	88.9	56.0
Unknown	0	2.8	0	0
Birth order				
Family with 1 girl	52.5	16.9	16.7	24.0
Family with 2 girls				
1st born girl	20.0	12.7	16.7	16.0
2nd born girl	5.0	11.3	11.1	8.0
Family with 3 or more girls				
1st born girl	12.5	22.5	27.8	4.0
Middle-born girl	10.0	31.0	27.8	36.0
Last-born girl	0	5.6	0	12.0
Status in 1900				
Professional	0	0	0	0
Business	2.5	2.8	0	4.0
Other white collar	15.0	14.1	22.2	12.0
Total white collar	17.5	16.9	22.2	16.0
Skilled (building)	0	0	0	0
Skilled (other)	2.5	7.0	11.1	8.0
Semiskilled	25.0	42.3	33.3	40.0
Unskilled	0	1.4	0	4.0
Total blue collar	27.5	50.7	44.4	52.0
Unemployed	55.0	32.4	33.3	32.0

Table 7. *Latin High School boy students* (*entered 1900–1*) *and English High School boy students* (*entered 1896–1905*) *according to nativity and ethnicity of household heads, by household characteristics* (%)

	N=56 LHS Yankee boys	N=40 EHS Yankee boys	N=28 LHS foreign boys	N=26 EHS foreign boys	N=71 EHS Eng. Can. boys	N=55 EHS Irish boys
Household head gender						
Male	100.0	100.0	100.0	100.0	97.2	94.5
Female	0	0	0	0	2.8	5.5
Household head marital status						
Married	98.2	100.0	100.0	100.0	94.4	90.9
Widow/er	1.8	0	0	0	5.6	9.1
Single	0	0	0	0	0	0
Household head occupation						
Professional	25.0	2.5	17.9	0	0	0
Business	37.5	32.5	46.4	11.5	23.9	25.5
Other white collar	19.6	22.5	7.1	11.5	9.9	3.6
Total white collar	82.1	57.5	71.4	23.1	33.8	29.1
Skilled (building)	1.8	10.0	7.1	11.5	29.6	14.5
Skilled (other)	10.7	22.5	7.1	42.3	16.9	18.2
Semiskilled	3.6	5.0	10.7	11.5	15.5	12.7
Unskilled	0	0	3.6	11.5	1.4	20.0
Total blue collar	16.1	37.5	28.6	76.9	63.4	65.5
Unemployed	1.8	5.0	0	0	2.8	5.4
Spouse employed	0	0	0	0	5.6	3.7
Household head literacy						
Can't read	0	0	0	0	0	5.5
Can't write	0	0	0	3.8	0	7.3
Spouse literacy						
Can't read	0	0	3.6	0	0	3.7
Can't write	0	0	3.6	0	0	3.7
Household head children						
1–3	69.6	70.0	35.7	42.3	52.1	30.9
4–6	28.6	27.5	42.9	42.3	42.3	41.8
7 or more	1.8	2.5	17.9	15.4	5.6	27.3
Head not parent	0	0	3.5	0	0	0
Household head home status						
Home owned	60.7	42.5	60.7	61.5	39.4	72.7

Table 7. (*cont.*)

	N = 56 LHS Yankee boys	N = 40 EHS Yankee boys	N = 28 LHS foreign boys	N = 26 EHS foreign boys	N = 71 EHS Eng. Can. boys	N = 55 EHS Irish boys
Home rented	39.3	57.5	39.3	38.5	59.2	25.5
Unknown	0	0	0	0	1.4	1.8
Birth order						
Family with 1 boy	37.5	50.0	21.4	23.1	36.6	25.5
Family with 2 boys						
1st born boy	26.8	20.0	10.7	19.2	15.5	7.3
2nd born boy	14.3	15.0	7.1	7.7	11.3	12.8
Family with 3 or more boys						
1st born boy	8.9	7.5	21.4	26.9	12.7	20.0
Middle-born boy	5.4	5.0	28.6	7.7	11.3	20.0
Last-born boy	7.1	2.5	10.7	15.4	12.7	14.5

Table 8. *Latin High School girl students (entered 1900–1) and English High School girl students (entered 1898–1902) according to nativity and ethnicity of household head, by household characteristics (%)*

	N = 40 LHS Yankee girls	N = 54 EHS Yankee girls	N = 17 LHS foreign girls	N = 33 EHS foreign girls	N = 61 EHS Eng. Can. girls	N = 42 EHS Irish girls
Household head gender						
Male	100.0	98.1	100.0	100.0	100.0	100.0
Female	0	1.9	0	0	0	0
Household head marital status						
Married	100.0	96.3	88.2	93.9	98.4	95.2
Widow/er	0	1.9	11.8	6.1	1.6	4.7
Single	0	1.9	0	0	0	0
Household head occupation						
Professional	12.5	3.7	29.4	3.0	3.3	0
Business	40.0	40.7	35.3	24.2	11.5	11.9
Other white collar	35.0	20.4	17.7	15.2	11.5	7.1
Total white collar	87.5	64.8	82.4	42.4	26.2	19.0

Table 8. (*cont.*)

	$N=40$ LHS Yankee girls	$N=54$ EHS Yankee girls	$N=17$ LHS foreign girls	$N=33$ EHS foreign girls	$N=61$ EHS Eng. Can. girls	$N=42$ EHS Irish girls
Skilled (building)	2.5	7.4	5.9	15.2	29.5	7.1
Skilled (other)	10.0	14.8	5.9	18.2	21.3	26.2
Semiskilled	0	7.4	0	15.2	9.8	28.6
Unskilled	0	1.9	0	9.1	4.9	16.7
Total blue collar	12.5	31.5	11.8	57.6	65.6	78.6
Unemployed	0	3.7	5.8	0	0	2.3
Spouse employed	2.5	0	0	0	1.6	0
Household head literacy						
Can't read	0	0	0	6.1	0	4.8
Can't write	0	0	0	6.1	0	4.8
Spouse literacy						
Can't read	0	0	0	3.0	0	2.4
Can't write	0	0	0	3.0	1.6	2.4
Household head children						
1–3	82.5	64.8	29.4	51.5	55.7	23.8
4–6	17.5	29.6	64.7	33.3	39.3	47.6
7 or more	0	5.6	5.9	15.2	4.9	28.6
Household head home status						
Home owned	50.0	38.9	64.7	42.4	36.1	66.7
Home rented	50.0	61.1	35.3	57.6	63.9	33.3
Unknown	0	0	0	0	0	0
Birth order						
Family with 1 girl	42.5	31.5	29.4	24.2	26.2	14.3
Family with 2 girls						
1st born girl	17.5	20.4	0	6.1	26.2	19.0
2nd born girl	17.5	11.1	11.8	15.2	1.6	2.4
Family with 3 or more girls						
1st born girl	10.0	16.7	11.8	15.2	34.4	61.9
Middle-born girl	10.0	14.8	35.3	27.3	6.6	0
Last-born girl	2.5	5.6	11.8	12.1	4.9	2.3

Appendix IV: Supplementary household data

Table 1. *Families of high school and grammar school students with boarders, servants, and other relatives*

	Families with boarders or relatives (%)	Families with servants (%)	N
Mid-nineteenth-century cohort			
Somerville High 1852–3			
Boys	81.2	0	16
Girls	61.1	0	36
Somerville High 1859–61			
Boys	56.0	36.0	25
Girls	38.6	36.4	44
Late-nineteenth-century cohort			
Somerville High 1871–2			
Boys	20.5	30.8	39
Girls	26.2	21.4	42
Somerville High 1879–81			
Boys	24.1	32.8	58
Girls	54.3	21.7	46
Grammar students, 1870 15–16 years old in 1870			
All boys	16.8	6.4	125
Yankee boys	25.0	11.4	44
FP boys	12.3	3.7	81
Irish boys	9.4	1.9	53
All girls	22.6	2.8	106
Yankee girls	40.0	10.0	30
FP girls	15.8	0	76
Irish girls	16.7	0	54

Table 1. (*cont.*)

	Families with boarders	Families with servants (%)	Families with relatives (%)	N
Turn of-the-century cohort				
Latin High 1900–1				
All boys	9.5	29.8	14.3	84
All girls	9.1	34.5	9.1	55
Yankee boys	10.7	33.9	12.5	56
FP boys	7.1	21.4	17.9	28
Yankee girls	7.7	35.9	10.3	39
FP girls	12.5	31.2	6.2	16
English High 1899				
All boys	10.8	15.4	15.4	65
All girls	12.9	10.6	11.8	85
Yankee boys	15.4	20.5	20.5	39
FP boys	3.8	7.7	7.7	26
Yankee girls	13.2	13.2	13.2	53
FP girls	12.5	6.2	9.4	32
English High 1896–1905				
Eng. Can. boys	4.3	7.2	8.7	69
Irish boys	7.8	3.9	9.8	51
Eng. Can. girls	10.5	5.3	15.8	57
Irish girls	5.0	7.5	5.0	40
Grammar students, 1900				
16 years old in 1900				
All boys	7.4	2.7	4.7	149
Yankee boys	13.6	9.1	6.8	44
FP boys	4.8	0	3.8	105
Eng. Can. boys	6.5	0	6.5	31
Irish boys	2.6	0	2.6	39
All girls	14.4	0.8	9.3	118
Yankee girls	14.9	2.1	14.9	47
FP girls	14.1	0	5.6	71
Eng. Can. girls	22.2	0	5.6	18
Irish girls	4.0	0	4.0	25

Note:
FP, of foreign parentage.
Eng. Can., English Canadian.

Table 2. *Status of sons and daughters, 12–20 years old, in families of the mid-nineteenth-century cohort, the late-nineteenth-century cohort, and the turn-of-the-century cohort*

	Sons (%)			Daughters (%)		
	School	Work	Home	School	Work	Home
Mid-nineteenth-century cohort						
Somerville High 1852–3						
Boys	72.2	22.2	5.6	62.5	0	37.5
Girls	56.0	44.0	0	84.8	0	15.2
Somerville High 1859–61						
Boys	72.7	21.2	6.1	68.4	0	31.6
Girls	66.7	20.0	13.3	83.1	0	16.9
Late-nineteenth-century cohort						
Somerville High 1871–2						
Boys	84.8	10.9	4.3	50.0	12.5	37.5
Girls	72.0	28.0	0	80.7	7.0	12.3
Somerville High 1879–81						
Boys	81.2	14.1	4.7	63.0	7.4	29.6
Girls	78.6	21.4	0	83.3	0	16.7
Grammar students, 1870 15–16 years old in 1870						
All boys	16.3	67.9	15.8	34.2	31.6	34.2
Yankee boys	23.9	52.2	23.9	40.7	29.6	29.6
FP boys	12.9	74.8	12.2	30.8	32.7	36.5
Irish boys	15.7	72.9	11.5	27.5	32.5	40.0
All girls	35.4	49.4	15.2	14.3	25.2	60.5
Yankee girls	44.4	50.0	5.6	13.9	8.3	77.8
FP girls	32.8	49.2	18.0	14.4	30.6	55.0
Irish girls	38.1	45.2	16.7	15.2	36.7	48.1
Turn-of-the-century cohort Latin High 1900–1						
All boys	84.6	12.0	3.4	81.6	5.3	13.2
All girls	71.4	28.6	0	97.2	1.4	1.4
Yankee boys	87.3	9.9	2.8	89.5	0	10.5
FP boys	80.0	15.6	4.4	73.7	10.5	15.8
Yankee girls	77.8	22.2	0	95.7	2.1	2.1
FP girls	60.0	40.0	0	100.0	0	0

Table 2. (*cont.*)

	Sons (%)			Daughters (%)		
	School	Work	Home	School	Work	Home
English High 1899						
All boys	84.7	14.1	1.2	67.6	21.6	10.8
All girls	64.9	29.7	5.4	84.7	11.7	3.7
Yankee boys	88.9	8.9	2.2	73.1	15.4	11.5
FP boys	81.0	19.0	0	54.5	36.4	9.1
Yankee girls	73.3	26.7	0	86.6	9.8	3.7
FP girls	59.1	31.8	9.1	81.8	14.5	3.6
English High 1896–1905						
Eng. Can. boys	75.7	21.6	2.7	70.6	14.7	14.7
Irish boys	67.5	32.5	0	61.9	26.2	11.9
Eng. Can. girls	44.8	48.3	6.9	75.8	11.6	12.6
Irish girls	63.2	31.6	5.3	71.6	17.9	10.4
Grammar students, 1900 16 years old in 1900						
All boys	21.1	68.9	10.0	43.2	36.4	20.3
Yankee boys	16.7	71.2	12.1	50.0	26.7	23.3
FP boys	22.5	68.1	9.3	40.9	39.8	19.3
Eng. Can. boys	22.6	69.4	8.1	35.5	38.7	25.8
Irish boys	25.0	70.0	5.0	31.0	48.3	20.7
All girls	31.8	51.1	17.0	22.0	50.5	27.4
Yankee girls	23.1	53.8	23.1	25.9	37.0	37.0
FP girls	36.1	50.8	13.1	20.4	56.1	23.5
Eng. Can. girls	33.3	55.6	11.1	27.3	51.5	21.2
Irish girls	36.4	45.5	18.2	9.1	68.2	22.7

Note:
FP, of foreign parentage.
Eng. Can., English Canadian.

Table 3. *Employment of siblings of high school and grammar school students mid-nineteenth century, late nineteenth century, and turn-of-the-century cohorts*

	Students with sibling 16–20 years old				Students with sibling 12–15 years old			
	% with working brother	N with brother	% with working sister	N with sister	% with working brother	N with brother	% with working sister	N with sister
Mid-nineteenth-century cohort								
Somerville High								
1852–3								
Boys	50.0	6	0	6	0	4	0	7
Girls	82.4	17	0	10	0	15	0	20
Somerville High								
1859–61								
Boys	80.0	5	0	9	0	7	0	7
Girls	66.7	6	0	13	16.7	12	7.7	13
Late-nineteenth-century cohort								
Somerville High								
1871–2								
Boys	40.0	10	22.2	9	16.7	6	0	3
Girls	58.3	12	28.6	14	0	11	0	8
Somerville High								
1879–81								
Boys	52.9	17	15.4	13	0	14	0	11
Girls	18.6	7	0	13	0	5	0	9

Table 3. (cont.)

	Students with sibling 16–20 years old				Students with sibling 12–15 years old			
	% with working brother	N with brother	% with working sister	N with sister	% with working brother	N with brother	% with working sister	N with sister
Grammar students, 1870								
15–16 years old in 1870								
Yankee boys	75.0	8	50.0	16	16.7	18	0	10
Yankee girls	85.7	7	28.6	7	20.0	10	0	3
FP boys	100.0	27	65.0	20	34.4	32	4.2	24
FP girls	86.4	22	57.9	19	22.6	31	0	24
Irish boys	100.0	15	64.3	14	31.8	22	5.6	18
Irish girls	83.3	12	66.7	12	25.0	24	0	18
Turn-of-the-century cohort								
Latin High 1900–1 and English High 1899								
Yankee boys	41.2	17	15.0	20	0	14	0	19
Yankee girls	46.2	13	25.0	24	0	16	0	17
FP boys	62.5	16	31.2	16	0	16	10.0	10
FP girls	57.1	14	33.3	21	0	10	0	14
All boys	51.5	33	22.2	36	0	30	3.5	29
All girls	51.9	27	28.9	45	0	26	0	31
English High 1896–1905								
Eng. Can. boys	75.0	16	18.7	16	14.3	16	7.7	13
Eng. Can. girls	81.2	16	38.2	34	10.0	10	0	38
Irish boys	82.4	17	47.4	19	0	23	14.3	14
Irish girls	60.0	15	47.6	21	0	17	0	30

252

Grammar students, 1900

16-years old in 1900								
Yankee boys	100.0	10	46.7	15	9.1	11	0	12
Yankee girls	78.6	14	50.0	6	14.3	7	0	13
FP boys	97.2	36	77.5	40	17.4	46	9.5	42
FP girls	84.6	26	82.8	29	25.9	27	7.1	28
Eng. Can. boys	100.0	12	85.7	14	23.1	13	6.7	15
Eng. Can. girls	100.0	3	83.3	6	33.3	6	0	10
Irish boys	100.0	15	70.6	17	18.8	19	10.0	10
Irish girls	76.9	13	83.3	12	26.7	15	25.0	4

Note:
FP, of foreign parentage.
Eng. Can., English Canadian.

Table 4. *Status of children in Detroit, Michigan, 1900*

	Sons 12–20 years (%)			Daughters 12–20 years (%)		
	School	Work	Home	School	Work	Home
Ethnicity						
Native white American	54.7	40.4	4.9	56.1	16.9	27.0
Black	50.0	50.0	0.0	45.5	40.9	13.6
English Canadian	54.7	39.6	5.7	40.7	27.8	31.5
French Canadian	46.2	48.7	5.1	28.2	43.6	28.2
British	45.0	49.2	5.8	53.4	27.1	19.5
Irish	43.2	48.6	8.1	43.2	39.8	17.0
German	30.5	59.5	10.0	29.2	45.1	25.8
Polish	26.4	63.5	10.1	26.1	56.2	17.6
Russian	53.3	30.0	16.7	17.4	60.9	21.7

Source: Olivier Zunz, *The Changing Face of Inequality: Urbanization, Industrial Development, and Immigrants in Detroit, 1880–1920* (Chicago, 1982), p. 234, Table 9.7.

Notes

Introduction

1 Somerville High School, *Radiator*, February 1900, pp. 3–4.
2 Hartmut Kaelble, *Historical Research on Social Mobility* (New York, 1981), pp. 79–80.
3 John Goldthorpe, *Social Mobility and Class Structure in Modern Britain* (Oxford, Eng., 1980), pp. 55–7; Samuel Bowles and Herbert Gintis, *Schooling in Capitalist America: Educational Reform and the Contradictions of Economic Life* (New York, 1975).
4 David B. Tyack, *The One Best System: A History of American Urban Education* (Cambridge, Mass., 1974); Diane Ravitch, *The Great School Wars, New York City, 1805–1973* (New York, 1974).
5 Robert S. Lynd and Helen Merrell Lynd, *Middletown: A Study in Modern American Culture* (New York, 1929), pp. 211–22.
6 Historiographic models of the family as a dynamic unit strategically employing resources and deploying roles are elaborated in Tamara Hareven, ed., *Transitions: The Family and the Life Course in Historical Perspective* (New York, 1978).
7 Joseph F. Kett, *Rites of Passage: Adolescence in America, 1790 to the Present* (New York, 1979); Oscar Handlin and Mary F. Handlin, *Facing Life: Youth and the Family in American History* (Boston, 1971); Paula S. Fass, *The Damned and the Beautiful: American Youth in the 1920s* (New York, 1977).
8 Burton J. Bledstein, *The Culture of Professionalism: The Middle Class and the Development of Higher Education in America* (New York, 1978).
9 Oscar Handlin, *Boston's Immigrants: A Study in Acculturation 1790–1880*, 2nd ed. (Cambridge, Mass., 1959); Stephan Thernstrom, *The Other Bostonians: Social Mobility in the American Metropolis, 1880–1970* (Cambridge, Mass., 1973); Sam B. Warner, Jr., *Streetcar Suburbs: The Process of Growth in Boston, 1870–1900* (Cambridge, Mass., 1962); Peter R. Knights, *The Plain People of Boston, 1830–1860: A Study in City Growth* (New York, 1971); Elizabeth H. Pleck, *Black Migration and Poverty: Boston 1865–1900* (New York, 1979).
10 Michael B. Katz, *The Irony of Early School Reform: Educational Innovation in Mid-Nineteenth Century Massachusetts* (Cambridge, Mass., 1968); Stanley K. Schultz, *The Culture Factory: Boston Public Schools, 1789–1860* (New York, 1972); Marvin Lazerson, *Origins of the Urban School: Public Education in Massachusetts, 1870–1915* (Cambridge, Mass., 1971); Carl F. Kaestle and Maris A. Vinovskis, *Education and Social Change in Nineteenth-Century Massachusetts* (Cambridge, Eng., 1980).

Chapter 1 Farm village to commuter suburb

1   Somerville, *Annual Reports*, 1872, pp. 3–13.
2   Edward A. Samuels and Henry H. Kimball, eds., *Somerville, Past and Present* (Boston, 1897), p. 50l; Samuel A. Drake, ed., *History of Middlesex County, Massachusetts* (Boston, 1880), Vol. II, p. 338.
3.   D. Hamilton Hurd, ed., *History of Middlesex County, Massachusetts* (Philadelphia, 1890), Vol. III, pp. 771–2.
4   *Acts and Resolves Passed by the Legislature of Massachusetts . . . 1842* (Boston, 1842), Chapter 76, pp. 528–9.
5   Samuels and Kimball, *Somerville, Past and Present*, p. 17.
6   Edwin P. Conklin, *Middlesex County and Its People* (New York, 1927), Vol. II, pp. 429–30.
7   United States Census Bureau, *Report on the Social Statistics of Cities* (Washington, D.C., 1886), Part I, p. 301.
8   Samuels and Kimball, *Somerville, Past and Present*, p. 81.
9   Conklin, *Middlesex County and Its People*, Vol. II, p. 430; James F. Hunnewell, *A Century of Town Life: A History of Charlestown, Massachusetts, 1775–1887* (Boston, 1888), pp. 31–9; Stephan Thernstrom, *Poverty and Progress: Social Mobility in a Nineteenth-Century City* (Cambridge, Mass., 1964), pp. 9, 11; Edward C. Kirkland, *Men, Cities, and Transportation: A Study in New England History, 1820–1900* (Cambridge, Mass., 1948), 2 Vol.
10   U.S. Census Bureau, *Report of the Social Statistics of Cities*, Part I, p. 301; Samuels and Kimball, *Somerville, Past and Present*, p. 77.
11   John G. Palfrey, *Statistics of the Condition of . . . Industry in Massachusetts . . . 1845 . . .* (Boston, 1846), p. 71.
12   Samuels and Kimball, *Somerville, Past and Present*, p. 78.
13   Henry C. Binford, *The First Suburbs: Residential Communities on the Boston Periphery, 1815–1860* (Chicago, 1985), pp. 40–3.
14   U.S. Census Bureau, *Report of the Social Statistics of Cities*, p. 300.
15   Samuels and Kimball, *Somerville, Past and Present*, pp. 78–9; The early development of Somerville and subsequent phases of physical expansion are described in City of Somerville, *Beyond the Neck: The Architecture and Development of Somerville, Massachusetts* (Somerville, n.d.).
16   The manuscript schedules of the United States Seventh Census of 1850 for Somerville show that laborers from these countries resided in the town.
17   Percy Wells Bidwell, "Rural Economy in New England at the Beginning of the Nineteenth Century," *Transactions of the Connecticut Academy of Arts and Sciences* 20(1916), pp. 383–91.
18   Oscar Handlin, *Boston's Immigrants: A Study in Acculturation*, 2nd ed. (Cambridge, Mass., 1959), pp. 187–8; Hurd, *History of Middlesex County, Massachusetts*, Vol. III, p. 761.
19   Samuel Eliot Morison, *Maritime History of Massachusetts, 1783–1860* (Boston, 1921), pp. 12, 52–95.
20   Handlin, *Boston's Immigrants*, pp. 5–7; Justin Winsor, *Memorial History of*

Boston, Including Suffolk County, 1630–1880 (Boston, 1881), Vol. IV, pp. 121, 149.

21 Handlin, *Boston's Immigrants*, p. 9.
22 Caroline Ware, *The Early New England Cotton Manufacture: A Study in Industrial Beginnings* (Cambridge, Mass., 1931), pp. 64–5, 227, 228–35; Thomas Dublin, *Women at Work: The Transformation of Work and Community in Lowell, Massachusetts, 1826–1860* (New York, 1979), pp. 23–57, 144–64.
23 Michael B. Katz, *The Irony of Early School Reform: Educational Innovation in Mid-Nineteenth Century Massachusetts* (Cambridge, Mass., 1968), p. 7; Hunnewell, *A Century of Town Life*, pp. 59–60.
24 Handlin, *Boston's Immigrants*, Table II, p. 239. The growth of towns and cities in antebellum New England is treated in Percy Wells Bidwell, "Population Growth in Southern New England, 1810–1860," *Quarterly Publications of the American Statistical Association*, New Series, no. 120, 15(1917), pp. 813–39, and Jeffrey G. Williamson, "Antebellum Urbanization in the American Northeast," *Journal of Economic History*, 25(1965), pp. 592–614.
25 Hunnewell, *A Century of Town Life*, p. 19.
26 Winsor, *Memorial History of Boston*, Vol. IV, p. 26.
27 Ibid., Vol. IV, pp. 25–6; George H. McCaffrey, "Political Disintegration and Reintegration of Metropolitan Boston." Ph.D. Thesis, 1937. Harvard University Archives, pp. 196–7.
28 Petitioners for separation in a referendum of 1841 had average property holdings of 23 acres and paid an average tax of $23 while those against had average holdings of 7 acres and paid an average tax of $11. Computed from "Petitioners for . . . Remonstrants against . . . Separation . . . ," document held by the Somerville Historical Society. Also see Samuels and Kimball, *Somerville, Past and Present*, p. 85; Conklin, *Middlesex County and Its People*, Vol. II, p. 430; Hurd, *History of Middlesex County*, Vol. III, p. 760.
29 Conklin, *Middlesex County and Its People*, Vol. II, p. 430.
30 Hurd, *History of Middlesex County*, Vol. III, p. 753.
31 Winsor, *Memorial History of Boston*, Vol. III, p. 284.
32 Sam B. Warner, Jr., *Streetcar Suburbs: The Process of Growth in Boston, 1870–1900* (Cambridge, Mass., 1962), pp. 18–19, 179; Binford, *The First Suburbs*, pp. 154–62.
33 Samuels and Kimball, *Somerville, Past and Present*, pp. 93–4.
34 John G. Palfrey, *Statistics of the Condition and Products of Certain Branches of Industry in Massachusetts . . . 1845* (Boston, 1846), pp. 71–2.
35 Francis DeWitt, *Statistical Information Relating to . . . Industry in Massachusetts . . . 1855 . . .* (Boston, 1856), pp. 339–41.
36 Oscar and Mary F. Handlin, *Commonwealth: A Study of the Role of Government in the American Economy, Massachusetts, 1774–1861* (New York, 1947), pp. 142–3.
37 John G. Palfrey, *Statistics*, p. 272; Francis DeWitt, *Statistical Information*, pp. 340–1.

38 Conklin, *Middlesex County and Its People*, Vol. II, p. 432; Mary A. Haley, *The Story of Somerville* (Boston, 1903), p. 113.

39 Somerville, *Annual Town Report*, 1857, p. 28.

40 *U.S. Seventh Census 1850* (Washington, D.C., 1853), p. 51; *U.S. Eighth Census 1860* (Washington, D.C., 1863), p. 224; *U.S. Ninth Census 1870* (Washington, D.C., 1873), Vol. I, p. 167.

41 DeWitt, *Statistical Information*, p. 341.

42 *Annual Town Reports*, 1868, p. 175; Massachusetts Board of Education *Thirty-Sixth Annual Report*, 1876, appendix.

43 Four members of the Tufts family were listed among the 36 largest holders of agricultural land in the 1850 U.S. Seventh Census manuscript schedules for Somerville.

44 Conklin, *Middlesex County and Its People*, Vol. II, p. 432.

45 Hurd, *History of Middlesex County*, Vol. III, p. 770.

46 U.S. Census Bureau, *Report on the Social Statistics of Cities*, Part I, p. 302.

47 Sample drawn from the manuscript schedules of the 1850 U.S. Seventh Census and the 1860 U.S. Eighth Census.

48 *U.S. Ninth Census 1870* (Washington, D.C., 1873), p. 167.

49 *Massachusetts Census 1875* (Boston, 1876), Vol. I, pp. 72–3, 364.

50 Computed from data in *Massachusetts Census 1875* (Boston, 1876), Vol. I, pp. 412–13.

51 *Massachusetts Census 1865* (Boston, 1867), p. 298.

52 Ibid., pp. 282–3, 295–6.

53 *U.S. Seventh Census 1850* (Washington, D.C., 1853), p. 51; *U.S. Eighth Census 1860* (Washington, D.C., 1863), p. 224. For frequency of family units in early industrializing communities, see Jonathan Prude, *The Coming of Industrial Order: Town and Factory Life in Rural Massachusetts, 1810–1860* (Cambridge, Eng., 1983), p. 192.

54 *Massachusetts Census 1865* (Boston, 1867), pp. 34–5.

55 The following tabular data were compiled from a sample of one out of three households from the U.S. Census manuscript schedules for Somerville in 1850 and a sample of one out of five households from the 1860 schedules. Because the 1850 and 1860 census schedules did not indicate relation to head of household, the tabulation of boarders included relatives with different surnames. This conflation applied to all data on boarders tabulated in this study until 1880 when the census began to specify relation to head of household. The classification of occupations here and in subsequent chapters is based upon the occupational classification tables in Stephan Thernstrom, *Poverty and Progress;* Thernstrom, *The Other Bostonians: Poverty and Progress in the American Metropolis, 1880–1970* (Cambridge, Mass., 1973), appendix B; Michael B. Katz, *The People of Hamilton, Canada West: Family and Class in a Mid-Nineteenth-Century City* (Cambridge, Mass., 1975), Appendix 2.

56 Cf. Katz, *People of Hamilton*, pp. 232, 235.

57 How early industrialization promoted the bifurcation of the social structure into a capital-owning class and a diversified, increasingly proletarianized working class is rigorously argued in Michael B. Katz, Michael J.

Doucet, and Mark J. Stern, *The Social Organization of Early Industrial Capitalism* (Cambridge, Mass., 1982), pp. 14–63.

58 Computed from sample of the 1860 U.S. Eighth Census manuscript schedules for Somerville.

59 Records of votes cast in Somerville in the late 1840s and early 1850s show that heavy majorities supported such Whig candidates as Benjamin Thompson and John G. Palfrey for U.S. Representative and John Henry Clifford, Horace Mann, and George N. Briggs for Governor. See Cambridge *Chronicle*, Nov. 12, 1846; Nov. 16, 1848; Nov. 13. 1852.

60 Lee Benson, *The Concept of Jacksonian Democracy: New York as a Test Case* (Princeton, 1961), pp. 86–109; Ronald P. Formisano, *The Birth of Mass Political Parties: Michigan 1827–1861* (Princeton, 1971), pp. 102, 169; Paul E. Johnson, *A Shopkeepers' Millenium: Society and Revivals in Rochester, New York, 1815–1837* (New York, 1978), pp. 7–8, 128–35. An examination of Whig ethics through a biographical case study is presented in Frank Otto Gatell, *John Gorham Palfrey and the New England Conscience* (Cambridge, Mass., 1963).

61 Carl F. Kaestle and Maris A. Vinovskis, *Education and Social Change in Nineteenth-Century Massachusetts* (Cambridge, England, 1980), pp. 228–32.

62 Binford, *The First Suburbs*, pp. 123–4.

63 Paul Goodman, "The Politics of Industrialism: Massachusetts, 1830–1870," in Richard Bushman et al., eds., *Uprooted Americans: Essays to Honor Oscar Handlin* (Boston, 1979), pp. 188–9.

64 Samuels and Kimball, *Somerville, Past and Present*, pp. 471, 501. The 1850 U.S. Seventh Census manuscript schedules listed Brastow as a "real estate dealer" owning $44,000 in property. The 1860 census schedules listed him as a "railroad agent," and the 1870 schedules as a "railroad contractor."

65 Samuels and Kimball, *Somerville, Past and Present*, p. 526; the manuscript schedules of the 1850 U.S. Seventh Census indicate that Edgerly was a "graindealer" owning $19,000 in real estate.

66 Katz, *Irony of Early School Reform*, pp. 11–14.

67 David Tyack and Elisabeth Hansot, *Managers of Virtue: Public School Leadership in America, 1820–1980* (New York, 1982), p. 56.

68 Horace Mann, *Life and Works of Horace Mann* (New York, 1891), Vol. IV, pp. 248, 251. A biography that places Mann's career in the context of social change is Jonathan Messerli, *Horace Mann: A Biography* (New York, 1972).

69 Charlestown *City Advertiser*, February 18, 1852, p.2.

70 Horace Mann, "Annual Report of the Secretary of the Board," in Massachusetts Board of Education, *Tenth Annual Report* (Boston, 1847), pp. 236–7; Mann, *Life and Works*, Vol. IV, p. 259. For an analysis of the vision of technological progress see John F. Kasson, *Civilizing the Machine: Technology and Republican Values in America, 1776–1900* (New York, 1976), pp. 39–51.

71 Samuels and Kimball, *Somerville, Past and Present*, pp. 226, p. 493.

72 See Somerville, *Annual School Committee Report,* 1855, p. 24. Carl F. Kaes-
    tle describes the ideological complex of Protestantism, republicanism, and
    capitalism that shaped the common-school movement in *Pillars of the Re-
    public: Common Schools and American Society, 1780–1860* (New York, 1983),
    pp. 102–3.
73 Somerville, *Annual School Committee Report,* 1851, p. 10.
74 Binford, *The First Suburbs,* pp. 176–9.
75 "Petition of Orr N. Towne and Others for a Grammar School," January
    25, 1843; "Petition of William A. Russell for School House," February 2,
    1843; "Petition of George W. Wyatt and Others for a New School House,"
    January 21, 1846; "Petition of Benjamin Woodman for School House Near
    the Residence of Isaac Tufts," February 1, 1851; "Petition of Clarke Ben-
    nett and others for Removal of Primary School House [at Spring Hill to
    western part of town near home of Thomas J. Leland]," March 14, 1851;
    "Petition of Jonathan Brown, Jr., for School House on Winter Hill," March
    14, 1854. These petitions were found in a file of town and city records
    compiled by Henry C. Binford and in the possession of the Somerville
    city clerk's office.
76 Binford, *The First Suburbs,* pp. 176–9.
77 *Annual School Committee Report,* 1854, p. 12.
78 *Annual School Committee Report,* 1851, p. 3; Cambridge *Chronicle,* May 1,
    1852, p. 2.
79 *Annual School Committee Report,* 1851, p. 12; Samuels and Kimball, *Somer-
    ville, Past and Present* p.189.
80 Stanley K. Schultz, *The Culture Factory: Boston Public Schools, 1789–1860*
    (New York, 1973), pp. 125–6, discusses the concept of graded classes but
    overemphasizes the mechanical utility of that system.
81 *Annual School Committee Report,* 1857, p. 6; in 1857, male grammar school
    teachers received $1,000 for their year's services and female grammar
    school teachers were paid $300.
82 *Annual School Committee Report,* 1851, p. 12.
83 Carl F. Kaestle, *The Evolution of an Urban School System: New York City,
    1750–1850* (Cambridge, Mass., 1973), pp. 83–4, 164–6; Kaestle, ed., *Jo-
    seph Lancaster and the Monitorial School Movement: A Documentary History*
    (New York, 1974).
84 *Annual School Committee Report,* 1851, p. 13.
85 Massachusetts Board of Education, *Fifteenth Annual Report,* 1852, appen-
    dix.
86 Massachusetts Board of Education, *Twenty-Fifth Annual Report,* 1861, ap-
    pendix.
87 Samuels and Kimball, *Somerville, Past and Present,* p. 226.

Chapter 2 The evolution of educational leadership

1 Somerville, *School Committee Minutes,* 1842, pp. 1–9.
2 Attendance rates were computed from *School Committee Minutes,* 1842,
   pp. 1–9 and Somerville, *Annual Town Reports,* 1845, p. 16.

3 *Annual Town Reports,* 1845, p. 16.
4 *Annual Town Reports,* 1847, p. 7.
5 *Annual Town Reports,* 1845, p. 1.
6 *Annual Town Reports,* 1845, pp. 1–2; 1847, p. 5–6.
7 *Annual Town Reports,* 1845, p. 3.
8 *Annual Town Reports,* 1845, p. 11.
9 Information on Jesse Kimball and Andrew Dearborn was derived from the manuscript schedules of the U.S. Seventh Census 1850 for Somerville.
10 *Annual Town Reports,* 1845, p. 10; *School Committee Minutes,* December 25, 1845.
11 Paul G. Faler, *Mechanics and Manufacturers in the Early Industrial Revolution: Lynn, Massachusetts, 1780–1860* (Albany, 1981), p. 119.
12 Carl F. Kaestle, "Social Change, Discipline, and the Common School in Early Nineteenth-Century America," *Journal of Interdisciplinary History* 9(1978), pp. 1–18.
13 *School Committee Minutes,* December 25, 1845.
14 *Annual Town Reports,* 1845, p. 10.
15 A similar confrontation between the parent of a punished student and school authorities in another mid-nineteenth-century urbanizing community that raised questions about the scope of local governmental authority is reported in Don Harrison Doyle, *The Social Order of a Frontier Community: Jacksonville, Illinois, 1825–1870* (Urbana, Ill., 1978), p. 207.
16 *Annual Town Reports,* 1845, p. 14.
17 *Annual Town Reports,* 1845, p. 13.
18 *Annual Town Reports,* 1845, p. 14.
19 *Annual Town Reports,* 1845, pp. 14–15.
20 *Annual Town Reports,* 1845, pp. 13, 14.
21 Massachusetts Board of Education, *Eleventh, Fourteenth, Twentieth, Twenty-Fifth, Thirtieth, and Thirty-Fifth Annual Reports,* 1848, 1851, 1857, 1861, 1866, 1875, appendices.
22 D. Hamilton Hurd, *History of Middlesex County, Massachusetts* (Philadelphia, 1890), Vol. III, p. 764. Five of the first nine Selectmen were members of this church.
23 Town investment in road improvements and construction helped build a sense of public interest and communal involvement in early industrial settlements in Massachusetts. Cf. Jonathan Prude, *The Coming of Industrial Order: Town and Factory Life in Rural Massachusetts, 1810–1860* (Cambridge, Eng., 1983), p. 240.
24 *Annual Town Reports,* 1842, p. 6.
25 *Annual Town Reports,* 1842–57.
26 Hurd, *History of Middlesex County,* Vol. III, p. 764.
27 Somerville, *Annual School Committee Report,* 1846, p. 11. For the influence of Protestant values on public schooling, see Timothy L. Smith, "Protestant Schooling and American Nationality, 1800–1850," *Journal of American History,* 53(1967), pp. 679–95; David Tyack, "Onward Christian Sol-

diers: Religion in the American Common School," in Paul Nash, ed., *History and Education: The Educational Uses of the Past* (New York, 1970).

28   The rise of newcomers to public leadership in an embryonic community was a repeated process in settlement patterns explained by Stanley Elkins and Eric McKitrick as a revision of Frederick Jackson Turner's frontier thesis. See Elkins and McKitrick, "A Meaning for Turner's Frontier," *Political Science Quarterly* 69(1954), pp. 321–53, 565–602.

29   *Annual School Committee Report*, 1857, pp. 19, 20.

30   Edward A. Samuels and Henry H. Kimball, *Somerville, Past and Present* (Boston, 1897), pp. 577, 581.

31   *Annual Town Reports*, 1845, p. 15.

32   Harvey J. Graff, "Literacy, Jobs, and Industrialization: The Nineteenth Century" in Graff, ed., *Literacy and Social Development in the West* (Cambridge, Eng., 1981), p. 258. Also cf. Alexander J. Field, "Educational Reform and Manufacturing Development in Mid-Nineteenth-Century Massachusetts," Ph.D. Thesis, University of California, Berkeley, 1974, ch. 2; Samuel Bowles and Herbert Gintis, *Schooling in Capitalist America: Educational Reform and the Contradictions of Economic Life* (New York, 1976), ch. 6; and Sydney Pollard, "Factory Discipline in the Industrial Revolution," *Economic History Review* 16(1963), pp. 254–71.

33   For an analysis of how statistical knowledge and popular numeracy became linked with national welfare, see Patricia Cline Cohen, *A Calculating People: The Spread of Numeracy in Early America* (Chicago, 1982).

34   Carl F. Kaestle and Maris A. Vinovskis, in *Education and Social Change in Nineteenth-Century Massachusetts* (New York, 1980), pp. 44–5.

35   David J. Rothman, *The Discovery of the Asylum: Social Order and Disorder in the New Republic* (Boston, 1971), ch. 4.

36   *Annual Town Reports*, 1845, p. 6. For the transformation of time in industrial society see Oscar Handlin, "The Modern City as a Field of Historical Study," in Oscar Handlin and John Burchard, eds., *The Historian and the City* (Cambridge, Mass., 1963), p. 14; Pitrim A. Sorokin and Robert K. Merton, "Social Time: A Methodological and Functional Analysis," *American Journal of Sociology* 42(1937), pp. 627–8; Herbert G. Gutman, *Work, Culture, and Society in Industrializing America* (New York, 1976), p. 3ff.; E. P. Thompson, "Time, Work-Discipline, and Industrial Capitalism," *Past and Present*, 38(1967), pp. 56–97.

37   *Annual School Committee Report*, 1846, p. 7.

38   *Annual School Committee Report*, 1846, p. 17.

39   *Annual School Committee Report*, 1846, p. 18.

40   *Annual School Committee Report*, 1846, pp. 18, 19.

41   Horace Mann, *Life and Works of Horace Mann* (New York, 1891), Vol. IV, p. 259.

42   Daniel Calhoun in *The Intelligence of a People* (Princeton, N. J., 1974), pp. 230–56, 291–306, describes the functional mental aptitudes of Americans in the nineteenth century, but he also discusses their superficial and formal, imitative propensities. Neil Harris in *Humbug: The Art of P. T. Barnum* (Boston, 1974), proposes that Americans of the mid-nineteenth century

developed a proclivity for empirically judging and manipulating their surroundings which he calls the "operational aesthetic."

43   Michael B. Katz points out the reformers' efforts to cultivate self-interest as a motivation for cognitive activity, by orienting study around practical problem-solving rather than rote recitation. See Katz, *The Irony of Early School Reform: Educational Innovation in Mid-Nineteenth Century Massachusetts* (Cambridge, Mass., 1968), pp. 131–6.

44   *Annual School Committee Report*, 1848, p. 3. The crucial influence of a teacher's "character" on pupil performance was described by James G. Carter, *Essays on Popular Education* (Boston, 1826), pp. 43–4.

45   For example, in 1845, the school committee complimented the teacher of the Prospect Hill School for avoiding "the infliction of corporeal punishment" for four years. See *Annual School Committee Report*, 1845, p. 7.

46   A stimulating discussion of the inculcation of "moral free agency" is found in Paul E. Johnson, *A Shopkeeper's Millenium: Society and Revivals in Rochester, New York, 1815–1837* (New York, 1978), pp. 3–8.

47   *Annual School Committee Report*, 1859, p. 14.

48   *Annual School Committee Report*, 1855, p. 4.

49   *Annual School Committee Report*, 1859, pp. 12–15.

50   *Annual School Committee Report*, 1855, p. 4.

51   Carl F. Kaestle and Maris A. Vinovskis, *Education and Social Change in Nineteenth-Century Massachusetts* (Cambridge, England, 1980), pp. 200ff.

52   Massachusetts Board of Education, *Eleventh Annual Report*, 1848, p. 25. Cf. Richard M. Bernard and Maris A. Vinovskis, "The Female School Teacher in Ante-Bellum Massachusetts," *Journal of Social History* 10(1977), pp. 332–45.

53   Michael B. Katz, Michael J. Doucet, and Mark J. Stern, *The Social Organization of Early Industrial Capitalism* (Cambridge, Mass., 1982), p. 363. Also cf. Kathryn Kish Sklar, *Catharine Beecher: A Study in American Domesticity* (New Haven, 1973), pp. 97–115.

54   *Annual School Committee Report*, 1849, p. 6. This change in policy toward female teachers also occurred in Boxford, Massachusetts. See Kaestle and Vinovskis, *Education and Social Change*, p. 155.

55   *Annual School Committee Report*, 1860, pp. 8–9.

56   *Annual School Committee Report*, 1849, p. 5. The problem of teacher turnover also plagued other Massachusetts towns in this decade. Cf. Kaestle and Vinovskis, *Education and Social Change*, pp. 153–4.

57   *Annual School Committee Report*, 1851, p. 4.

58   *Annual School Committee Report*, 1853, pp. 7–12.

59   *Annual School Committee Report*, 1849, p. 5.

60   *Annual School Committee Report*, 1851, pp. 4, 5.

61   Samuels and Kimball, *Somerville, Past and Present*, p. 230; The creation of a teaching profession is treated as an integral part of common-school reform in Carl F. Kaestle, *The Evolution of an Urban School System: New York City, 1750–1850* (Cambridge, Mass., 1973), pp. 179–84; Katz, *Irony*, pp. 153–60.

62   *Annual School Committee Report*, 1855, p. 24.

Chapter 3 The free high school

1 George L. Baxter, "Early High School History," Somerville *Journal*, February 5, 1915, p. 11.

2 Michael B. Katz discovered the controversy in Beverly in 1860 that culminated in a popular referendum to abolish the high school. He supplied an influential interpretation of the vote that found class conflict at its heart. See *The Irony of Early School Reform: Educational Innovation in Mid-Nineteenth Century Massachusetts* (Cambridge, Mass., 1968), pp. 19–93. Maris A. Vinovskis has reanalyzed the Beverly dispute in terms of a wider set of factors involved in educational change that indicate the greater importance of district needs and resources. See his *The Origins of Public High Schools: A Reexamination of the Beverly High School Controversy* (Madison, 1985).

3 Cf. Michael Zuckerman, *Peaceable Kingdoms: New England Towns in the Eighteenth Century* (New York, 1970).

4 Baxter, "Early High School History."

5 Cambridge *Chronicle*, May 1, 1852; Alexander J. Inglis, *The Rise of the High School in Massachusetts* (New York, 1911), p. 46.

6 Katz, *Irony of Early School Reform*, pp. 227–8.

7 Carl F. Kaestle, *Pillars of the Republic: Common Schools and American Society, 1780–1860* (New York, 1983), pp. 119–20.

8 Somerville, *Annual School Committee Report*, 1857, p. 13; Baxter, "Early High School History."

9 *Annual School Committee Report*, 1846, p. 22.

10 Ibid., p. 23.

11 *Annual School Committee Report*, 1857, p. 13.

12 Recordbook of Somerville High School, Vol. I.

13 James McLachlan, *American Boarding Schools* (New York, 1970), pp. 19–48.

14 Baxter, "Early High School History."

15 Somerville, *Annual Town Reports*, 1845, p. 7.

16 Cf. Michael B. Katz, Michael J. Doucet, and Mark J. Stern, *The Social Organization of Early Industrial Capitalism* (Cambridge, Mass., 1982), pp. 253–54. A similar decline in school attendance was caused by labor-market expansion in Hamilton, Ontario, Canada from 1851 to 1871.

17 George L. Baxter, "A Brief History of the High School," *Somerville High School Radiator* 4(1895), No. 5, p. 5; *Annual School Committee Report*, 1860, p. 102.

18 *Annual School Committee Report*, 1857, pp. 8–9, 12–18.

19 *Annual School Committee Report*, 1852, pp. 3, 5; 1857, p. 15.

20 *Annual School Committee Report*, 1857, pp. 13–14.

21 *Annual School Committee Report*, 1857, p. 19.

22 The historical problem of the relationship between family and schooling was stated in a seminal way in Bernard Bailyn, *Education in the Forming of American Society: Needs and Opportunities for Study* (Chapel Hill, 1960).

23 Pathbreaking historiographic use of student records is found in Katz,

Irony; Carl F. Kaestle, *The Evolution of an Urban School System: New York City, 1750–1850* (Cambridge, Mass., 1973). Also see Michael B. Katz, "Who Went to School?" *History of Education Quarterly* (Fall 1972), pp. 432–54. For an earlier model for analysis of high school enrollment, see George S. Counts, *The Selective Character of American Secondary Education* (Chicago, 1922).

24 Cf. Stephan Thernstrom, *Poverty and Progress: Social Mobility in a Nineteenth Century City* (Cambridge, Mass., 1964), p. 141.

25 Kaestle, *Pillars*, p. 121. For artisans' support of the public high school in another industrial community in Massachusetts, see Carl F. Kaestle and Maris A. Vinovskis, *Education and Social Change in Nineteenth-Century Massachusetts* (Cambridge, Eng., 1980), p. 173; Artisans' fear of downward mobility had a basis in reality. See Stuart Blumin, "Mobility and Change in Ante-Bellum Philadelphia," in Stephan Thernstrom and Richard Sennet, eds., *Nineteenth-Century Cities: Essays in the New Urban History* (New Haven, 1969), pp. 165–208.

26 Harvey J. Graff, *The Literacy Myth: Literacy and Social Structure in the Nineteenth-Century City* (New York, 1979), pp. 314–15.

27 Wages of laborers in Somerville were recorded in the 1850 U.S. Seventh Census manuscript schedules for Somerville.

28 James A. Henretta, "The Study of Social Mobility: Ideological Assumptions and Conceptual Bias," *Labor History* 18(1977), pp. 165–78.

29 Patrick J. Harrigan, *Mobility, Elites, and Education in French Society* (Waterloo, Ontario, Canada, 1980).

30 Joseph Kett, *Rites of Passage: Adolescence in America, 1790 to the Present* (New York, 1977), pp. 111–43, and Michael B. Katz, *People of Hamilton, Canada West: Family and Class in a Mid-Nineteenth Century City* (Cambridge, Mass., 1975), pp. 256–7, discuss the nuances of "semi-dependency" and "semi-autonomy" in the transition to adulthood.

31 "Middle-born" refers to one child or any number of children born between the first-born and last-born children.

32 Cf. Katz, *People of Hamilton*, p. 272.

33 A theory of exchange relations in the family is elaborated by Michael Anderson, *Family Structure in Nineteenth-Century Lancashire* (Cambridge, Eng., 1971), pp. 5–16. A wise modification of Anderson's model that stresses the non-economic principle of "reciprocity" over self-interest is presented in Tamara K. Hareven, *Family Time and Industrial Time: The Relation Between the Family and Work in a New England Industrial Community* (Cambridge, Eng., 1982), pp. 107–12.

34 Resident extended relatives were identified by surnames similar to the head of household. This is a crude procedure that undercounts resident relatives without similar names and includes them as boarders. See footnote 55 in Chapter 1.

35 Kathryn Kish Sklar, *Catharine Beecher, A Study in American Domesticity* (New Haven, 1973), pp. 151–67; Nancy F. Cott, *The Bonds of Womanhood: "Woman's Sphere" in New England, 1780–1835* (New Haven, 1977), pp. 63–100.

36 *Annual School Committee Report*, 1857, p. 17.

37 Kett, *Rites of Passage*, p. 138.

38 Economists have defined the "opportunity cost of education" as income forgone by an individual during school attendance. The willingness of individual students or parents to pay the opportunity cost of education has been treated as a vital ingredient in the formation of "human capital." Theodore W. Schultz in his seminal "Investment in Human Capital," *American Economic Review* 51(1961), pp. 1–17, defined human capital as "skill, knowledge, and similar attributes that affect particular human capabilities to do productive work." Mary Jean Bowman supplied an enlightening history of "human capital" theory in "The Human Investment Revolution in Economic Thought," *Sociology of Education* 39(1966), pp. 111–38.

39 Kaestle and Vinovskis, *Education and Social Change*, pp. 74–5, 77ff; Oscar Handlin and Mary F. Handlin, *Facing Life: Youth and the Family in American History* (Boston, 1971), p. 96.

40 Carroll Smith-Rosenberg and Charles Rosenberg, "The Female Animal: Medical and Biological Views of Woman and Her Role in Nineteenth-Century America," *Journal of American History* 50(1973), pp. 332–56. Many physicians argued that at menstrual periods, women were unable to think or act normally. See E. H. Clarke, *Sex in Education or a Fair Chance for the Girls* (Boston, 1873), pp. 127–9; Richard Reece, *The Lady's Medical Guide* (Philadelphia, 1833), p. 71; H. C. Storer, *Criminal Abortion* (Boston, 1868), p. 101.

41 *Fiftieth Anniversary of the Somerville High School, 1852–1902* (Somerville, 1902), p. 60.

42 Records of Somerville High School linked to 1860 U. S. Census schedules for Somerville.

Chapter 4 The rise of Yankee city and the prolongation of schooling

1 Samuel Adams Drake, *History of Middlesex County, Massachusetts* (Boston, 1880), Vol. II, p. 322.

2 Edwin P. Conklin, *Middlesex County and Its People* (New York, 1927), Vol. II, p. 432.

3 Francis De Witt, *Statistical Information Relating to . . . Industry in Massachusetts . . . 1855 . . .* (Boston, 1856), pp. 339–41; Oliver Warner, *Statistical Information Relating to . . . Industry in Massachusetts . . . 1865 . . .* (Boston, 1866), pp. 390–2.

4 Oliver Warner, *Abstract of the Census of Massachusetts, 1865 . . .* (Boston, 1867), pp. 72–3; *United States Ninth Census 1870* (Washington, D.C., 1873), Vol. I, p. 167.

5 Somerville, *Annual Town Reports*, 1867, p. 13.

6 *Annual Town Reports*, 1865, pp. 18–19; Edward A. Samuels and Henry H. Kimball, eds., *Somerville: Past and Present* (Boston, 1897), p. 125.

7 Drake, *History of Middlesex County*, Vol. II, p. 324.

8 Samuels and Kimball, *Somerville, Past and Present*, p. 126.

9   *Annual Town Reports,* 1867, p. 13.

10 D. Hamilton Hurd, *History of Middlesex County, Massachusetts* (Philadelphia, 1890), Vol. III, p. 771.

11 Drake, *History of Middlesex County,* Vol. II, p. 324.

12 Geoffrey Blodgett, *The Gentle Reformers: Massachusetts Democrats in the Cleveland Era* (Cambridge, Mass., 1966), p. 33.

13 *Municipal Charter of the City of Somerville* (Boston, 1872), pp. 3–7.

14 Somerville *Journal,* December 11, 1880, p. 1. The *Journal* was established in 1870 as Somerville's first newspaper. It was a firm supporter of the Republican Party and frequently voiced its views. It approvingly reported "regular ticket" or Republican victories in the annual city elections. Cf. *Journal,* December 9, 1876, p. 1; December 11, 1880, p. 1; December 8, 1883, p. 1; December 6, 1884, p. 1; and December 10, 1892, p. 1. The *Journal* also reported Somerville's consistent support of Republican candidates for state and national offices. Cf. *Journal,* November 4, 1876, p. 1; November 6, 1880, p. 1; November 10, 1888, p. 1; November 12, 1892, p. 1.

15 Somerville *Journal,* December 6, 1892, p. 1; December 10, 1892, p. 1.

16 Blodgett, *The Gentle Reformers,* pp. 61–3.

17 Harold R. Taylor, "Somerville Politics, 1921–1929." Honors Thesis (Harvard University, 1939), pp. 35–6.

18 Somerville *Journal,* May 27, 1876, p. 4. The status implications of temperance are examined in Joseph R. Gusfield, *Symbolic Crusade: Status Politics and the American Temperance Movement* (Urbana, 1963).

19 City of Somerville, *Fiftieth Anniversary of the City of Somerville* (Somerville, 1922), p. 34.

20 *Massachusetts Census 1885* (Boston, 1887), Vol. I, pt. 1, p. 94.

21 Officeholders traced in listings of city officials, *Annual Reports,* 1880–1893.

22 Somerville *Journal,* December 10, 1892, p. 1. Quincy E. Dickerman and Giles W. Bryant won seats on the School Committee as Citizens Republican candidates.

23 Samuels and Kimball, *Somerville, Past and Present,* p. 130.

24 Somerville, *Annual Reports,* 1882–1895, "Building Permits."

25 *Annual Reports,* 1891, p. 375; 1892, p. 481; 1893, p. 559; 1894, p. 550; 1895, Sec. S, p. 3.

26 Samuels and Kimball, *Somerville, Past and Present,* pp. 134, 145–280.

27 Samuels and Kimball, *Somerville, Past and Present,* pp. 165–6; *Annual Reports,* 1881, pp. 12–13; 1891, p. 19.

28 Massachusetts Board of Education, *Forty-fifth, Fiftieth, Fifth-fifth, and Sixtieth Annual Reports,* 1880–1, 1885–6, 1890–1, 1895–6, appendices.

29 Oscar Handlin, *Boston's Immigrants: A Study in Acculturation,* 2nd ed. (New York, 1959), pp. 211–15.

30 Computed from *Massachusetts Census 1875* (Boston, 1876), Vol. I, pp. 412–13.

31 Computed from Somerville, *Annual Reports,* 1880, p. 258; 1890, p. 452; 1900, p. 441.

32 Computed from *Massachusetts Census 1885,* Vol. I, pt. 2, pp. 263–6; Ste-

phan Thernstrom, *The Other Bostonians: Poverty and Progress in the American Metropolis, 1880–1970* (Cambridge, Mass., 1973), p. 131, Table 6.9.

33 Computed from *Massachusetts Census 1875*, Vol. I, pp. 279–81; *U.S. Eleventh Census 1890* (Washington, D.C., 1895), Vol. I, pt. 1, p. 536.
34 Alaric B. Start, ed., *History of Tufts College* (Medford, Massachusetts, 1896), pp. 20–1.
35 *U.S. Eleventh Census 1890* (Washington, D.C., 1895), Vol. V, pt. 2, p. xxx.
36 Ibid., pp. 68–79.
37 *U.S. Twelfth Census 1900* (Washington, D.C., 1902), Vol. IX, pt. 3, p. 392.
38 Mary A. Haley, *The Story of Somerville* (Boston, 1903), p. 123.
39 *U.S. Eleventh Census 1890*, Vol. V, pt. 2, p. 5; *U.S. Thirteenth Census 1910* (Washington, D.C., 1912), Vol IX, p. 528.
40 The adverse impact of mechanization upon artisanship depended upon the type of skilled work. The construction trades were especially adaptive to technological innovation in the late nineteenth century. See Andrew Dawson, "The Paradox of Dynamic Technological Change and the Labor Aristocracy in the United States, 1880–1914," *Labor History* 20(1979), pp. 334–5.
41 Thernstrom, *The Other Bostonians*, p. 50.
42 H. W. Crispin, "The Traction Age in Greater Boston, 1895–1915," Honors Thesis (Harvard University, 1938), pp. 32, 49–50.
43 Samuels and Kimball, *Somerville, Past and Present*, p. 472.
44 Sam B. Warner, Jr., *Streetcar Suburbs: The Process of Growth in Boston, 1870–1900* (Cambridge, Mass., 1962), p. 56.
45 Taylor, "Somerville Politics," p. 40.
46 *Annual Reports*, 1880, p. 218.
47 Computed from Somerville, *Annual Reports*, 1875, p. 204; 1885, p. 314; 1895, sec. Z, p. 6; *Massachusetts Census 1875*, Vol. I, part 1, pp. 72–3; *Massachusetts Census 1885*, Vol. I, pt. 1, p. 342; *Massachusetts Census 1895* (Boston, 1897), Vol. II, p. 273.
48 William P. Jones, *Somerville Fifty Years Ago* (Somerville, 1933), p. 62. The establishment of a city board of health helped greatly to improve sanitation practices. See *Annual Reports*, 1889, p. 240.
49 Taylor, "Somerville Politics," pp. 35–6.
50 Samuels and Kimball, *Somerville, Past and Present* pp. 439–42.
51 Ibid., pp. 333–438.
52 Ibid., pp.333–45.
53 Ibid., p. 427.
54 See Francis G. Couvares, *The Remaking of Pittsburgh: Class and Culture in an Industrializing City, 1877–1919* (Albany, 1984), p. 99.
55 Massachusetts Bureau of Labor Statistics, *Annual Report*, 1876, pp. 70–77. A survey of 3,675 male wage laborers conducted by the bureau revealed that the average workingman with dependents received $481.81 in yearly wages, while his minor children contributed $239.19 annually in earnings to the family income.
56 *Annual Reports*, 1874, pp. 115–16.
57 *Annual Reports*, 1874, p. 114; 1877, p. 121.

58 *Annual Reports,* 1875, pp. 100–1.
59 *Annual Reports,* 1875, p. 102.
60 Warner, *Streetcar Suburbs,* p. 8.
61 Burton J. Bledstein, *The Culture of Professionalism: The Middle Class and the Development of Higher Education in America* (New York, 1976), pp. 31–9.
62 Alan Dawley, *Class and Community: The Industrial Revolution in Lynn* (Cambridge, Mass., 1976), pp. 73–96, describes the erosive effects of high-speed machinery on the shoemaker's craft; Joseph F. Kett, *Rites of Passage: Adolescence in America, 1790 to the Present* (New York, 1977), p. 138.
63 Massachusetts Bureau of Statistics of Labor, *Annual Report,* 1906, pt. 1, pp. 3–5. The bureau lamented, "From the introduction of the first labor-saving machine dates the decline of the apprentice. . . . Up to the present day the need of apprentices has not been felt to any apparent extent, but now on all sides is heard the statement that skilled labor is difficult to obtain, and the introduction of laws and resolutions in State Legislatures looking toward a technical or trade education for the young persons who are growing up in our midst indicates a desire to return to old conditions." The bureau's report of 1906 cited the observations of Director Back, a German expert on industrial training, sent by his government to America to study labor conditions. He wrote, "In America a young man has much less opportunity than in Germany to learn in a practical way all the details of a trade, and thus to become a skilled workman in a thorough sense of the term. This is largely due to a difference of systems, the general tendency in the United States being to reduce prices by entirely substituting machinery for handwork, by using a limited number of designs, and by manufacturing in immense quantities. . . . The scarcity of such skilled workmen is now being complained of more and more in the United States. Most owners of small establishments which still employ handworkers, especially those in large cities, are unwilling to take the trouble and assume the responsibility of training apprentices." Also see Carroll D. Wright, *The Apprenticeship System in Its Relation to Industrial Education,* U.S. Bureau of Education, Bulletin No. 6 (Washington, D.C., 1908), pp. 9ff.
64 Thernstrom, *The Other Bostonians,* p. 300. Also see Alexander Keyssar, *Out of Work: The First Century of Unemployment in Massachusetts* (Cambridge, Eng., 1986), pp. 54–5, 308–13.
65 This development is evidenced by the increasing share of high school students from artisan families and their high rate of entry into white-collar jobs. See Chapters 5 and 7.
66 *Annual Reports,* 1872, pp. 102–3; 1886, p. 159.
67 *Annual Reports,* 1873, pp. 97–9; 1882, pp. 145–7.
68 *Annual Reports,* 1882, p. 145.
69 *Annual Reports,* 1893, p. 254.
70 *Annual Reports,* 1886, p. 157.
71 *Annual Reports,* 1873, p. 99.
72 *Annual Reports,* 1881, p. 136.
73 *Annual Reports,* 1884, p. 168.

74 *Annual Reports,* 1877, p. 144.
75 *Annual Reports,* 1875, p. 142; 1877, p. 112.
76 *Annual Reports,* 1884, p. 166.
77 *Annual Reports,* 1875, p. 107; 1877, pp. 114–15.
78 *Annual Reports,* 1877, p. 117.
79 *Annual Reports,* 1888, pp. 159–61; 1891, pp. 149–50.
80 *Annual Reports,* 1888, p. 106; 1899, pp. 90–1.
81 *Annual Reports,* 1872, p. 104; 1888, p. 182.
82 *Annual Reports,* 1872, p. 103; 1886, p. 160.
83 Marvin Lazerson, *Origins of the Urban School: Public Education in Massa-chusetts, 1870–1915* (Cambridge, Mass., 1971), pp. 74–5.
84 Massachusetts Board of Education, *Fifty-ninth Annual Report,* 1894–5, pp. 367–8.
85 Massachusetts Board of Education, *Fifty-ninth Annual Report,* pp. 498–9; Thomas M. Baillet, "The Psychology of Manual Training," *Journal of Education* 38(1893), pp. 364–5.
86 Massachusetts Board of Education, *Fifty-ninth Annual Report,* pp. 382, 385.
87 *Annual Reports,* 1894, p. 220; 1896, p. 288.
88 *Annual Reports,* 1875, p. 104.
89 *Annual Reports,* 1888, pp. 170, 173.
90 *Annual Reports,* 1889, pp. 157–8; 1890, pp. 156–60; Massachusetts Board of Education, *Fifty-fifth Annual Report,* 1890–1, pp. 365–96; *Sixtieth Annual Report,* 1895–6, pp. 382–433. Drawing lessons were standardized by grade level and based on a series of texts called "Prang's drawing books." See *Annual Reports,* 1891, p. 186.
91 *Annual Reports,* 1888, p. 180.
92 *Annual Reports,* 1888, pp. 176–7.
93 *Annual Reports,* 1896, p. 288.
94 Civil Service Commission of Massachusetts, *Fifth Annual Report* (Boston, 1889), pp. 124–9.
95 Richard Henry Dana, *Civil Service Reform in Massachusetts* (Boston, 1888), p. 2.
96 *Annual Reports,* 1874, p. 111.
97 Lazerson, *Origins of the Urban School,* p. 3.
98 *Annual Reports,* 1875, p. 119.
99 *Annual Reports,* 1882, p. 149; 1888, p. 152.
100 *Annual Reports,* 1890, p. 220.
101 Massachusetts Board of Education, *Fifty-fifth Annual Report,* 1890–1, pp. 18–47; *Fifty-sixth Annual Report,* 1891–2, pp. 11–12.
102 *Annual Reports,* 1893, p. 250.
103 *Annual Reports,* 1888, p. 15.
104 A model for the reorganization of urban public schools in the late nineteenth century that typologizes the bureaucratic and centralizing innovations discussed in this section is presented in Michael B. Katz, *Class, Bureaucracy, and Schools: The Illusion of Educational Change in America* (New York, 1975), Expanded Edition, pp. 56–104.

105 Computed from *Annual Reports,* 1875, p. 204; *Massachusetts Census 1875,*
     Vol. I, p. 364; *Massachusetts Census 1895,* Vol. II, p. 273.
106 Stanley K. Schultz, *The Culture Factory: Boston Public Schools, 1789–1860*
     (New York, 1973), pp. 92–100.
107 *Annual Reports,* 1883, pp. 157–60.
108 Samuels and Kimball, *Somerville, Past and Present,* pp. 185–6.
109 *Annual Reports,* 1884, p. 146.
110 *Annual Reports,* 1875, p. 144.
111 *Annual Reports,* 1873, p. 87; 1890, pp. 220–4.
112 Computed from *Annual Reports,* 1873, pp. 82, 89; 1880, pp. 120, 126;
     1890, pp. 220–4, 225.
113 Lazerson, *Origins of the Urban School,* p. 11.
114 Boston, *Annual Report of School Committee,* 1891, appendix, pp. 110, 118.
115 *Annual Reports,* 1882, p. 131.
116 Massachussets Board of Education, *Forty-fifth, Fiftieth, Fifty-fifth, and
     Sixtieth Annual Reports,* 1880–1, 1885–6, 1890–1, 1895–6, appendices.
117 Lazerson, *Origins of the Urban School,* p. 3.
118 Somerville, *Annual Reports,* 1873, p. 89; 1880, p. 126; 1890, p. 225.
119 *Annual Reports,* 1876, pp. 126–7.
120 Computed from *Annual Reports,* 1874, p. 109; 1880, p. 130; 1885, p. 144;
     1891, pp. 179–83.
121 Boston, *Annual Report of School Committee,* 1891, appendix, p. 7.

Chapter 5 Popularizing high school: "the college of the people"

1   Somerville, *Annual Reports,* 1876, p. 108.
2   Students could also elect to take a five-year course that required fewer
    subjects each term. Nearly all students chose the four-year option be-
    cause many intended to leave for work before graduation or because the
    opportunity cost for an additional year was too high. See *Annual Reports,*
    1921, p. 146.
3   *Annual Reports,* 1870, pp. 55–6; 1921, pp. 144–5.
4   Oscar Handlin and Mary F. Handlin, *Commonwealth: A Study of the Role
    of Government in the American Economy: Massachusetts, 1774–1861* (New
    York, 1947), p. 207; Rush Welter, *Popular Education and Democratic Thought
    in America* (New York, 1962), pp. 60–73.
5   *Annual Reports,* 1877, p. 116.
6   *Annual Reports,* 1876, p. 127.
7   *Annual Reports,* 1890, p. 153.
8   *Annual Reports,* 1889, p. 154.
9   *Annual Reports,* 1892, p. 180.
10 Edward A. Samuels and Henry H. Kimball, *Somerville, Past and Present*
    (Boston, 1897), p. 202; *Annual Reports,* 1892, p. 180.
11 *Annual Reports,* 1889, p. 155.
12 *Annual Reports,* 1892, p. 181.
13 *Annual Reports,* 1895, part E, p. 36.

14 *Annual Reports,* 1892, p. 179.
15 Somerville *Journal,* March 5, 1892, p. 1.
16 *Annual Reports,* 1892, p. 182.
17 Massachusetts Board of Education, *Fifty-fifth Annual Report,* 1890–1, p. 407.
18 Harry Braverman, *Labor and Monopoly Capital: The Degradation of Work in the Twentieth Century* (New York, 1974), p. 297; Belton M. Fleisher, *Labor Economics: Theory and Evidence* (Englewood Cliffs, N.J., 1970), p. 219, Table 13–8, data computed from *Historical Statistics of the United States, Colonial Times to 1957* (Washington, D.C., 1960), pp. 91–2.
19 Somerville High School *Radiator,* January 1901, p. 76.
20 *Annual Reports,* 1921, p. 144ff.
21 *Annual Reports,* 1894, p. 227.
22 Massachusetts Board of Education, *Sixtieth Annual Report,* 1895–6, p. 373.
23 Ibid., pp. 357ff.
24 The poor articulation between the high school and college received considerable attention in the 1880s, at the local as well as the national level. It was declared "a serious evil" by the Massachusetts Classical and High School Teachers' Association. See "Meeting of Classical and High School Teachers," *Journal of Education* (April 17, 1884), p. 252. The National Council of Education of the National Education Association also began to investigate ways to improve linkage. James C. Mackenzie of the N.E.A.'s Committee of Ten, which helped establish guidelines for a uniform secondary preparation for college, complained about the "utter chaos into which college entrance requirements have fallen" in "The Report of the Committee of Ten," *School Review* 2(1894), p. 148. The best study of the Committee of Ten is Theodore R. Sizer, *Secondary Schools at the Turn of the Century* (New Haven, 1964). Also see Edward A. Krug, *The Shaping of the American High School* (New York, 1964), pp. 18–65; Frederick Rudolph, *The American College and University: A History* (New York, 1962), pp. 283–6.
25 *Annual Reports,* 1889, pp. 150ff.
26 *Annual Reports,* 1892, p. 2.
27 Somerville *Journal,* March 5, 1892, p. 1.
28 Somerville *Journal,* April 2, 1892, p. 1.
29 Somerville *Journal,* March·5, 1892, p. 2.
30 Ibid.
31 Six aldermen and common councilmen were listed from 1891–3 as large taxpayers, those paying $100 or more. Three school committeemen were listed as large taxpayers. The average payment of the aldermen and common councilmen was $208.25 and that of the school committeemen was $172.33. See Somerville *Journal,* August 13, 1892, p. 1; August 20, 1892, p. 1.
32 Aldermen William Hunnewell, an advocate for immediate construction of the English High School, and Charles B. Osgood and S. Walker Janes, advocates of a trial two-session plan, were all businessmen. See Somerville *Journal,* May 28, 1892, p. 2.

33 Somerville *Journal*, April 2, 1892, p. 2; May 14, 1892, p. 4.
34 Somerville *Journal*,, April 30, 1892, p. 2.
35 Somerville *Journal*, May 14, 1892, p. 4; May 28, 1892, p. 4.
36 Somerville *Journal*, May 28, 1892, p. 4.
37 Somerville *Journal*, September 9, 1893, p. 1.
38 Ibid., p. 4.
39 Somerville *Journal*, May 28, 1892, p. 2.
40 *Annual Reports*, 1892, pp. 30–1.
41 Somerville *Journal*, September 9, 1893, p. 1.
42 Somerville *Journal*, September 16, 1893, p. 1. The depression of 1893 appears to have had a negligible effect on Somerville's economy. Businessmen and industrialists of the city were sanguine about future economic prospects. Most reported little or no decline in business; some even anticipated significant gains in the fall. The outlook of the business community encouraged the City Council to plan an investment in the English High School. See Somerville *Journal*, August 26, 1893, p. 1.
43 *Annual Reports*, 1895, part E, p. 37. This term or its variant was popular among high school promoters. Cf. David B. Tyack, ed., *Turning Points in American Educational History* (New York, 1967), pp. 352–63, 386–92; Tyack, *The One Best System: A History of American Urban Education* (Cambridge, Mass., 1974), p. 57.
44 *Annual Reports*, 1895, part E, pp. 38–47.
45 *Annual Reports*, 1897, p. 307.
46 *Annual Reports*, 1896, pp. 298–301.
47 *Annual Reports*, 1896, p. 316; 1900, p. 208.
48 Enrollments and attendance were also enhanced by a reorganization of electric car routes that improved access to the high school. Somerville High School *Radiator*, March 1899, p. 4.
49 John O. Norris, "The High School in Our System of Education," *Education* (March, 1883), p. 332; H. C. Missimer, "Something for the Educational Iconoclast," *Academy* (April, 1889), p. 121; "Notes," *Academy* (March, 1891), p. 114.
50 Tyack, *The One Best System*, pp. 57–8.
51 David M. Hoyt, "Relation of the High School to the Community," *Education* 6(1886), p. 430.
52 A study of birth order and examination performance in twentieth-century Holland suggests that priority of birth may result in higher intellectual achievement. See Lillian Belmont and Francis A. Marolla, "Birth Order, Family Size, and Intelligence," *Science* 182(1972), pp. 1096–101.
53 John Modell, "Patterns of Consumption, Acculturation, and Family Income Strategies in Late Nineteenth-Century America," Tamara K. Hareven and Maris A. Vinovskis, eds., *Family and Population in Nineteenth-Century America* (Princeton, 1978), p. 230.
54 Cf. Frank W. Notestein, "Trends in the Size of Families Completed Prior to 1910 in Various Social Classes," *American Journal of Sociology* 38(1932), pp. 398–408; Richard Easterlin, "On the Relation of Economic Factors to Recent and Projected Fertility Changes," *Demography* 3(1966), pp. 131–

53; Paula S. Fass, *The Damned and the Beautiful: American Youth in the 1920's* (New York, 1977), pp. 58–64; W. Elliot Brownlee, *The Dynamics of Ascent: A History of the American Economy,* 2nd ed. (New York, 1979), pp. 284–6.

55   The rationality of investment in secondary schooling was substantiated by the high rate of entry into white-collar jobs of high-school students. See Chapter 7.

56   Computed from records of the Somerville High School for 1896–1910.

57   John Modell and Tamara K. Hareven concluded from a study of boarding practices in Boston, 1885, that immigrant families rarely took in boarders. See Modell and Hareven, "Urbanization and the Malleable Household: An Examination of Boarding and Lodging in American Families," Michael Gordon, ed., *The American Family in Social-Historical Perspective* (New York, 1978), 2nd ed., p. 56.

58   Modell, "Patterns of Consumption," p. 227.

59   Stephan Thernstrom, *Poverty and Progress: Social Mobility in a Nineteenth Century City* (Cambridge, Mass., 1964), p. 155; Thernstrom, *The Other Bostonians: Poverty and Progress in the American Metropolis, 1880–1970* (Cambridge, Mass., 1973), p. 175; Josef J. Barton, *Peasants and Strangers: Italians, Rumanians, and Slovaks in an American City, 1890–1950* (Cambridge, Mass., 1975), p. 123.

60   This family history was reconstructed from the data for the James Kenney family in the U.S. Twelfth Census of 1900 manuscripts for Somerville, Massachusetts.

61   Joel Perlmann, "Curriculum and Tracking in the Transformation of the American High School: Providence, Rhode Island, 1880–1930," *Journal of Social History* 19(Fall 1985), pp. 29–55.

62   Ibid., p. 35.

63   Cf. Irwin Yellowitz, *The Position of the Worker in American Society, 1865–1896* (Englewood Cliffs, N.J., 1969), p. 21; James A. Henretta, "The Study of Social Mobility: Ideological Assumptions and Conceptual Bias," *Labor History* 18(1977), pp. 165–78; Virginia Yans-McLaughlin, *Family and Community: Italian Immigrants in Buffalo, 1880–1930* (Ithaca, 1977), pp. 194–7; John Bodnar, "Schooling and the Slavic American Family, 1900–1940," Bernard J. Weiss, ed., *American Education and the European Immigrant, 1840–1940* (Urbana, 1982); Bodnar, *The Transplanted: A History of Immigrants in Urban America* (Bloomington, 1985), p. 196. For the view that sponsorship of education is determined chiefly by ethnic culture see Thomas Kessner, *The Golden Door: Italian and Jewish Immigrant Mobility in New York City, 1880–1915* (New York, 1977), pp. 95–9.

64   Cf. Patrick J. Harrigan, "The Social Origins, Ambitions, and Occupations of Secondary Students in France During the Second Empire," in Lawrence Stone, ed., *Schooling and Society: Studies in the History of Education* (Baltimore, 1976), p. 228.

65   Anthony Giddens, *Class Structure of the Advanced Societies* (London, 1973), pp. 107–11, 177–97.

66   Stuart M. Blumin, "The Hypothesis of Middle-Class Formation in Nine-

teenth-Century America: A Critique and Some Proposals," *American His-torical Review* 90(1985), pp. 309–38; Olivier Zunz, "American History and the Changing Meaning of Assimilation," *Journal of American Ethnic History* 4(1985), pp. 66–9.

Chapter 6 The origins of high school youth culture

1 Social scientists studying the historical emergence of youth culture have identified its two major peer-centered characteristics: "inward-lookingness" – "young people, whatever segment of the youth culture they choose, look very largely to one another. Their friends are young people and a large fraction of their communications come from young people"; "intimate psychic bonds with one another" – "A second element that characterizes the culture of youth is similar to the first, but not the same: it is the psychic attachment of youth to others their own age." Panel on Youth, *Youth: Transition to Adulthood* (Chicago, 1974), pp. 112–47.

2 Ibid., p. 24.

3 Paula S. Fass, *The Damned and the Beautiful: American Youth in the 1920s* (New York, 1977), pp. 208–21; cf. Robert S. Lynd and Helen Merrell Lynd, *Middletown: A Study in American Culture* (New York, 1929), pp. 211–2, and August B. Hollingshead, *Elmtown's Youth and Elmtown Revisited* (New York, 1949), pp. 119–50.

4 For an example of the application of this procedure see Warren Leon, "High School: A Study of Youth and Community in Quincy, Massachus-sets," Ph.D. Thesis, 1979, Harvard University Archives.

5 John Franklin Brown, *The American High School* (New York, 1909), ch. 10–11; Horace A. Hollister, *High School Administration* (Boston, 1909), ch. 10; Franklin W. Johnson, "The Social Organization of the High School," *School Review* 17(1909), pp. 665–80.

6 Joseph Kett, *Rites of Passage: Adolescence in America, 1790 to the Present* (New York, 1977), p. 187.

7 Somerville High School *Radiator*, May 1895, p. 3; June 1895, p. 11.

8 *Radiator*, January 1898, pp. 3–4. Alexander Roberts and Edgar Draper, *Extraclass and Intramural Activities in High Schools* (Boston, 1928), ch. 3, and Hollister, *High School Administration*, pp. 198–201, also point out the improvement of general discipline in the student body resulting from student government.

9 *Radiator*, June 1895, p. 11; June 1899, p. 22.

10 The representation of boys and girls on the *Radiator* was determined by a count of editorial staff members every year from 1897 to 1905.

11 *Radiator*, June 1895, p. 15.

12 *Radiator*, June 1899, "English High School Notes."

13 *Radiator*, June 1899, p. 22.

14 *Radiator*, June 1895, p. 19.

15 *Radiator*, June 1904, p. 246. Brown, *The American High School*, pp. 318–27

and Spencer R. Smith, "Report of the Committee on the Influence of Fraternities in the High School," *School Review* 13(1905). pp. 1–10 reflect widespread criticism of the anti-democratic character of fraternities.

16 *Radiator,* June 1899, p. 16.

17 *Radiator,* June 1900, p. 29.

18 *Radiator,* June 1906, p. 187.

19 For the numerous socials and dances that were part of the official academic calendar see *Radiator,* June 1900, p. 31; June 1902, p. 233; June 1904, p. 256. Cf. Hollingshead, *Elmtown's Youth,* pp. 151–79, and Elaine Tyler May, *Great Expectations: Marriage and Divorce in Post-Victorian America* (Chicago, 1980), p. 68.

20 *Radiator,* May 1899, p. 4.

21 *Radiator,* June 1895, p. 16.

22 *Radiator,* March 1898, p. 4

23 *Radiator,* March 1898, pp. 3–4

24 *Radiator,* January 1900, p. 4; February 1900, p. 4.

25 A major sociological analysis of the rise of peer-group dependency is David Riesman, Nathan Glazer, and Reuel Denney, *The Lonely Crowd: A Study of American Character,* abridged edition (New Haven, 1975), pp. 126–60.

26 *Radiator,* November 1897, p. 3. Cf. Charles Dillon, *Journalism for High Schools* (New York, 1918). Brown and Draper, *Extramural,* pp. 163–80, supplies a brief history of high school journalism and its functions.

27 *Radiator,* October 1902, p. 4.

28 *Radiator,* April 1899, p. 4.

29 *Radiator,* June 1895 p. 4.

30 *Radiator,* April 1896, p. 4.

31 *Radiator,* May 1901, p. 186; October 1902, p. 4.

32 *Radiator,* March 1902, p. 128.

33 *Radiator,* December 1901, p. 52.

34 *Radiator,* March 1903, p. 126.

35 *Radiator,* December 1902, p. 52.

36 *Radiator,* June 1899, p. 4.

37 *Radiator,* April 1902, p. 156; March 1903, p. 126.

38 *Radiator,* June 1895, p. 21.

39 *Radiator,* February 1895, p. 3.

40 Somerville *Journal,* December 5, 1896, p. 2; December 3, 1897, p. 6; November 25, 1898, p. 1; November 30, 1900, p. 8; November 27, 1903, p. 8; November 25, 1904, p. 1; *Radiator,* December 1898, p. 3.

41 Somerville *Journal,* July 16, 1897, p. 2; June 24, 1898, p. 10; June 7, 1901, p. 12; June 13, 1902, p. 10; June 12, 1903, p. 9; July 1, 1904, p. 9.

42 *Radiator,* June 1895, p. 21; November 1896, p. 4.

43 *Radiator,* June 1897, p. 13.

44 *Radiator,* June 1897, pp. 13–15. Cf. L. H. Gulick, "Team Games and Civic Loyalty," *School Review* 14(1906), pp. 676–8.

45 *Radiator,* January 1899, p. 4.

46 *Radiator,* February 1896, p. 3.

47 *Radiator*, April 1895, p. 4.
48 *Radiator*, May 1895, p. 3. Cf. Roberts and Draper, *Extraclass*, pp. 191–6; Kett, *Rites of Passage*, p. 176.
49 *Radiator*, March 1896, p. 3.
50 *Radiator*, December 1898, p. 4.
51 *Radiator*, October 1903, p. 6.
52 *Radiator*, June 1896, p. 14.
53 *Radiator*, November 1898, p. 4.
54 *Radiator*, November 1899, p. 4.
55 *Radiator*, December 1899, p. 2; June 1900, p. 4.
56 *Radiator*, January 1896, p.4; March 1898, p. 5, "A Crisis in France," by English High School student William H. Burgess; January 1904, "A Review of the Past Year," p. 86; May 1904, "World Events," p. 190.
57 *Radiator*, January 1896, p. 5; February 1896, p. 4.
58 *Radiator*, January 1903, p. 76; June 1902, p. 208; February 1903, p. 100.
59 *Radiator*, February 1904, pp. 114–15.
60 *Radiator*, February 1902, p. 103; March 1904, p. 114.
61 *Radiator*, November 1903, p. 35.
62 *Radiator*, October 1901, p. 4.
63 *Radiator*, March 1901, p. 134. Cf. M. Kent Jennings and Richard G. Niemi, *The Political Character of Adolescence: The Influence of Families and Schools* (Princeton, 1974), pp. 334–5. Attachment to ideals of the Republican Party among turn-of-the-century middle-class youth is recalled in Henry Seidel Canby, *American Memoir* (Boston, 1947), pp. 122–4.
64 *Radiator*, June 1895, p. 18.
65 *Radiator*, June 1897, p. 13.
66 *Radiator*, June 1895, p. 15.
67 *Radiator*, March 1901, p. 134.
68 *Radiator*, June 1902, p. 238.
69 *Radiator*, June 1904, p. 249.
70 *Radiator*, January 1896, p. 4.
71 *Radiator*, June 1902, p. 236; June 1904, pp. 241–3.
72 *Radiator*, November 1903, p. 35.
73 *Radiator*, June 1897, p. 12.
74 *Radiator*, April 1896, p. 4; January 1902, p. 80.
75 *Radiator*, December 1902, p. 52.
76 *Radiator*, March 1903, p. 126. Bertha Lee Gardner, "Debating in the High School," *School Review* 19(1911), pp.534–45 criticizes the mercenary degradation of debate into a mere contest for victory.
77 *Radiator*, December 1898, p. 4.
78 *Radiator*, April 1903, p. 150.
79 *Radiator*, November 1902, p. 28.
80 *Radiator*, December 1897, p. 3.
81 *Radiator*, December 1898, p. 4. See R.S. Morrill, "The Coach and the School," *School Review* 32(1924), pp. 380–7.
82 *Radiator*, June 1897, p. 14; Roberts and Draper *Extraclass*, p. 195.
83 *Radiator*, March 1902, p. 128.

84   Stephen Steinberg, *The Ethnic Myth: Race, Ethnicity, and Class in America* (New York, 1981), pp. 230–8.
85   *Radiator,* December 1896, p. 4.
86   *Radiator,* January 1896, p. 4.
87   *Radiator,* March 1902, p. 128.
88   *Radiator,* December 1896, p. 4.
89   Somerville *Journal,* March 17, 1916, p. 1.
90   *Radiator,* January 1901, p. 75.
91   *Radiator,* May 1902, p. 180.
92   *Radiator,* May 1901, p. 185.
93   *Radiator,* February 1900, p. 4.
94   *Radiator,* June 1903, "Ivy Day Oration."
95   *Radiator,* June 1904, p. 233.
96   *Radiator,* June 1903, p. 76.
97   Ibid., "The Class Ode."
98   *Radiator,* June 1904, p. 233.
99   *Radiator,* January 1903, p. 76.
100 *Radiator,* January 1902, p. 79.
101 *Radiator,* June 1903, "The Golden Passport."
102 *Radiator,* June 1904, p. 231.
103 *Radiator,* June 1903, "The Class Ode."
104 *Radiator,* October 1903, p. 6.
105 *Radiator,* June 1904, p. 250.
106 See Chapter 5 and Chapter 7.
107 *Radiator,* February 1895, pp. 6–7.
108 In the early twentieth century, G. Stanley Hall idealized adolescence with similar themes couched in complex theoretical schema. Because Hall believed adolescence to be the "golden stage when life glisters and crepitates," "the apical stage of human development . . . before the decline of the highest powers of the soul in maturity and age," he advocated that it be prolonged and treasured. See Hall, *Adolescence: Its Psychology and Its Relations to Anthropology, Sociology, Sex, Crime, Religion and Education* (New York, 1905), Vol. I, chapters 4–6, and Vol. II, pp. 132, 361.
109 Oscar Handlin, *John Dewey's Challenge to Education* (New York, 1959), pp. 27–39. An important argument for the dramaturgical presentation of personality is Erving Goffman, *The Presentation of Self in Everyday Life* (New York, 1959). Erik H. Erikson, *Young Man Luther: A Study in Psychoanalysis and History* (New York, 1958), pp. 14–15, defines adolescence as a problematic stage of identity formation, but I am less persuaded than he is that it constitutes a "crisis."
110 Goffman, *Presentation,* pp. 1–4, 77–80, 84–5, 104–5, ch. 6. Goffman distinguishes between "communication in both its narrow and broad sense." He explains, "The expressiveness of the individual (and therefore his capacity to give impressions) appears to involve two radically different kinds of sign activity: the expression that he *gives,* and the expression that he *gives off.* The first involves verbal symbols or their substitutes

which he uses admittedly and solely to convey the information that he and the others are known to attach to these symbols. This is communication in the traditional and narrow sense. The second involves a wide range of action that others can treat as symptomatic of the actor, the expectation being that the action was performed for reasons other than the information conveyed in this way." See Chapter 5 for tabular data on the demographic dominance of students from white-collar Yankee families.

111   The ethnic and occupational-class determinants of dropping out of high school are discussed at length in the following chapter.

Chapter 7 Educational opportunity and social mobility

1   Somerville High School *Radiator*, June 1904, p. 233.
2   Somerville *Journal*, "High School Reminiscences," May 17, 1935.
3   *Radiator*, June 1903, "Ivy Day Oration."
4   Cf. Charles H. Thurber, "Is the Present High-School Course a Satisfactory Preparation for Business? If Not, How Should It Be Modified?" *Journal of Proceedings and Addresses, National Education Association* (Chicago, 1897), pp. 808–18.
5   Oscar Handlin and Mary F. Handlin, *Facing Life: Youth and the Family in American History* (Boston, 1971), pp. 157–63.
6   Joseph F. Kett, *Rites of Passage: Adolescence in America, 1790 to the Present* (New York, 1977), pp. 152–3.
7   Michael B. Katz, *Class, Bureaucracy, and Schools: The Illusion of Educational Change in America*, Expanded Edition (New York, 1975), p. 42.
8   Oscar and Mary Handlin, *The Dimensions of Liberty* (Cambridge, Mass., 1961), pp. 142–4; Katz, *Class, Bureaucracy, and Schools*, Expanded Edition, pp. 42–3; Samuel Bowles and Herbert Gintis, *Schooling in Capitalist America: Educational Reform and the Contradictions of Economic Life* (New York, 1976), pp. 48, 147–8, 181, 199; Diane Ravitch, *The Revisionists Revised: A Critique of the Radical Attack on the Schools* (New York, 1977), pp. 73–99.
9   Josef J. Barton, *Peasants and Strangers: Italians, Rumanians, and Slovaks in an American City, 1890–1950* (Cambridge, Mass., 1975), p. 135. Barton built a useful model for the study of education in the historical process of mobility. Cf. George S. Counts, *The Selective Character of American Secondary Education* (Chicago, 1922); and C. Arnold Anderson, "A Skeptical Note on the Relation of Vertical Mobility to Education," *American Journal of Sociology* 66(1961), pp. 560–1.
10   Stephan Thernstrom, *The Other Bostonians: Poverty and Progress in the American Metropolis, 1880–1970* (Cambridge, Mass., 1973), Appendix B, pp. 289–302.
11   Cf. Michael B. Katz, *The People of Hamilton, Canada West: Family and Class in a Mid-Nineteenth-Century City* (Cambridge, Mass., 1975), pp. 136–75.
12   Michael B. Katz, Michael J. Doucet, and Mark J. Stern, *The Social Organization of Early Industrial Capitalism* (Cambridge, Mass., 1982), ch. 1, 2.

Katz and his colleagues rigorously argue the analytical difference between class and social stratification.

13 Oscar Handlin and Mary F. Handlin, *Facing Life: Youth and the Family in
American History* (Boston, 1971), pp. 157–63. Also see George E. Gay,
"Why Pupils Leave the High School Without Graduating," *Education*
22(1901–2), pp. 300–7. In a survey of 1,436 male and female high school
leavers in Massachusetts, Gay found that over a third dropped out due
to their families' need for their service or earnings.

14 Students who dropped out of high school, who graduated from high
school, and who graduated and went to college were traced to their last
job as adults in Somerville. "Last job" in this study is defined as the
occupation held by a person closest to 15 years after entry into high school,
and when that person was near 30 years of age or older. Studies of career
mobility have shown that as an individual turns thirty a levelling off
usually occurs in occupational mobility. Cf. Thernstrom, *The Other Bostonians*, p. 62. Professional and other white-collar occupations were combined to form the category of white-collar jobs, and skilled and low-manual
jobs were combined to form the category of blue-collar jobs. Although
this formulation of two status categories is crude, it covers the major
dimension of intergenerational occupational mobility that would have
been appreciably influenced by a high school education.

15 An important study of the influence of parental status on the social mobility of high school students is Robert K. Merton and Bryce Ryan, "Paternal Status and the Economic Adjustment of High-School Graduates,"
Social Forces 22(1943), pp. 302–6. After studying the employment patterns
of a sample of graduates of 14 Boston high schools from 1916 to 1934,
Merton and Ryan concluded that students with equal amounts of schooling tended to inherit the social status of their parents. Their study, however, traced sample members only to the first occupation they took in
the labor market, thereby giving only a partial reconstruction of career
lines.

16 Burton J. Bledstein, *The Culture of Professionalism: The Middle Class and the
Development of Higher Education in America* (New York, 1976), provides a
tendentious and over-reified cultural history of this growing linkage between higher education and professionalization at the turn of the century.

17 Thomas Dublin, "Women Workers and the Study of Social Mobility,"
Journal of Interdisciplinary History (1979), pp. 647–8.

18 *The Fiftieth Anniversary of the Somerville High School, 1852–1902* (Somerville, 1902), listed the maiden names, married names, and addresses in
1902 of all female graduates who could be contacted.

19 Dublin, "Women Workers," p. 648, shows that one third of a sample of
175 New Hampshire women of the mid-nineteenth century whose husbands could be traced married "urban men and settled permanently in
cities." Dublin suggests that marriage leading to geographic mobility –
especially moves to urban centers – may have facilitated the social mobility of women, since rising men often moved to cities.

20 By utilizing the techniques and findings of large statistical studies, Samuel Bowles and Herbert Gintis, *Schooling in Capitalist America*, pp. 131–41, and Christopher Jencks, *Inequality: A Reassessment of the Effect of Family and Schooling in America* (New York, 1972), pp. 185–8, have challenged the assumption that grades and test scores predict career success. Since their arguments are based on data drawn from twentieth-century surveys, they do not provide a reliable historical baseline against which to judge the changing relationship between scholastic achievement and occupational mobility.

21 These figures were compiled from the records of the Somerville High School.

22 Douglas Lamar Jones, *Village and Seaport: Migration and Society in Eighteenth Century Massachusetts* (Hanover, N.H., 1981), pp. 112–13.

23 Thernstrom, *The Other Bostonians*, p. 229. For other relevant discussions of the relationship between migration and industrial social structure, see Katz, *The People of Hamilton* and *Social Organization*; Peter R. Knights, *The Plain People of Boston, 1830–1860: A Study in City Growth* (New York, 1971); Howard Chudacoff, *Mobile Americans: Residential and Social Mobility in Omaha, 1880–1920* (New York, 1972).

24 Stephan Thernstrom, "Urbanization, Migration, and Social Mobility in Late Nineteenth-Century America," in Barton J. Bernstein, *Towards a New Past: Dissenting Essays in American History* (New York, 1967), p. 171.

25 John Goldthorpe, *Social Mobility and Class Structure in Modern Britain* (Oxford, 1980), p. 54.

26 Ibid., p. 57.

27 Seymour Martin Lipset and Reinhard Bendix in *Social Mobility in Industrial Society* (Berkeley, 1964), p. 93, argue that the "absence of pressure for entry into the labor market is in itself a major facilitation of upward mobility."

28 Bowles and Gintis, *Schooling in Capitalist America*.

29 Cf. Perlmann, Joel, "Who Stayed in School? Social Structure and Academic Achievement in the Determination of Enrollment Patterns, Providence, Rhode Island, 1880–1925," *Journal of American History*, 72(1985), pp. 588–614.

Chapter 8 The birth of progressive reform and the junior high school

1 Somerville, *Annual Reports*, 1929, "Elections."

2 Sam B. Warner, Jr., *Streetcar Suburbs: The Process of Growth in Boston, 1870–1900* (Cambridge, Mass., 1962), p. 66; David Ward, *Cities and Immigrants: A Geography of Change in Nineteenth-Century America* (New York, 1971), pp. 141–2; Robert A. Woods and Albert J. Kennedy, *The Zone of Emergence* (Cambridge, Mass., 1962), pp. 1–2, 21–5.

3 *United States Twelfth Census 1900* (Washington, D.C., 1901), Vol. I, pt. 1, p. 660; *U.S. Fifteenth Census 1930* (Washington, D.C., 1932), Vol. III, pt. 1, p. 1111.

4 J. Joseph Huthmacher, *Massachusetts People and Politics, 1919–1933* (Cambridge, Mass., 1959), pp. 1–14.

5 Harold R. Taylor, "Somerville Politics, 1921–1929," Senior Honors Thesis, Harvard University, 1939, p. 8.

6 *Official Catholic Directory*, 1900 (Milwaukee, Wisc., 1900), p. 27; 1910 (New York, 1910), p. 51; 1921 (New York, 1921), p. 37; 1926 (New York, 1926), p. 43; 1930 (New York, 1930), p. 38.

7 Interview with W. S. Howe in Taylor, "Somerville Politics," p. 12.

8 Lyman Hodgdon, former alderman from ward one and ex-chairman of the Republican City Committee, remarked, "Some people say that the influx of the Irish Catholics into Somerville was part of a deliberate colonizing scheme, inspired by the Catholic clergy. In this way, cities around Boston were gradually brought under control of the church." See Taylor, "Somerville Politics," p. 40.

9 Taylor, "Somerville Politics," p. 9.

10 "Up the hill" was a catchphrase used by the Irish in early-twentieth-century Somerville to describe the move from a working-class neighborhood to a middle-class neighborhood. Interview with John J. Murphy, former Mayor of Somerville, April 1938, in Taylor, "Somerville Politics," p. 15.

11 *U.S. Thirteenth Census 1910* (Washington, D.C., 1913), Vol. II, p. 895; *U.S. Fourteenth Census 1920* (Washington, D.C., 1922), Vol. II, p. 468.

12 Taylor, "Somerville Politics," p. 36.

13 Huthmacher, *Massachusetts People and Politics*, pp. 1–18.

14 Taylor, "Somerville Politics," p. 15.

15 *U.S. Twelfth Census 1900*, Vol. I, pt. 1, p. 802; *U.S. Fifteenth Census 1930* (Washington, D.C., 1932), Vol. III, pt. 1, p. 1099.

16 Computed from data in *Massachusetts Census 1915* (Boston, 1918), p. 262, and *U.S. Fifteenth Census 1930* (Washington, D.C., 1933), Vol. IV, pp. 743, 746.

17 Zane L. Miller, *The Urbanization of Modern America: A Brief History* (New York, 1973), p. 84.

18 Somerville *Journal*, December 30, 1898, p. 12.

19 Somerville *Journal*, January 13, 1899, p. 1.

20 Somerville *Journal*, October 31, 1896, p. 1.

21 Somerville *Journal*, December 30, 1898, p. 12.

22 Somerville *Journal*, September 22, 1899, p. 8.

23 Somerville *Journal*, September 15, 1899, p. 3.

24 Somerville *Journal*, September 15, 1899, p. 3; Edward A. Samuels and Henry H. Kimball, *Somerville: Past and Present* (Boston, 1897), p. 650.

25 Somerville *Journal*, September 29, 1899, p. 1.

26 Average family size was computed from *Massachusetts Census 1905* (Boston, 1909), Vol. I, pp. 772–3. The number of rooms in a dwelling place was derived from the *Massachusetts Census 1915*, p. 93.

27 *U.S. Thirteenth Census 1910* (Washington, D.C., 1913), Vol. I, p. 666; *U.S. Fourteenth Census 1920* (Washington, D.C., 1921), Vol I, p. 231.

28 The *Massachusetts Census 1915,* p. 504, reported that only 5 percent of married women in Somerville were employed.

29 Massachusetts State Board of Education, *Sixty-fifth Annual Report,* 1900– 1, appendix; *Seventy-fifth Annual Report,* 1910–1, appendix.

30 *Annual Reports,* 1900, p. 207; 1924, p. 215. Enrollment figures refer to the number of students enrolled, 5 to 15 years old.

31 The number of foreign-born male operatives grew from 614 in 1900 to 1,664 in 1930. They comprised 48 percent of factory workers in 1900 and 54 percent in 1930. Cf. *U.S. Twelfth Census 1900, Special Reports, Occupations* (Washington, D.C., 1904), p. 734; *U.S. Fifteenth Census 1930,* Vol. IV, p. 743–5.

32 Theodore Sizer, *Secondary Schools at the Turn of the Century* (New Haven, 1964), pp. 209–71.

33 Edward A. Krug, *The Shaping of the American High School* (New York, 1964), pp. 391–2.

34 Enrollment percentages for other cities were based on enrollment in all of their secondary schools: Latin high schools, English high schools, technical high schools, and commercial high schools. In 1915 Boston's secondary schools enrolled 34.2 percent of the city's high-school-age population, Lynn 32.4 percent, Lawrence 18.8 percent, Lowell 23.4 percent, and Cambridge 37.2 percent. Enrollment figures obtained from Somerville, *Annual Reports,* 1915, p. 154; Boston, *Annual Reports of the School Committee,* 1915, Document 12, pp. 8, 20; Cambridge, *City Documents,* 1915–16, pp. 311–2; Lawrence, *Annual Reports of the School Committee,* 1915, p. 43; Lowell, *Annual Reports of the School Committee,* 1915–16, pp. 20, 49; Lynn, *Annual Reports of the School Committee,* 1916, pp. 67, 68; *Massachusetts State Census,* 1915, pp. 184–285.

35 U.S. Office of Education, *Biennial Survey of Education in the United States* (Washington, D.C., 1957), part 1, p. 26.

36 The numbers of graduates were obtained from Somerville, *Annual Reports,* 1915, p. 154, and 1930, p. 186.

37 *Annual Reports,* 1910, p. 168; 1911, p. 182.

38 Marvin Lazerson, *Origins of the Urban School: Public Education in Massachusetts, 1870–1915* (Cambridge, Mass., 1971), pp. 175–6. A disappointing but usable biography of Snedden is Walter Drost, *David Snedden and Education for Social Efficiency* (Madison, 1967). Snedden's influential ideas are presented in *The Problem of Vocational Education* (Boston, 1910). Also cf. U.S. Bureau of Labor, *Twenty-fifth Annual Report* (Washington, D.C., 1911), pp. 96–106.

39 *Annual Reports,* 1913, pp. 160, 161.

40 *Annual Reports,* 1909, p. 174.

41 Lazerson, *Origins of the Urban School,* pp. 142–3. Susan Kingsbury wrote the "Report of the Sub-Committee on the Relation of Children to the Industries" for the Massachusetts Commission on Industrial and Technical Education, *Report* (Boston, 1906).

42 *Annual Reports,* 1909, p. 168.

43   *Annual Reports,* 1913, p. 221; 1920, p. 139.
44   For a brief historical survey of the junior-high-school movement, see Edward A. Krug, *The Shaping of the American High School* (New York, 1964), pp. 327–35. In 1910, the first recognized junior high school was established in Berkeley, California. Within the next ten years, nearly a thousand other cities across the nation introduced the junior high school into their public school systems. See Frank F. Bunker, "The Better Articulation of the Parts of the Public School System," *Educational Review* (March 1914), pp. 253–5, 260–1; Somerville, *Annual Reports,* 1920, p. 183; W. A. Smith, "Junior High School Practices in Sixty-Four Cities," *Educational Administration and Supervision* (March 1920), p. 139. Theoretical discussion of the social functions of the junior high school are found in Charles Hubbard Judd, *The Evolution of a Democratic School System* (Boston, 1918); Thomas H. Briggs, *The Junior High School* (Boston, 1920); Leonard V. Koos, *The Junior High School* (New York, 1921); William A. Smith, *The Junior High School* (New York, 1926); Francis T. Spaulding, *The Small Junior High School* (Cambridge, Mass., 1927); Joseph K. Van Denburg, *The Junior High School Idea* (New York, 1922). The provision of equal educational opportunity by the junior high school is summarized in F. G. Bonser, "Democratizing Secondary Education by the Six-Three-Three-Plan," *Educational Administration and Supervision,* 1(1915), pp. 567–76. Emma V. Thomas-Tindal and Jessie DuVal Myers, two Philadelphia secondary teachers, enthusiastically described the cultural milieu of the junior high school in *Junior High School Life* (New York, 1927).
45   The expansion of the white-collar sector of the labor force is described in Nelson N. Foote and Paul K. Hatt, "Social Mobility and Economic Advancement," *American Economic Review,* 43(1958), pp. 364–78. Stephan Thernstrom in *The Other Bostonians: Poverty and Progress in the American Metropolis* (Cambridge, Mass., 1973), pp. 50–1, shows that the white-collar sector in Boston has grown very gradually, but steadily, from 1880, when it comprised 32 percent of the male labor force, to 1970 when it was 51 percent.
46   *Annual Reports,* 1920, pp. 185–9.
47   Somerville, *School Committee Minutes, 1911–1913* (Somerville, 1923), February 7, 1912.
48   *Annual Reports,* 1913, pp. 167–8.
49   *Annual Reports,* 1914, p. 187.
50   Ibid., pp. 183–5.
51   Ibid., pp. 186–7. The fact that Forster Intermediate was located in affluent Winter Hill accounts heavily for the high percentage of commercial and preparatory majors.
52   *Massachusetts Census 1915,* pp. 84–6. Somerville's population density of 22,078 to a square mile was second in the state to Chelsea's, which was 22,856.
53   *Annual Reports,* 1912–1915, "School Department," Table 14a.
54   Somerville *Journal,* April 7, 1916, p. 1; *School Committee Minutes,* April 14, 1916, p. 6.

55 Somerville *Journal,* April 14, 1916, p. 6.
56 *Annual Reports,* 1912–1930, "Elections."
57 Interview with Robert C. Harriss, February 1939, given to Harold R. Taylor, and summarized in his senior thesis, "Somerville Politics, 1921–1929," p. 54. David Fulton, Albert Hughes, Waldo Phelps, Robert Harriss, and Elmer Hayes – all prominent Irish Catholic politicians – joined the Republican Party to improve their political chances and connections.
58 Taylor, "Somerville Politics," p. 43.
59 This pattern emerged from a rough count of Irish, Swedish, and Italian surnames among the lists of graduates in intervals from 1913 to 1930. *Annual Reports,* 1913, 1915, 1917, 1920, 1925, 1930, "School Department," lists of graduates.
60 Somerville *Journal,* April 7, 1916, p. 4; September 1, 1916, p. 2; September 14, 1917, p. 1; April 30, 1918, p. 3.
61 *Annual Reports,* 1924, p. 226.
62 *Annual Reports,* 1915–1921, "School Department," Table 19a.
63 *Annual Reports,* 1912–1924, "School Department," Tables 10 and 14a. The percentage of pupils truant or absent was obtained by taking the ratio of absentees and truancies to the number of pupils in grades.
64 Computed from *Annual Reports,* 1917–1921, "Police Reports."
65 Somerville *Journal,* May 16, 1919, p. 6.
66 Somerville *Journal,* June 13, 1919, p. 3.
67 Somerville *Journal,* January 30, 1920, p. 1.
68 Ibid., p. 6.
69 Somerville *Journal,* May 14, 1920, p. 6.
70 Somerville *Journal,* March 12, 1920, p. 3.
71 Somerville *Journal,* May 14, 1920, p. 1.
72 Somerville *Journal,* May 21, 1920, p. 1.
73 See *Beyond the Neck: The Architecture and Development of Somerville, Massachusetts* (Somerville, 1982), p. 48.
74 Somerville *Journal,* May 14, 1920, p. 1.
75 Somerville *Journal,* May 21, 1920, p. 12.
76 *Annual Reports,* 1924, p. 226.
77 Somerville *Journal,* May 21, 1920, p. 12.
78 *School Committee Minutes,* May 29, 1916; Somerville *Journal,* March 17, 1916, p. 4.
79 Somerville *Journal,* February 25, 1921, p. 1; October 1, 1920, p. 1.
80 Somerville *Journal,* August 4, 1916. William McCarthy, whose tax was $276.06 for the year, was listed as one of the city's large taxpayers.
81 Somerville *Journal,* May 28, 1920, p. 1.
82 *School Committee Minutes,* June 11, 1920.
83 Somerville *Journal,* May 28, 1920, p. 1.
84 Somerville *Journal,* June 11, 1920, p. 9.
85 Ibid., p. 9.
86 Somerville *Journal,* July 23, 1920, p. 2.
87 Somerville *Journal,* February 4, 1921, p. 11; June 17, 1921, p. 9.
88 Somerville *Journal,* June 10, 1921, p. 1; June 17, 1921, p. 9.

89 Somerville *Journal*, June 17, 1921, p. 9.
90 See "Elections" in *Annual Reports*, 1912–1921.
91 Pioneering studies of the class origins of school board members were George S. Counts, *The Social Composition of Boards of Education* (Chicago, 1927), and Scott Nearing, "Who's Who in Our Boards of Education?" *School and Society* 5(1917), pp. 89–90. A discussion of the method of class analysis is W. W. Charters, "Social Class Analysis and the Control of Public Education," *Harvard Educational Review*, 23(1953), pp. 268–83.
92 Huthmacher, *Massachusetts People and Politics*, pp. 5–6.
93 "Lists of Big Tax Payers" in Somerville *Journal*, August 8, 1913; August 13, 1915; August 4, 1916; September 5, 1919.
94 Somerville *Journal*, June 30, 1922, pp. 17–20.
95 A check was made in the city directory to identify the occupations of these individuals. There were 3 lawyers, 3 physicians, 1 reporter, 1 post office clerk, 1 teacher, 1 police court clerk, and 2 clerks.
96 Tamara K. Hareven, *Family Time and Industrial Time* (Cambridge, Eng., 1982), pp. 360–1.
97 John M. Hoban, Irish alderman from ward two, fought unsuccessfully to abolish the examination. He contended that it discriminated against Catholics.
98 *Official Catholic Directory* (New York, 1926), p. 43.
99 The key figure in this coalition was Joseph Borgatti, who persuaded Italians to transfer their allegiance to the Democratic Party in the 1920s.
100 Huthmacher, *Massachusetts People and Politics*, p. 257–69.
101 Oscar Handlin, *Al Smith and His America* (Boston, 1958). The pluralistic character of reform coalitions in the Progressive Era and the 1920s is described in John D. Buenker, *Urban Liberalism and Progressive Reform* (New York, 1973), pp. 217–31.
102 The development of the latter political pattern in central cities has been well established by historical research. Cf. Samuel P. Hays, "The Politics of Reform in Municipal Government in the Progressive Era," *Pacific Northwest Quarterly*, 55(1964), pp. 157–69; David B. Tyack, *The One Best System: A History of American Urban Education* (Cambridge, Mass., 1974), pp. 126–76; Diane Ravitch, *The Great School Wars: A History of the Public Schools as Battlefield for Social Change* (New York, 1974), pp. 107–58.

Conclusion: The high school in the light of history

1 C. Wright Mills, *White Collar: The American Middle Classes* (New York, 1951), p. ix.
2 Joel Perlmann, "Who Stayed in School? Social Structure and Academic Achievement in the Determination of Enrollment Patterns, Providence, Rhode Island, 1880–1925," *Journal of American History*, 72(December 1985), pp. 588–614.
3 Oscar and Mary Handlin, *The Dimensions of Liberty* (Cambridge, Mass., 1961), p. 140.

4 Michael B. Katz, "Who Went to School?" *History of Education Quarterly* (Fall 1972), pp. 432–54.
5 Cf. Daniel Walker Howe, "Victorian Culture in America," in Howe, ed., *Victorian America* (New York, 1976), p. 11.
6 Cf. Harry Braverman, *Labor and Monopoly Capital: The Degradation of Work in the Twentieth Century* (New York, 1974).
7 Landmark works calling for the reform of the high school include James Bryant Conant, *The American High School Today: A First Report to Interested Citizens* (New York, 1959); Ernest L. Boyer, *A Report on Secondary Education in America* (New York, 1983); Theodore R. Sizer, *Horace's Compromise: The Dilemma of the American High School* (Boston, 1984).

Index

ability grouping, in intermediate school, 200–1
academies (private schools), 21, 42, 44, 223
activists
  transitional newcomers as, 193–4
  see also political participation; voluntary asssociations
adolescence
  Hall on, 150, 278 *n*108
  see also peer-group culture
Adrian, Michigan, student-origin studies in, 101
adulthood, transition to, 150–1, 166
age grading, 52
age priority, *see* birth order
American Protective Association, 72, 189
analytic thought, and Somerville curriculum, 34–5, 77–8
Anglo-Saxons
  games of, 128
  see also Yankees
apprenticeship
  decline of, 269 *n*63
  difficulty in finding, 76
  high school competition from, 42, 90
  for high school leavers, 55
aptitude grouping, and junior high school, 201
artisans
  Boston–Somerville flight of, 71–2
  on common council, 64
  and English High establishment, 92, 94
  insecurity of, 70, 76
  as parents of high schoolers, 42, 45, 46, 47, 49, 57, 58, 76, 89, 108
  second-generation Irish as, 68
  and semiskilled workers, 69

  see also blue-collar workers; skilled workers
assimilation
  and high school, 221
  in junior high school, 201
  in zone of emergence, 193
athletics, high school, *see* sports, high school
attendance by enrolled students
  as decreased by epidemics, 84
  in Somerville schools (1842–45), 23–4, 28
  in Somerville schools (1850s), 43
  in Somerville schools (late 1800s), 86–7, 88
  see also enrollment in high school
autonomous cognitive abilities, as educational objective, 35–6, 39
"average ability," as teaching basis, 77

Baker, May, 146
baseball, high school, 126–8, 132, 140
basketball teams, girls', 129, 147
Baxter, George L., 40, 98, 132
Bell, Luther V., 17
Beverly, Massachusetts, high school opposed in, 40
Bingham, Norman W., 95–6, 97
birth order, and high school attendance, 52–3, 109–10, 111
birth rate
  for foreign-born, 10, 67
  see also family size
blacks, in Somerville, 9
blue-collar workers
  and high school as occupational mobility, 166–8, 171, 177–85
  migration regimes of, 174–6
  as parents of high schoolers, 102,

DATE DUE